Contents

Table of Cases

List of Cases with Principle of Law

2 Processing of Juveniles by the Police

Haley v. State of Ohio, 68 S. Ct. 302 (1948): Coerced confessions are not admissible as evidence in adult proceedings against juveniles.

Gallegos v. Colorado, 370 U.S. 49 (1962): The isolation of a juvenile for prolonged periods of time by the police may result in confessions that are deemed involuntarily obtained.

Fare v. Michael C., 442 U.S. 707 (1979): A request by a juvenile to see his or her probation officer is not equivalent to asking for a lawyer.

New Jersey v. T.L.O., 469 U.S. 325 (1985): Public school officials need only "reasonable grounds" to search juveniles; they do not need a warrant or probable cause.

Harling v. United States, 295 F.2d 161 (D.D.C. 1961): Confessions made to police are not admissible if the juvenile is subsequently tried as an adult.

United States v. Miller, 453 F.2d 634 (4th Cir. 1972): Handwriting samples and fingerprints obtained without coercion in a noncustodial setting are admissible in court.

United States v. Ramsey, 367 F. Supp. 1307 (W.D. Mo. 1973): Statements obtained by state officers in violation of state statutes are admissible if they do not violate the Constitution.

United States v. Barfield, 507 F.2d 53 (5th Cir. 1975): Advice to tell the truth, given in a noncustodial setting, does not amount to coercion.

United States v. Sechrist, 640 F.2d 81 (7th Cir. 1981): Fingerprints may be taken based on less than probable cause if the juvenile is legally detained.

United States v. Bernard S., 795 F.2d 749 (9th Cir. 1986): Despite language barriers, incriminating statements made by a juvenile are admissible in court as long as the juvenile understands his rights and waives them voluntarily.

Cason v. Cook, 810 F.2d 188 (8th Cir. 1987): "Reasonable grounds" instead of "probable cause" is the standard used in searches made by public school officials. This is the same standard used even if the search was conducted with the assistance of a police officer.

Smith v. State, 623 So. 2d 369 (Ala. Cr. App. 1992): A juvenile's request during questioning that his grandmother be called invoked his right to remain silent.

In the Interest of J.L., A Child, 623 So. 2d 860 (Fla. App. 1993): Police must have a reason to stop and frisk a juvenile; a juvenile's mere presence in an area does not justify an investigatory search.

In the Interest of S.A.W., 499 N.W.2d 739 (Iowa App. 1993): Reasonable suspicion justifies a stop in an area where a crime is alleged to have happened.

In re Starvon J., 29 Cal. Rptr. 2d 471 (Cal. App. 1994): Detention of a juvenile for purposes other than an investigation does not affect the voluntariness of statements made should that juvenile become a suspect.

In re Gilbert E., 38 Cal. Rptr. 2d 866 (Cal. App. 1995): A police officer's continued questioning of a juvenile after the juvenile unequivocally refuses to waive his or her *Miranda* rights is a violation of the right to remain silent.

State v. Sugg, 456 S.E.2d 469 (W. Va. 1995): A juvenile may waive *Miranda* rights even in the absence of his or her parents, as long as the juvenile knowingly, voluntarily, and intelligently waives such rights.

3   Curfew Ordinances and Juveniles

Bykosky v. Borough of Middletown, 410 F. Supp 1242 (M.D. Pa. 1975): Curfew ordinances that provide a wide range of exceptions are nonetheless constitutional.

Illinois v. Chambers, 360 N.E.2d 55 (Ill. 1976): Curfew laws imposed statewide for the welfare of juveniles within the boundaries of the state are constitutional.

Johnson v. City of Opelousas, 658 F.2d 1065 (5th Cir. 1981): Curfew ordinances that restrict all movement of juveniles during the specified hours are unconstitutional.

Waters v. Barry, 711 F. Supp. 1121 (D.D.C. 1989):   Overly restrictive curfew ordinances violate the fundamental rights of juveniles and are unconstitutional. However, a properly crafted curfew ordinance does not restrict the government's right to search and seize material from juveniles who violate such curfews.

Panora v. Simmons, 445 N.W.2d 363 (Iowa 1989):   Curfew ordinances that provide for parentally approved exceptions do not infringe on the autonomy of the family or parental rights in general.

People in Interest of J.M., 768 P.2d 219 (Colo. 1989):   Curfew ordinances for juveniles enacted for order maintenance are constitutional as long as they do not unduly infringe on liberty interests.

Brown v. Ashton, 611 A.2d 599 (Md. App. 1992):   Curfew ordinances that do not match their specified intent in law are unconstitutional on their face; however, officials who enforce previously unchallenged curfew ordinances are immune from civil liability.

City of Maquoketa v. Russell, 484 N.W.2d 179 (Iowa 1992):   Curfew ordinances that restrict all movement of juveniles, with no exceptions, are too broad and are unconstitutional.

Qutb v. Strauss, 11 F.3d 488 (5th Cir. 1993):   Carefully crafted juvenile curfew ordinances do not violate the equal protection clause, nor do they unconstitutionally infringe parental rights of privacy.

State v. Bean, 869 P.2d 984 (Utah App. 1994):   Reasonable suspicion of curfew violation and the fact that a minor might be in possession of alcohol allows officials a limited period of time to question the suspect without infringement of constitutional rights.

Matter of Appeal in Maricopa County, 887 P.2d 599 (Ariz. App. 1994):   A juvenile's walk in the park in violation of a curfew ordinance is not protected as a First Amendment activity.   The ordinance itself did not violate the fundamental rights of juveniles and could be enforced.

4   Detention of Juveniles

Schall v. Martin, 104 S. Ct. 2403 (1984):   Preventive detention of juveniles is constitutional.

Baldwin v. Lewis, 300 F. Supp. 1220 (E.D. Wis. 1969): Juveniles are entitled to a hearing on the existence of probable cause for continued detention subsequent to arrest.

Martarella v. Kelley, 349 F. Supp. 575 (S.D.N.Y. 1972): Punitive, hazardous, and unhealthy conditions of confinement violate juveniles' constitutional rights.

Cox v. Turley, 506 F.2d 1347 (6th Cir. 1974): Denial of statutory provisions in juvenile arrest and detention processes is unconstitutional.

Martin v. Strasburg, 689 F.2d 365 (2d Cir. 1982): Preventive detention of a juvenile is unconstitutional.

D.B. v. Tewksbury, 545 F. Supp. 896 (D. Or. 1982): It is a violation of constitutional rights to hold juveniles in adult jails if they are status offenders, pending adjudication or held in circumstances that constitute punishment.

Horn by Parks v. Madison County Fiscal Court, 22 F.3d 653 (6th Cir. 1994): Detention officials who exercise reasonable caution in protecting juveniles detained in facilities primarily dedicated to the housing of adults are not liable for injuries.

5   Intake and Court Process Before Adjudication

In re Frank H., 337 N.Y.S.2d 118 (1972): Juveniles do not have a right to counsel at intake.

Wansley v. Slayton, 487 F.2d 90 (4th Cir. 1973): Spontaneous statements made by a juvenile while under the exclusive jurisdiction of the juvenile court can be used in adult criminal proceedings.

Moss v. Weaver, 525 F.2d 1258 (5th Cir. 1976): Pretrial detention of juveniles without a probable cause determination is unconstitutional.

In re Wayne H., 596 P.2d 1 (Cal. 1979): Information gathered at intake cannot be used in any guilt-finding process, be it juvenile or adult.

Washington v. Chatham, 624 P.2d 1180 (Wash. App. 1981): Juveniles do not have a constitutional right to diversion.

United States v. Nash, 620 F. Supp. 1439 (S.D.N.Y. 1985): If the requirements of the Federal Juvenile Delinquency Act concerning admonition of legal rights, notification of a responsible adult, and presentment to a magistrate are not satisfied, any post-arrest statements made prior to presentment before the magistrate must be suppressed.

Washington v. Chavez, 761 P.2d 607 (Wash. 1988): Local court rules establishing time frames for juvenile processing do not violate the separation of powers doctrine.

Christopher P. v. New Mexico, 816 P.2d 485 (N.M. 1991): A juvenile has a Fifth Amendment privilege to remain silent that applies during a psychological evaluation to determine amenability to juvenile treatment. Evidence obtained in violation of that right is not admissible in court.

In the Matter of Jason J., 590 N.Y.S.2d 893 (A.D. 1992): Minor mistakes are allowed in a juvenile delinquency petition as long as they do not jeopardize the integrity of the petition.

United States v. A.R., 38 F.3d 699 (3d Cir. 1994): Psychiatric evaluation for the purpose of determining amenability to juvenile treatment is not a critical stage in the juvenile justice process and therefore the Fifth and Sixth Amendments do not apply.

R.R. v. Portsey, 629 So. 2d 1059 (Fla. App. 1994): Conducting detention hearings by electronic means must be formally established either through legislation or by court rules, otherwise it is not an acceptable alternative to physical presence in the courtroom.

State v. K.K.H., 878 P.2d 1255 (Wash. App. 1994): A probable cause hearing generally must be held within 48 hours after arrest.

6   Waiver of Juvenile to Adult Court

Kent v. United States, 383 U.S. 541 (1966): A juvenile must be given due process before being transferred from a juvenile court to an adult court.

Breed v. Jones, 421 U.S. 517 (1975): Juveniles are entitled to the constitutional right against double jeopardy.

Summers v. State, 230 N.E.2d 320 (Ind. 1967): Juveniles cannot be denied the rights guaranteed in the transfer process under *Kent*.

United States v. Howard, 449 F.2d 1086 (D.C. Cir. 1971): A transfer hearing must involve a full review of all relevant issues in determining fitness for transfer to adult court.

People v. Fields, 199 N.W.2d 217 (Mich. 1972): Juvenile transfer statutes must contain standards to be constitutional.

Fain v. Duff, 488 F.2d 218 (5th Cir. 1973): It is double jeopardy to adjudicate a juvenile as a delinquent on an offense, and to then transfer him or her to adult court to face criminal charges on the same offense.

United States ex rel. Bombacino v. Bensinger, 498 F.2d 875 (7th Cir. 1974): Transfer hearing processes that do not include presentation of evidence and a statement of the reasons for transfer are constitutional.

In re Mathis, 537 P.2d 148 (Or. App. 1975): A decision to transfer based on the strength of the evidence, the child's age, and the need for long-term care is constitutional.

Russell v. Parratt, 543 F.2d 1214 (8th Cir. 1976): The practice of a prosecutor holding unreviewable discretion to charge a juvenile as an adult without holding an evidentiary hearing is constitutional.

United States v. J.D., 517 F. Supp. 69 (S.D.N.Y. 1981): Evaluative information to be used in a transfer hearing cannot include information that would violate the privilege against self-incrimination.

Matter of Seven Minors, 664 P.2d 947 (Nev. 1983): Transfer decisions should be made based on clear and convincing evidence, using such factors as seriousness, criminal history, and social history of the juvenile.

State v. Muhammad, 703 P.2d 835 (Kan. 1985): If a juvenile is notified of a transfer hearing, is given the right to be present, and is represented by counsel, due process is not violated if that juvenile does not appear at the hearing and is transferred to criminal court.

R.H. v. State, 777 P.2d 204 (Alaska App. 1989): The privilege against self-incrimination is violated when a juvenile is forced to participate in a psychological evaluation as part of transfer proceedings.

People v. P.H., 582 N.E.2d 700 (Ill. 1991): The gang-transfer provision of a transfer statute is constitutional.

People v. R.L., 634 N.E.2d 733 (Ill. 1994): The required prosecution in adult court of juveniles charged with possession or possession with intent to sell of drugs within 1,000 feet or on the property of public housing does not discriminate against a class, despite its disparate impact, and is constitutional.

C.M. v. State, 884 S.W.2d 562 (Tex. App. 1994): The trial judge holds discretion in assessing the weight to be given to the various factors considered by the court in a transfer hearing.

Laswell v. Frey, 45 F.3d 1101 (6th Cir. 1995): Admitting to charges pending in the course of a detention hearing does not turn that detention hearing into an adjudication hearing; thus, jeopardy does not attach.

7   Adjudication

In re Gault, 387 U.S. 1 (1967): Juveniles must be given four basic due process rights in adjudication proceedings that can result in confinement in an institution in which their freedom would be curtailed.

In re Winship, 397 U.S. 358 (1970): Proof beyond a reasonable doubt, not simply a preponderance of the evidence, is required in juvenile adjudication hearings in cases in which the act would have been a crime if it had been committed by an adult.

McKeiver v. Pennsylvania, 403 U.S. 528 (1971): Juveniles have no constitutional right to trial by jury, even in a delinquency proceeding.

Ivan v. City of New York, 407 U.S. 203 (1972): The decision in *Winship*—that juveniles are entitled to proof beyond a reasonable doubt in adjudication hearings—should be applied retroactively to all cases in the appellate process.

Goss v. Lopez, 419 U.S. 565 (1975): Due process must be given to juveniles even in short-term suspension cases.

United States v. Torres, 500 F.2d 944 (2d Cir. 1974): The federal Juvenile Delinquency Act does not violate a juvenile's rights when it holds that a juvenile who consents to an adjudication hearing gives up the right to trial by jury.

In re Montrail M., 601 A.2d 1102 (Md. 1992): The merger doctrine applies to all juvenile cases and does not constitute double jeopardy.

Boyd v. State, 853 S.W.2d 263 (Ark. 1993): When a juvenile is to be tried as an adult, the rules in adult criminal trials apply.

In re Marven C., 39 Cal. Rptr. 2d 354 (Cal. App . 1995): The state carries a clear burden to prove that, based on such factors as age, experience, conduct, and knowledge, a juvenile under the age of 14 clearly has the capacity to appreciate the wrongfulness of his or her conduct.

8   Disposition of Juveniles

Eddings v. Oklahoma, 455 U.S. 104 (1982): Mitigating circumstances, including age and relevant social history, must be considered in juvenile capital cases.

Thompson v. Oklahoma, 487 U.S. 815 (1988): It is unconstitutional to sentence a juvenile to death if he or she was 15 years of age or younger at the time of the commission of the offense.

Stanford v. Kentucky, 492 U.S. 361 (1989): It is constitutional for a state to impose the death penalty on a juvenile who was 16 years old or older at the time the crime was committed.

Board of Managers of Arkansas Training School for Boys v. George, 377 F.2d 228 (8th Cir. 1967): Disposition placements based solely on race are unconstitutional.

United States ex rel. Murray v. Owens, 465 F.2d 289 (2d Cir. 1972): The New York statute that permitted a 15-year-old juvenile who had committed an act equivalent to a serious crime to be tried without a jury and sent to a correctional facility used for adult offenders did not constitute a denial of due process and was therefore constitutional.

Baker v. Hamilton, 345 F. Supp. 345 (W.D. Ky. 1972): Placement in an adult jail, without total separation from adults, is unconstitutional.

State in the Interest of D.G.W., 361 A.2d 513 (N.J. 1976): The juvenile court is authorized to impose restitution as long as due process is observed.

Thompson v. Carlson, 624 F.2d 415 (3d Cir. 1980): The subsequent adult conviction of a juvenile supersedes any youthful offender provisions attached to an earlier sentence.

In re Marcellus L., 278 Cal. Rptr. 901 (Cal. App. 1991): Evidence obtained from an otherwise illegal search may be introduced in juvenile court because the minor was subject to search at any time as a condition of probation and therefore had no reasonable expectation of privacy.

In re Binh L., 6 Cal. Rptr. 2d 678 (Cal. App. 1992): Unjustified searches can be valid if the juvenile is subject to search as a condition of probation.

Matter of Shawn V., 600 N.Y.S.2d 393 (A.D. 1993): When determining appropriate disposition placement under a least restrictive standard, a balance must be struck between the needs of the juvenile and the need for public safety.

P.W. v. State, 625 So. 2d 1207 (Ala. Cr. App. 1993): Reasonable court costs and fines can be assessed in juvenile court as long as issues of indigency, when relevant, are addressed.

In re Jamont C., 17 Cal. Rptr. 2d 336 (Cal. App. 1993): The probation condition that permitted searches without individualized suspicion did not violate the juvenile's Fourth Amendment right to privacy.

G.A.D. v. State, 865 P.2d 100 (Alaska App. 1993): Public protection prevails over a juvenile's right to a least restrictive placement.

A.S. v. State, 627 So. 2d 1265 (Fla. App. 1993): Parents of a convicted juvenile are not responsible for restitution to the victim unless the court finds evidence of a lack of good faith effort on the part of the parents to raise the juvenile.

United States v. Juvenile No. 1 (LWQ), 38 F.2d 470 (9th. Cir. 1994): A probation condition prohibiting a juvenile from carrying a gun is valid under the First Amendment.

State in Interest of T.L.V., 643 So. 2d 290 (La. App. 1994): Juvenile courts are not bound by the state's mandatory adult sentencing guidelines.

In re Tyrell J., 876 P.2d 519 (Cal. 1994): Evidence obtained by the police in a questionable search may be admissible in court if the juvenile was subject to a probation condition to submit to a search with or without a warrant.

9   Conditions of Confinement and Liability for Failure to Protect

Inmates of Boys' Training School v. Affleck, 346 F. Supp 1354 (D.R.I. 1972): Cruel and unusual conditions of confinement are anti-rehabilitative and unconstitutional.

Morales v. Turman, 383 F. Supp. 53 (E.D. Tex. 1974): Conditions of confinement in Texas constituted cruel and unusual punishment and were unconstitutional. Moreover, juveniles enjoy a constitutional right to treatment.

Nelson v. Heyne, 492 F.2d 352 (7th Cir. 1974): Conditions of confinement that constituted cruel and unusual punishment were declared unconstitutional.

Cruz v. Collazo, 450 F. Supp. 235 (D.P.R. 1978): Transferring a juvenile from a non-secure facility into a secure facility is constitutional.

C.J.W. by and through L.W. v. State, 853 P.2d 4 (Kan. 1993): The state has a duty to protect the juveniles who come under its care and custody. Failure to provide information that results in the injury of a minor places potential liability on the state.

State ex rel. Southers v. Stuckey, 867 S.W.2d 579 (Mo. App. 1993): Public administrators are immune from civil liability in the performance of discretionary duties.

10   Release and Revocation of Juveniles

Reed v. Duter, 416 F.2d 744 (7th Cir. 1969): Juveniles seeking release from institutionalization have the same right to indigency appeal and counsel as adults.

Majchszak v. Ralston, 454 F. Supp. 1137 (W.D. Wis. 1978): Denial of parole as an adult inmate cannot be based on juvenile adjudications that were conducted without legal assistance to the juvenile.

United States v. Riggans, 746 F.2d 1379 (9th Cir. 1984): Due process is not violated by long delays in the service of a probation violation warrant as long as the delay is within statutory guidelines.

Watts v. Hadden, 627 F. Supp. 727 (D. Colo. 1986): Offenders sentenced under special laws are to be afforded the benefits of those laws until no other such offenders remain in the system.

J.K.A. v. State, 855 S.W.2d 58 (Tex. App. 1993): Full due process proceedings are not required when the court reviews a violation of a probation condition for revocation purposes.

In the Matter of Lucio F.T., 888 P.2d 958 (N.M. App. 1994): The use of an adult conviction in the revocation of a juvenile's probation does not constitute double jeopardy.

Matter of Tapley, 865 P.2d 12 (Wash. App. 1994): Different release policies do not violate the equal protection clause as long as they do not establish an expectation that the minimum release date is the actual release date.

J.R.W. v. State, 879 S.W.2d 254 (Tex. App. 1994): A trial court does not exceed its authority by transferring a juvenile to prison on his or her eighteenth birthday, as allowed by state law.

In re Interest of Thomas W., 530 N.W.2d 291 (Neb. App. 1995): A detailed written statement of evidence relied upon in a probation revocation proceeding is not essential as long as the record is preserved in some manner for appeal.

In the Interest of D.S. and J.V., Minor Children, 652 So. 2d 892 (Fla. App. 1995): Probation restrictions on juvenile association are allowable as long as they can be reasonably enforced.

11 Privacy and Confidentiality of Juvenile Records and Proceedings

Davis v. Alaska, 415 U.S. 308 (1974): Despite state confidentiality laws, the probation status of a juvenile witness may be brought out by the opposing lawyer on cross-examination.

Smith v. Daily Mail Publishing Co., 443 U.S. 97 (1979): A state law making it a crime to publish the name of a juvenile charged with a crime is unconstitutional.

In re Smith, 310 N.Y.S.2d 617 (1970): It is unconstitutional to keep juvenile records when the petitions were withdrawn because of lack of evidence.

In re J.D.C., 594 A.2d 70 (D.C. App. 1991): A juvenile does not have to prove that continued exposure in the press would cause future harm before the press is excluded from the juvenile's hearing.

United States v. Three Juveniles, 862 F. Supp. 651 (D. Mass. 1994): The federal Juvenile Delinquency Act does not violate the First Amendment in mandating the closure of juvenile court proceedings.

State v. Acheson, 877 P.2d 217 (Wash. App. 1994): Juveniles can be required by state law to register under sex offender registration statutes.

The Origins of American Juvenile Justice— An Overview 1

Early America and Troubled Children

In the American colonies, children were treated in the legal system much as they were in England under English Common Law. Children age six and younger were thought to be incapable of committing a crime because of their young age; children who were between the ages of seven and 14 were also considered incapable of criminal conduct unless it could be shown that the child possessed criminal intent. Older children were legally considered to be adults.[1] There was no separate juvenile system; whether juveniles were treated in the adult system was determined by their age and/or whether they had criminal intent. Once in the adult system, the juveniles were subjected to adult sanctions.

By the early 1800s, American society experienced changing social conditions as the result of industrialization, immigration, urban growth, and new economic opportunities.[2] One response to rapidly changing and seemingly out-of-control societal problems was to turn to the legal system and laws, and to use the newly founded correctional institutions.[3] Because this resulted in increased numbers of juveniles being housed in adult prisons, reformers were concerned about what happened to troubled children who came through the adult legal system.[4]

In 1822, the New York City Society for the Prevention of Pauperism stated in its publication, "Report on the Penitentiary System in the United States," that housing children in adult prisons resulted in a "contamination of innocence."[5] The next year, that same reform group urged that action be taken that would address the issue of troubled children who offended society with their "ragged and uncleanly appearance, the vile language, and the idle and miserable habits."[6] The efforts of the reformers resulted in the 1825 opening of the New York House of Refuge—the first institution designed to hold only juveniles.[7]

The House of Refuge admitted juveniles who committed crimes, were homeless or lived in poverty, and were judged to be salvageable, or, in the words of the act itself, "proper objects" for rescue.[8] The concept of building an alternative institution housing only juveniles flourished, resulting in the opening of houses of refuge in many major American cities.[9]

Parens Patriae

Eventually, concern arose as to where houses of refuge received the legal authority to institutionalize troubled children. The answer was found in the doctrine of *parens patriae*, literally meaning "the state as parent." It "refers traditionally to the role of the state as sovereign and guardians of persons under legal disability."[10] Based on English Chancery Court law, *parens patriae* gives the state access to intervene in the lives of children.[11]

In 1838, the Pennsylvania Supreme Court found in *Ex parte Crouse*[12] that under the *parens patriae* doctrine the courts had a right to intervene in the life of a juvenile. In this case, a young girl, Mary Ann Crouse, was committed to the Philadelphia House of Refuge for incorrigibility based on her mother's testimony. Mary Ann's father sought his daughter's release by arguing that Mary Ann had received no jury trial before her incarceration, and that violated her rights. The Court held that juveniles were not entitled to the protections afforded adults under the Bill of Rights.[13] The court stated:

> The object of charity is reformation by training of inmates; by imbuing their minds with principles of morality and religion; by furnishing them with a means to earn a living; and, above all, by separating them from the corrupting influences of improper associates. *To this end, may not the natural parents, when unequal to the task of education, or unworthy of it, be superseded by the* parens patriae, *or common guardian of the community?*[14]

The court, acting as parent to the child under the doctrine of *parens patriae*, was to administer the benevolent care and training that the child missed at home. However, the ruling of the Pennsylvania Supreme Court did not state how all courts would interpret the roles of the parents, courts, and institutions.

In 1870, the Illinois Supreme Court held in *People v. Turner*[15] that *parens patriae* should not be stronger than the parents' natural rights to take care of their children. However, this decision was not followed by lower courts.[16]

In 1905, the Pennsylvania Supreme Court held in *Commonwealth v. Fisher*[17] that the courts could intervene in the life of a child for that child's good. A child, the Court stated, had the *right* to state intervention if the parents were not providing care. The legal precedent seemed to be that troubled children would be guided by the state if their parents were remiss in their obligations as parents. The state had acquired authority for intervention in the lives of its troubled children.[18]

Changing Directions in Juvenile Institutions

Although the houses of refuge were widely employed, the goals of the institutions were not fully realized. Houses of refuge were run like adult prisons, which included the trappings of security and the same routines and regulations.[19] Eventually, the houses began to experience problems that led reformers to question their effectiveness. One writer states:

> While the houses of refuge had many prominent supporters, the new youth prisons also suffered the problems that would plague later juvenile correctional facilities. For example, there is ample evidence of the use of solitary confinement, whipping, and other forms of corporal punishment. The labor system within the houses of refuge was managed by outside contractors who sometimes abused the children. . . . Violence was commonplace in these prisons and one historian estimates that 40 percent of the children escaped from the institutions or from their post-release placements.[20]

By the mid-1800s, the houses of refuge were eventually assimilated by state and local governments, and the concept of the state training, industrial, or reform school was born.[21] The first state training school opened in Massachusetts in 1847.[22] By 1890, every northern state in the United States had a refuge or reform school in operation.[23] However, although some suggest that the training schools were designed to protect the best interests of juveniles, the schools had critics.[24] These critics urged reformers to continue seeking better solutions to the problems of troubled children.

Juvenile Court

In 1899, Illinois created the first juvenile court to deal exclusively with the problems of all "troubled" children—from lawbreakers to those abused or neglected.[25]   The court was founded on the belief that the child's inappropriate behavior was the result of both family background and surroundings.[26]   The court operated informally, was considered civil in nature, focused on the child and not the offending behavior, and was designed to rehabilitate.[27]   With that mandate, it is not surprising that the processes of the court were also informal, participation of lawyers was not desired, and formal rules of evidence were not employed.[28]   The juvenile court saw no need for juveniles to be afforded constitutional protections because the court served as a surrogate parent to the child. In the words of one writer:

> Many believed that the creation of the juvenile court established the best of all possible circumstances. The interests of the individual child and the state were one and the same. The court, armed with a vision of adolescence and how adolescents and parents should and should not behave, with legal definitions of adolescence, with legal jurisdiction to intervene, and with technologies of intervention, was in place.[29]

The concept of a separate court to handle troubled children became so popular that within 25 years of the creation of the first court in Illinois, all remaining states, except two, had followed suit.[30]   For the next 67 years, the courts operated under the premise of *parens patriae*, and the belief that the juvenile justice system operated in the best interests of the child. Ensuring that juveniles were entitled to be helped and that their best interests were the guiding light, the court assumed the right to intervene in the individual children's lives; yet it gave scant attention to monitoring the system it had created.[31]   It was not until the 1960s that the public and media scrutiny of the juvenile justice system prompted significant procedural changes.

Providing Due Process Rights

A significant period of change and reform in the juvenile justice system occurred in the 1960s and 1970s as the juvenile justice system, the courts, and the institutions came under criticism from numerous sides. As stated by one observer:

> Critics of the juvenile court became more vocal and more organized. The most politically potent attack on the court charged that judges were overly lenient with violent and serious offenders. Some critics questioned the court's practice of mixing dependent and neglected youth with serious criminal offenders, while others alleged that the court was particularly punitive in handling female status offenders. The mounting attacks on the court were

fueled by periodic reports of scandals and child abuse in juvenile correctional facilities.[32]

Historically, the U.S. Supreme Court had left the juvenile court alone. In the 1960s, however, a number of cases were sent to the Supreme Court. The Supreme Court perhaps realized that the juvenile justice system was in no position to reform itself. The Supreme Court abandoned its "hands-off" policy and decided to intervene in juvenile proceedings.[33] From 1966 to 1975, it handed down a series of decisions that reshaped the juvenile justice court process. In *Kent v. United States*,[34] the Supreme Court gave juveniles the right to a hearing, to counsel, and to a statement of the reasons for transferring a juvenile to adult court in certification cases. Though the focus of the *Kent* case was on the certification process, the Court expressed concern about other aspects of juvenile court. Justice Abe Fortas stated:

> While there can be no doubt of the original laudable purpose of the juvenile courts, studies and critiques of recent years raise serious questions as to whether actual performances measure well enough against purpose to make tolerable the immunity of the process from the reach of constitutional guarantees applicable to adults. There is much evidence that some juvenile courts . . . lack the personnel, facilities and techniques to perform adequately as representatives of the State in a *parens patriae* capacity, at least with respect to children charged with law violation. There is evidence, in fact, that there may by grounds for concern that the juvenile receives the worst of both worlds: that he gets neither the protections accorded to adults nor the solicitous care and regenerative treatment postulated for children.[35]

The following year, the landmark juvenile case of *In re Gault*[36] gave juveniles the basic rights afforded adults during adjudication of cases that might result in confinement in an institution in which their freedom would be curtailed. Specifically, juveniles were given the right against self-incrimination, the right to notice of charges, the right to confront and cross-examine witnesses, and the right to counsel. Perhaps the significance of *Gault* is best summarized in the Court opinion, in which the Court said that: ". . . neither the Fourteenth Amendment nor the Bill of Rights is for adults alone."[37] *Gault* gave juveniles certain due process rights in juvenile adjudication proceedings. Correspondingly, more than any case, *Gault* signaled the demise of the pure *parens patriae* approach to juvenile justice.

In 1970, in *In re Winship*,[38] the Court held that juveniles had to be afforded the same level of proof that was given an adult—proof beyond a reasonable doubt. In 1971, in *McKeiver v. Pennsylvania*,[39] the Supreme Court did not extend to juveniles the right to trial by jury. The Court stressed that it did not want the juvenile court to lose all of the distinctions that kept it separate from the criminal court. In 1975, in *Breed v. Jones*,[40] the Court held that adjudicating a juvenile delinquent, and then transferring that juvenile to the adult system to stand trial for the same offense constituted double jeopardy and was unconstitutional. What was once considered a purely civil case was now considered a criminal case under the double jeopardy provision of the Constitution.

During the due process era, the Supreme Court afforded juveniles several constitutional rights. The Court's decisions also created an adversarial system of juvenile justice and therefore reshaped the juvenile court process. The legal approach, however, did not cure the problems of the juvenile justice system.

A Plethora of Reform Movements

While the Supreme Court was handing down significant decisions affording juveniles constitutional rights, other reform movements surfaced. Many were aimed at the allegations of the lack of success of juvenile correctional institutions and rehabilitative programs. In 1973, the National Advisory Commission on Criminal Justice Standards and Goals stated that "[t]he failure of major juvenile and youth institutions to reduce crime is incontestable."[41] Furthermore, the Commission asserted that "the primary purpose to be served in dealing with juveniles is their rehabilitation and reintegration, a purpose that cannot be served satisfactorily by state institutions."[42]

Congress and some states employed various reforms to lessen reliance on juvenile institutions. These reforms included the Juvenile Justice and Delinquency Prevention Act of 1974, deinstitutionalization, decriminalization, diversion, and judicial intervention.[43] Although many states were in the midst of juvenile justice reforms by the time the Juvenile Justice and Delinquency Prevention Act was passed in 1974, the Act was important because it indicated that Congress agreed that the "present system of juvenile justice [was] failing miserably."[44] On a more practical level, the Act required that juveniles be removed from adult jails, and that programs be created to provide alternatives to youth who were in inappropriate institutional placements.[45]

Deinstitutionalization involves the concept of moving away from reliance on institutions, meaning either moving juveniles out of the facilities completely or into smaller institutions based in a community setting.[46] By contrast, decriminalization refers to the process of taking status offenders and their offenses—such as running away from home, skipping school, and disobeying parents, out of the realm of delinquent conduct.[47] States generally have not removed status offenders from their juvenile court jurisdiction, but they have reclassified status offender categories.[48] Now juvenile statutes include provisions to differentiate status offenders, such as Children in Need of Supervision (CHINS), from delinquent children.[49] Diversion programs redirect youth who are not appropriate candidates for juvenile court into other directions.[50] Though diversion programs were prevalent in the 1970s, they had virtually disappeared by the 1980s due to lack of funding, changing philosophies, and arguments about their effectiveness.[51]

The focus of all these movements was to get children out of juvenile correctional facilities if their placement was inappropriate, non-beneficial, or in violation of their constitutional rights. The main goal of these programs—to curb the increasing numbers of inappropriate placements into juvenile institutions—was not realized. At a time when crime statistics showed a decrease in juvenile crime rates, juvenile institutions continued to increase in population.[52]

In sum, the 1960s and 1970s were a time of reform in juvenile justice. The Supreme Court changed juvenile court practices, while other reforms addressed issues related to the most effective way to deal with children after they came through juvenile court. By the mid-1970s, however, the sentiment toward the handling of juvenile offenders began to shift.

Getting Tougher with Juvenile Offenders

The effectiveness of the juvenile justice system and its previous course of rehabilitative ideals ran afoul of the conservative agenda of the late 1970s and the 1980s.[53] Public concern about juvenile crime may have motivated state governments to change the direction of juvenile justice policy—and to "get tough" when dealing with juvenile offenders.[54]

Reformers called for various measures, among them: "(1) vigorous prosecution of serious and violent juvenile offenders, (2) a new focus on the plight of 'missing children,' (3) mandatory and harsher sentencing laws for young offenders, (4) national crusades against drugs and pornography, and (5) programs to reduce school violence."[55] Many changes began to take place in the juvenile justice arena that were "motivated by the concepts of deterrence and deserts."[56] Substantial changes resulted primarily in more transfers to criminal court and in increasing numbers of juveniles in correctional facilities.[57] Legislators changed transfer statutes by lowering the age when jurisdiction could be waived, or excluding certain acts from the jurisdiction of the juvenile court.[58]

Today and Beyond

This trend from the late 1970s and the 1980s has continued unabated in the field of juvenile justice today. It is fueled by reports of increasing juvenile crime rates and the recurring belief that the juvenile justice system cannot eradicate, or even slow down, juvenile crime, especially violent juvenile crime. According to James Fox:

> A growing number of teens and preteens see few feasible or attractive alternatives to violence, drug use and gang membership. For them, the American Dream is a nightmare: There may be little to live for and to strive for, but plenty to die and even kill for. . . . Even if the recent surge in teenage homicide rates slows, our nation faces a future juvenile violence problem that may make today's epidemic pale in comparison.[59]

Backed by reported increases in juvenile crime and public demand, virtually every state legislature has continued their "get tough" approach to juvenile crime by initiating some type of governmental response—whether legislative or executive in nature.[60] According to recent research conducted by the Office of Juvenile Justice and Delinquency Prevention, since 1992 there have been five areas that these responses have addressed. They are: (1) the continued expansion of the use of transfer to the adult court, (2) the creation of new correctional programs, (3) the creation of new alternatives in judicial dispositions, (4) opening up the juvenile court by eroding the once-strict confidentiality mandates, and (5) allowing the victims of juvenile crime to have a voice in the juvenile justice system.[61] Nationwide, the underlying philosophy of the juvenile court appears to be shifting from treatment to punishment.[62] This trend is likely to continue in the immediate future. Whether this is the answer to the enduring problem of juvenile offenders and juvenile crime remains a topic of great debate.

The juvenile justice system has adopted its own language in an effort to remove itself philosophically from the trappings of the adult criminal court. Below is a chart that notes the differences. It is important to understand that this chart reflects the traditional juvenile justice system, much of which, however, is currently undergoing tremendous changes philosophically and procedurally.

Differences in Terminology Between Adult and Juvenile Court Proceedings

Adult Proceedings	Juvenile Proceedings
1. Criminal in nature	1. Civil in nature
2. Arrested	2. Taken into custody
3. Charged	3. Prosecutor petitions the court for juvenile to be adjudicated
4. Accused of crime under penal code	4. Alleged violation comes under the juvenile or family code
5. Given a public trial—formal	5. Given a private hearing—more informal
6. Found guilty of a criminal offense by an impartial judge or jury	6. Found to have engaged in delinquent conduct—adjudicated delinquent by a judge acting as a kindly parent
7. Sentenced	7. Dispositioned
8. Might get probation	8. Might get probation
9. Might be sent to jail, penitentiary, or other place of incarceration	9. Might be committed to state facility for juveniles
10. If incarcerated, serves sentence	10. If committed, most likely for an indeterminate amount of time—longest possible—until age of majority
11. Judge or jury determines length of stay	11. Facility determines when released—based on when rehabilitated
12. Purpose of incarceration—punishment and deterrence	12. Purpose of commitment—rehabilitation and salvation
13. Released on parole	13. Released on aftercare

Notes

1   James F. Short, *Delinquency and Society* (1990). George Kelling, "The Historical Legacy." In *From Children to Citizens: Volume I: The Mandate for Juvenile Justice* (Mark Harrison Moore, ed., 1987).

2   George Kelling, "The Historical Legacy." In *From Children to Citizens: Volume I: The Mandate for Juvenile Justice* (Mark Harrison Moore, ed. 1987).

3   George Kelling, "The Historical Legacy." In *From Children to Citizens: Volume I: The Mandate for Juvenile Justice* (Mark Harrison Moore, ed. 1987).

4   Cliff Roberson, *Exploring Juvenile Justice: Theory and Practice* (1996).

5   Cited in Stanford Fox, "Juvenile Justice Reform: An Historical Perspective," 22 *Stanford Law Review* 1187–1239 (1970) at 1189.

6   Cited in Stanford Fox, "Juvenile Justice Reform: An Historical Perspective," 22 *Stanford Law Review* 1187–1239 (1970) at 1189.

7   Cliff Roberson, *Exploring Juvenile Justice: Theory and Practice* (1996).

8   Cited in Stanford Fox, "Juvenile Justice Reform: An Historical Perspective," 22 *Stanford Law Review* 1187–1239 (1970) at 1190.

9   Cliff Roberson, *Exploring Juvenile Justice: Theory and Practice* (1996).

10   *Black's Law Dictionary* (1979) at 1003.

11   James F. Short, *Delinquency and Society* (1990).

12   *Ex parte Crouse*, 4 Whart. 9 (Pa. 1838).

13   John Whitehead and Stephen Lab, *Juvenile Justice: An Introduction* (1990).

14   Cited (emphasis added) in Barry Krisberg, *The Juvenile Court: Reclaiming the Vision*. Washington, DC: The National Council on Crime and Delinquency (1988).

15   *People v. Turner*, 55 Ill. 280 (1879).

16   John Whitehead and Stephen Lab, *Juvenile Justice: An Introduction* (1990).

17   *Commonwealth v. Fisher*, 213 Pa. 48 (1905).

18   John Whitehead and Stephen Lab, *Juvenile Justice: An Introduction* (1990).

[19]   Cliff Roberson, *Exploring Juvenile Justice: Theory and Practice* (1996).

[20]   Barry Krisberg, *The Juvenile Court: Reclaiming the Vision*. Washington, DC: The National Council on Crime and Delinquency (1988) at 3.

[21]   Barry Krisberg, *The Juvenile Court: Reclaiming the Vision*. Washington, DC: The National Council on Crime and Delinquency (1988).

[22]   George Kelling, "The Historical Legacy." In *From Children to Citizens: Volume I: The Mandate for Juvenile Justice* (Mark Harrison Moore, ed. 1987).

[23]   Barry Krisberg, *The Juvenile Court: Reclaiming the Vision*. Washington, DC: The National Council on Crime and Delinquency (1988).

[24]   Allen Breed and Barry Krisberg, "Juvenile Corrections: Is There a Future?" *Corrections Today*. December, 48:8:14-20 (1986).

[25]   Barry Krisberg, *The Juvenile Court: Reclaiming the Vision*. Washington, DC: The National Council on Crime and Delinquency (1988) at 3.

[26]   George Kelling, "The Historical Legacy." In *From Children to Citizens: Volume I: The Mandate for Juvenile Justice* (Mark Harrison Moore, ed. 1987).

[27]   George Kelling, "The Historical Legacy." In *From Children to Citizens: Volume I: The Mandate for Juvenile Justice* (Mark Harrison Moore, ed. 1987).

[28]   Cliff Roberson, *Exploring Juvenile Justice: Theory and Practice* (1996).

[29]   George Kelling, "The Historical Legacy." In *From Children to Citizens: Volume I: The Mandate for Juvenile Justice* (Mark Harrison Moore, ed. 1987) at 42.

[30]   Barry Krisberg and James Austin, *Reinventing Juvenile Justice* (1993).

[31]   George Kelling, "The Historical Legacy." In *From Children to Citizens: Volume I: The Mandate for Juvenile Justice* (Mark Harrison Moore, ed. 1987).

[32]   Barry Krisberg, *The Juvenile Court: Reclaiming the Vision*. Washington, DC: The National Council on Crime and Delinquency (1988) at 6.

[33]   Cliff Roberson, *Exploring Juvenile Justice: Theory and Practice* (1996).

[34]   *Kent v. United States*, 383 U.S. 541 (1966).

[35]   *Kent v. United States*, 383 U.S. 541 (1966) at 555-556.

36   *In re Gault*, 387 U.S. 1 (1967).

37   *In re Gault*, 387 U.S. 1 (1967) at 13.

38   *In re Winship*, 397 U.S. 358 (1970).

39   *McKeiver v. Pennsylvania*, 403 U.S. 548 (1971).

40   *Breed v. Jones*, 421 U.S. 519 (1975).

41   Cited in Ira Schwartz, In *Justice for Juveniles: Rethinking the Best Interests of the Child* (1989) at 6.

42   Cited in Ira Schwartz, In *Justice for Juveniles: Rethinking the Best Interests of the Child* (1989) at 6-7.

43   Barry Krisberg, *The Juvenile Court: Reclaiming the Vision*. Washington, DC: The National Council on Crime and Delinquency (1988). Allen Breed and Barry Krisberg, "Juvenile Corrections: Is There a Future?" *Corrections Today*. December, 48:8:14-20 (1986). Ira Schwartz, In *Justice for Juveniles: Rethinking the Best Interests of the Child* (1989).

44   Birch Bayh quoted in Ira Schwartz, In *Justice for Juveniles: Rethinking the Best Interests of the Child* (1989) at 4.

45   Ira Schwartz, In *Justice for Juveniles: Rethinking the Best Interests of the Child* (1989).

46   Cliff Roberson, *Exploring Juvenile Justice: Theory and Practice* (1996). Barry Krisberg, *The Juvenile Court: Reclaiming the Vision*. Washington, DC: The National Council on Crime and Delinquency (1988).

47   Cliff Roberson, *Exploring Juvenile Justice: Theory and Practice* (1996).

48   Barry Krisberg, *The Juvenile Court: Reclaiming the Vision*. Washington, DC: The National Council on Crime and Delinquency (1988).

49   Barry Krisberg, *The Juvenile Court: Reclaiming the Vision*. Washington, DC: The National Council on Crime and Delinquency (1988).

50   Barry Krisberg, *The Juvenile Court: Reclaiming the Vision*. Washington, DC: The National Council on Crime and Delinquency (1988).

[51]   Barry Krisberg, *The Juvenile Court: Reclaiming the Vision*. Washington, DC: The National Council on Crime and Delinquency (1988).

[52]   Barry Krisberg, *The Juvenile Court: Reclaiming the Vision*. Washington, DC: The National Council on Crime and Delinquency (1988).

[53]   Barry Krisberg, *The Juvenile Court: Reclaiming the Vision*. Washington, DC: The National Council on Crime and Delinquency (1988).

[54]   Ira Schwartz, In *Justice for Juveniles: Rethinking the Best Interests of the Child* (1989).

[55]   Barry Krisberg, *The Juvenile Court: Reclaiming the Vision*. Washington, DC: The National Council on Crime and Delinquency (1988) at 11.

[56]   Barry Krisberg, *The Juvenile Court: Reclaiming the Vision*. Washington, DC: The National Council on Crime and Delinquency (1988) at 12.

[57]   Barry Krisberg and James Austin, *Reinventing Juvenile Justice* (1993).

[58]   Barry Krisberg, *The Juvenile Court: Reclaiming the Vision*. Washington, DC: The National Council on Crime and Delinquency (1988).

[59]   James Fox, *Trends in Juvenile Violence: A Report to the United States Attorney General on Current and Future Rates of Juvenile Offending*. Washington, DC: Bureau of Justice Statistics, United States Department of Justice (1996) at 2-3.

[60]   Patricia Torbet, Richard Gable, Hunter Hurst IV, Imogene Montgomery, Linda Szymanski, and Douglas Thomas, *State Responses to Serious and Violent Juvenile Crime*. Washington, DC: National Center for Juvenile Justice. Office of Juvenile Justice and Delinquency Prevention. U.S. Department of Justice, Office of Justice Programs (1996).

[61]   Patricia Torbet, Richard Gable, Hunter Hurst IV, Imogene Montgomery, Linda Szymanski, and Douglas Thomas, *State Responses to Serious and Violent Juvenile Crime*. Washington, DC: National Center for Juvenile Justice. Office of Juvenile Justice and Delinquency Prevention. U.S. Department of Justice, Office of Justice Programs (1996).

[62]   Patricia Torbet, Richard Gable, Hunter Hurst IV, Imogene Montgomery, Linda Szymanski, and Douglas Thomas, *State Responses to Serious and Violent Juvenile Crime*. Washington, DC: National Center for Juvenile Justice. Office of Juvenile Justice and Delinquency Prevention. U.S. Department of Justice, Office of Justice Programs (1996).

Processing of Juveniles by the Police

2

I. United States Supreme Court Cases

Haley v. State of Ohio (1948)
Gallegos v. Colorado (1962)
Fare v. Michael C. (1979)
New Jersey v. T.L.O. (1985)

II. Lower Court Cases

Harling v. United States (1961)
United States v. Miller (1972)
United States v. Ramsey (1973)
United States v. Barfield (1975)
United States v. Sechrist (1981)
United States v. Bernard S. (1986)
Cason v. Cook (1987)
Smith v. State (1992)
In the Interest of J.L., A Child (1993)
In the Interest of S.A.W. (1993)
In re Starvon J. (1994)
In re Gilbert E. (1995)
State v. Sugg (1995)

Introduction

Police officers play a vital role in all communities in the prevention and control of crime and delinquency. Their presence at public gatherings where juveniles are present, such as sporting events, dances, or concerts, is designed to serve as a deterrent to destructive and violent behavior. They have broad discretion in the handling of juveniles observed or reported committing unlawful acts, and serve as the major source of referral to juvenile courts. They are frequently the first contact a juvenile has with the criminal justice system.[1]

Handling juveniles can produce major role conflicts for police officers and their agencies. In many cases they find their primary duty, law enforcement, undercut by their legal and moral obligation to act in the best interests of the child. Many officers dislike getting involved in juvenile matters because law enforcement involving juveniles is likely to be held in low regard by fellow police officers. Police officers are prone to use informal procedures in dealing with juveniles. It is estimated that between 40 and 50 percent of all juveniles taken into custody by the police are handled informally within the agency itself or referred to community service agencies that specialize in juvenile offenders.[2]

The major areas of police efforts in dealing with juveniles include discovery and investigation of delinquency, disposition of cases, protection of juveniles, and delinquency prevention. While rarely bringing rewards in the way of promotions or job satisfaction to police officers, most major police agencies are renewing their efforts in dealing with juvenile crime in an effort to contain the overall crime rates in their areas.[3] As a result, more and more officers will be assigned to deal with juvenile delinquency issues, their interaction extending from street encounters to juvenile court appearances. Officer awareness of the special circumstances of juveniles will enhance the quality of interactions with juveniles early in criminal justice processing.

This chapter focuses on the variety of contacts between juveniles and police. It presents the fundamental rights enjoyed by juveniles and the differences in police treatment of juveniles when no landmark cases are established to guide such interaction.

Haley, Gallegos, Fare, and *T.L.O.*, all United States Supreme Court cases, set the constitutional rights available to all juveniles in these proceedings. *Haley* prohibits the use of coerced confessions in adult judicial proceedings against juveniles. *Gallegos* further explores the proper use of juvenile confessions, the Court saying that isolation of a juvenile for prolonged periods is in fact coercion and renders any incriminating statements made by the juvenile inadmissible in court. *Fare* further defines the line between voluntary and involuntary statements made by juveniles while in police custody, determining that a juvenile who asks for a probation officer is not, by that request, asking for a lawyer.

Each situation involving a juvenile must be weighed on its own merits so as to distinguish between voluntary statements and involuntary statements.

T.L.O. is a search and seizure case involving the search of a juvenile on school property. The Court found that due to the need to maintain order and control in schools, school officials need only have reasonable grounds to search a juvenile and his or her property when suspected of violating school rules. Warrants and probable cause, both required in police searches, are not required in school searches conducted by school administrators.

Lower court cases briefed in the chapter cover the gamut from the acquisition of fingerprints to the role of police liaison officers in school settings. Street stops and resulting frisk searches were questioned in *In the Interest of J.L., A Child* and *In the Interest of S.A.W.*, while later cases revisit issues involving the Fifth Amendment, the Fourth Amendment, age deception, and deception concerning involvement in a crime.

These later cases, although from lower courts and therefore lacking the authority of landmark Supreme Court cases, paint a picture of the continuing conflict between the law and juveniles who come in contact with the criminal justice system.

Notes

[1]   Peter C. Kratcoski and Lucille D. Kratcoski, *Juvenile Delinquency* (1996).

[2]   Larry J. Siegel and Joseph J. Senna, *Juvenile Delinquency: Theory, Practice & Law* (1991).

[3]   Peter C. Kratcoski and Lucille D. Kratcoski, *Juvenile Delinquency* (1996).

I.   UNITED STATES SUPREME COURT CASES

Haley v. State of Ohio
68 S. Ct. 302 (1948)

Coerced confessions are not admissible as evidence in adult proceedings against juveniles.

FACTS: At midnight on October 14, 1945, a confectionery store was robbed and its owner shot and killed. Five days later, Haley, a 15-year, eight-month-old black male, was arrested for his alleged participation in the robbery/murder. He was taken to police headquarters for questioning. For five hours Haley was questioned by various police officers, usually in teams of two. At no time during the questioning was Haley informed of his right to legal counsel and legal counsel was not sought for Haley. After being shown documents that were alleged to be confessions of the other two participants in the robbery, Haley confessed. Haley was then held incommunicado for three days before formal charges were filed. An attorney retained by Haley's mother attempted to see him twice during this period and was turned away. Haley's mother attempted to see him but was denied access for five days after his arrest. At Haley's trial the defense objected to the admission of the confession on the grounds that the process by which it was acquired violated Haley's due process rights under the Fourteenth Amendment.

ISSUE: Does the due process clause of the Fourteenth Amendment prohibit the use of coerced confessions against juveniles? YES.

DECISION: The Fourteenth Amendment prohibits police from violating the due process clause in obtaining admissions or confessions from adults and juveniles. Coerced confessions cannot be used in court.

REASON: "We do not think the methods used in obtaining this confession can be squared with the due process of law which the Fourteenth Amendment commands.

"What transpired would make us pause for careful inquiry if a mature man was involved. And when, as here, a mere child—an easy victim of the law—is before us, special care in scrutinizing the record must be used. Age 15 is a tender and difficult age for a boy of any race. He cannot be judged by more exacting standards of maturity.

"No friend stood at the side of this 15-year-old boy as the police, working in relays, questioned him hour after hour, from midnight until dawn. No lawyer stood guard to make sure that the police went so far and no farther, to see that they stopped short of the point where he became the victim of coercion . . .

"This disregard of the standards of decency [is] underlined by the fact that he was held incommunicado for over three days during which the lawyer retained to represent him twice tried to see him and twice was refused admission. A photographer was admitted at once, but his closest friend—his mother—was not allowed to see him for over five days after his arrest. It is said that these events are not germane to the present problem because they happened after the confession was made. But they show such a callous attitude of the police towards the safeguards which respect for ordinary standards of human relationships compels that we take with a grain of salt their present apologia that the five-hour grilling of this boy was conducted in a fair and dispassionate manner."

CASE SIGNIFICANCE: In this case, the Court, for the first time, suggested that, despite *parens patriae* (the doctrine stating that the state serves as the "parent" of the juvenile), there are constitutional requirements that protect all accused persons, whether they are adults or juveniles. The Court did not go so far as to say that juveniles had constitutional rights, but it held that police dealings with juveniles cannot be held to a lower standard than police dealings with adults. Juveniles cannot protect themselves against police misconduct as adults can, hence it is only reasonable that a juvenile be given the same, if not greater protection, against coercion than adults.

This case was decided in 1948—long before the exclusionary rule was extended to the states by the Supreme Court. In 1961, in the case of *Mapp v. Ohio*, 367 U.S. 643 (1961), the Court applied the exclusionary rule, which provides that evidence obtained illegally is inadmissible as evidence in a court of law, to the states. Had this case been decided after 1961, the Court would certainly have used the exclusionary rule to reject the evidence instead of resorting to the due process clause of the Fourteenth Amendment.

This decision is easy to accept today, but was not as easily reached in 1948 under the pure *parens patriae* philosophy. At present, the concept that juveniles deserve better protection than adults against possible police abuses is accepted. This was not the case in 1948 when *parens patriae* insulated police and courts from judicial scrutiny on the ground that these agencies were entitled to greater authority when dealing with juveniles.

Gallegos v. Colorado
370 U.S. 49 (1962)

The isolation of a juvenile for prolonged periods of time by the police may result in confessions that are involuntarily obtained.

FACTS: Gallegos, a 14-year-old, and a juvenile companion followed an elderly male to his hotel, entered his room on a ruse, assaulted and overpowered him, stole $13.00 from his pockets, and fled. Gallegos was picked up by the police and admitted his part in the assault and robbery. After his arrest, Gallegos was isolated from his family for five days, even though his mother attempted to see him. He was held at Juvenile Hall, where he was kept in security, although he was allowed to eat with the other inmates. Formally questioned by police while in confinement, Gallegos gave a confession that an officer recorded in longhand. There is no record of Gallegos having received his *Miranda* warnings or any other advice by a friendly adult. Gallegos was found delinquent, based on the assault and robbery incident, and was committed to the Boys' Industrial School for an indeterminate period. The victim, who had been hospitalized since the assault and robbery, subsequently died. Gallegos was then charged with first degree murder. The jury found him guilty based primarily on the confession signed by Gallegos after he had been held incommunicado for five days.

ISSUE: May police isolation of a juvenile for prolonged periods result in confessions that are considered involuntary? YES.

DECISION: The isolation of a juvenile for prolonged periods by the police may result in confessions that are deemed involuntarily obtained and in violation of the juvenile's due process rights.

REASON: "Confessions obtained by 'secret inquisitorial processes' are suspect since such procedures are conducive to the use of physical and psychological pressure.

"The fact that petitioner was only 14 years old puts this case on the same footing as *Haley v. Ohio*, 68 S. Ct. 302 (1948). There was no evidence of prolonged questioning. But the five-day detention—during which time the boy's mother unsuccessfully tried to see him and he was cut off from contact with any lawyer or adult advisor—gives the case an ominous cast. The prosecution says that the boy was advised of his right to counsel but that he did not ask either for a lawyer or for his parents. But a 14-year-old boy, no matter how sophisticated, is unlikely to have any conception of what will confront him when he is made accessible only to the police.

"The prosecution says that the youth and immaturity of the petitioner and the five-day detention are irrelevant because the basic ingredients of the confession came tumbling out as soon as he was arrested. But if we took that position, it would, with all deference, be in callous disregard of this boy's constitutional rights. He cannot be compared with an adult in full possession of his senses and knowledgeable of the consequences of his admissions. He would have no way of knowing what the consequences of his confession were without advice as to his rights—from someone concerned with securing him those rights—and without the aid of more mature judgment as to the steps he should take in the predicament in which he found himself. A lawyer or an adult relative or friend could have given the petitioner the protection which his own immaturity could not. Adult advice would have put him on less unequal footing with his interrogators. Without some adult protection against this inequality, a 14-year-old boy would not be able to know, let alone assert, such constitutional rights as he had. To allow this conviction to stand would, in effect, be to treat him as if he had no constitutional rights.

"The youth of the petitioner, the long detention, the failure to send for his parents, the failure immediately to bring him before the judge of the Juvenile Court, the failure to see to it that he had the advice of a lawyer or a friend—all these combine to make us conclude that the formal confession on which this conviction may have rested . . . was obtained in violation of due process."

CASE SIGNIFICANCE: This case established age as a factor in determining whether coercion was used in focused accusatory questioning. The youthful age of the defendant and the length of isolation imposed by the police made it tempting for the juvenile to confess. The defendant in this case was only 14 years old. It is difficult to believe that he fully understood his constitutional right to counsel during questioning. It is also difficult to believe that he had the will to withstand the pressure during the five days of isolation. Given these circumstances, it is easy to conclude that the confession of the juvenile was coerced.

Fare v. Michael C.
442 U.S. 707 (1979)

A request by a juvenile to see his or her probation officer is not equivalent to asking for a lawyer.

FACTS: Michael C., a juvenile, was taken into police custody under suspicion of murder. Prior to questioning by two police officers, Michael C. was advised of his *Miranda* rights. When asked if he wanted to waive his right to have an attorney present during questioning, he responded by asking for his probation officer. He was informed by the police that the probation officer would be contacted later, but that he could talk to the police if he wanted. Michael C. agreed to talk and during questioning made statements and drew sketches that incriminated him. He was charged with murder in juvenile court. Michael C. moved to suppress the incriminating sketches, alleging that they were obtained in violation of his *Miranda* rights and that his request to see his probation officer was, in effect, an assertion of his right to remain silent and that this was equivalent to his having requested an attorney.

ISSUE: Is the request by a juvenile probationer to see his or her probation officer during police questioning the same as a request for the assistance of an attorney, thus invoking the Fifth Amendment right to remain silent pursuant to *Miranda*? NO.

DECISION: The request by a juvenile probationer during police questioning to see his or her probation officer, after having received the *Miranda* warnings by the police, is not equivalent to asking for a lawyer and therefore is not considered an assertion of the right to remain silent. Evidence voluntarily given by the juvenile probationer is therefore admissible in court in a subsequent criminal trial.

REASON: "The rule in *Miranda*, . . . was based on this Court's perception that the lawyer occupies a critical position in our legal system because of his unique ability to protect the Fifth Amendment right of a client undergoing custodial interrogation. Because of this special ability of the lawyer to help the client preserve his Fifth Amendment rights once the client becomes enmeshed in the adversary process, the Court found that 'the right to have counsel present at the interrogation is indispensable to the protection of the Fifth Amendment privilege under the system' established by the Court.

"A probation officer is not in the same posture [as is a lawyer] with regard to either the accused or the system of justice as a whole. Often he is not trained in the law, and so is not in a position to advise the accused as to his legal rights. Neither is he a trained advocate, skilled in the representation of the interests of his client before police and court. He does not assume the power to act on behalf of his client by virtue of his status as advisor, nor are the communications of the accused to the probation officer shielded by the lawyer-client privilege.

"Moreover, the probation officer is the employee of the State which seeks to prosecute the alleged offender. He is a peace officer, and as such is allied, to a greater or lesser extent, with his fellow peace officers. He owes an obligation to the State notwithstanding the obligation he may also owe the juvenile under his supervision. In most cases, the probation officer is duty-bound to report wrongdoing by the juvenile when it comes to his attention, even if by communication from the juvenile himself."

CASE SIGNIFICANCE: Although this case involved a juvenile probationer, the Court's decision should apply to adult probationers and parolees as well. In essence, the Court said that a probation officer does not perform the same function as a lawyer, therefore a request by a probationer to see his or her probation officer is not equivalent to a request to see a lawyer. The Court then proceeded to distinguish between a probation officer and a lawyer. First, the Court stated that communications of the accused to the probation officer are not shielded by the lawyer-client privilege. This means that information given by a client to the probation officer may be disclosed in court, unlike information shared by a client with a lawyer. Second, the Court makes clear that a probation officer's loyalty and obligation is to the state, despite any obligation he or she may also have to the probationer. This means that, despite an officer's feelings for or rapport with the client, there should be no question of where his or her loyalties lay. Professionalism requires that these two obligations not be confused and that it be made clear to the probationer and the officer, particularly in situations in which confidences are shared, that the officer's loyalty is ultimately with the state, not with the probationer.

———

New Jersey v. T.L.O.
469 U.S. 325 (1985)

Public school officials need only "reasonable grounds" to search juveniles; they do not need a warrant or probable cause.

FACTS: A 14-year-old girl was discovered smoking cigarettes in a school lavatory in violation of school rules. She was taken to the principal's officer by a high school teacher. When the student denied that she had been smoking, the assistant vice principal demanded to see her purse. Inside the purse, a pack of cigarettes and a package of cigarette rolling papers, commonly associated with the use of marijuana, were discovered. The assistant vice principal then proceeded to search the purse thoroughly and found marijuana, a pipe, plastic bags, a substantial amount of money, an index card containing a list of names of students who owed her money, and two letters that implicated her in marijuana dealing. The state brought delinquency charges against the student in juvenile court. She moved to have the evidence found in her purse suppressed, alleging that the search was illegal.

ISSUE: Do public high school officials need probable cause or a warrant in order to search juveniles? NO.

DECISION: Public school officials do not need a warrant or probable cause before conducting a search. For a search to be valid, all they need are "reasonable grounds" to suspect that the search will produce evidence that the student has violated or is violating either the law or the rules of the school.

REASON: "Today's public school officials do not merely exercise authority voluntarily conferred on them by individual parents; rather, they act in furtherance of publicly mandated educational and disciplinary policies.

"It is evident that the school setting requires some easing of the restrictions to which searches by public authorities are ordinarily subject. The warrant requirement, in particular, is unsuited to the school environment: requiring a teacher to obtain a warrant before searching a child suspected of an infraction of school rules (or of the criminal law) would unduly interfere with the maintenance of the swift and informal disciplinary procedures needed in the schools.

"The school setting also requires some modification of the level of suspicion of illicit activity needed to justify a search. . . . Under ordinary circumstances, a search of a student by a teacher or other school official will be 'justified at its inception' when there are reasonable grounds for suspecting that the search will turn up evidence that the student has violated or is violating either a law or the rules of the school. Such a search will be permissible in its scope when the measures adopted are reasonably related to the objectives of the search and not excessively intrusive in light of the age and sex of the student and the nature of the infraction."

CASE SIGNIFICANCE: This case clarifies the issue of whether public school officials must obtain a warrant and have probable cause before conducting a search and what degree of certainty is needed for a valid search by public school officials. The Court said that public school officials are representatives of the state and as such are governed by the provisions of the Fourth Amendment. But the Court also recognized that in order to maintain an environment in which learning can take place, some restrictions placed on public authorities by the Fourth Amendment had to be eased. Therefore, the Court ruled that public school officials: (1) need not obtain a warrant before conducting a search; and (2) do not need probable cause to justify a search. All they need are reasonable grounds—a lower standard of certainty.

Whether the ruling applies to college students or to students attending private high schools was not addressed by the Court. It would be reasonable to assume, however, that this ruling would also apply to public elementary school students, although the age of the students searched would probably have relevance to the court. On the other hand, lower court decisions have usually held that college students, regardless of age, are considered adults and therefore this case probably does not apply to college students or campuses. It is noted that this case applies to high school teachers and administrators who are conducting a search. It does not apply to police officers who are bound by the "probable cause" requirement even in school searches. The only possible exception might be if the officers are to perform the search at the request of public school authorities for non-criminal activities.

II. LOWER COURT CASES

Harling v. United States
295 F.2d 161 (D.D.C. 1961)

Confessions made to police are not admissible if the juvenile is subsequently tried as an adult.

FACTS: Harling, 17 years old, was taken into custody on charges of assault with a dangerous weapon and robbery. He was placed in a lineup and identified as one of the two participants in the robbery and the individual who stabbed a clerk during the robbery. Harling was charged as a delinquent in juvenile court. He was later identified by a second witness as one of two assailants in the crime, whereupon he made statements that implicated him in the crime. Harling was returned to the Receiving Home to await juvenile court proceedings. Two weeks later, the Juvenile Court waived jurisdiction and ordered Harling to stand trial as an adult in circuit court.

ISSUE: Are statements made by a juvenile to police while in the jurisdiction of the juvenile court, prior to any waiver proceedings, admissible in adult criminal court proceedings? NO.

DECISION: Damaging admissions by a juvenile while in police custody cannot be used as evidence in adult criminal proceedings if the juvenile is subsequently waived to adult court.

REASON: "The decision in *Pee v. United* States, 274 F.2d 556 (1959) . . . 'makes plain that from the moment a child commits an offense in effect he is exempt from the criminal law unless and until the Juvenile Court waives its jurisdiction. During that period the juvenile rules govern;' . . .

. . . "[T]he principles of 'fundamental fairness' govern in fashioning procedures and remedies to serve the best interests of the child. It would offend these principles to allow admissions made by the child in the non-criminal and non-punitive setting of juvenile proceedings to be used later for the purpose of securing his criminal conviction and punishment. Such a practice would be tantamount to a breach of faith with the child, since he cannot be charged with knowledge of either his privilege against self-incrimination or the Juvenile Court's power to waive its jurisdiction and subject him to criminal penalties.

. . . "[I]f admissions obtained in juvenile proceedings before waiver of jurisdiction may be introduced in an adult proceeding after waiver, the juvenile proceedings are made to serve as an adjunct to and a part of the adult criminal process. This would destroy the Juvenile Court's *parens patriae* relation with the child and would violate the non-criminal philosophy . . .

"In *United States v. Dickerson*, 271 F.2d 487, 491 (1959), we strongly intimated that any 'departure in practice from that philosophy would require the application of procedural safeguards observed in criminal proceedings.' These strict safeguards, however, are wholly inappropriate for the flexible and informal procedures of the Juvenile Court which are essential to its *parens patriae* function. To avoid impairment of this function, the juvenile proceeding must be insulated from the adult proceeding."

CASE SIGNIFICANCE: This case reinforced the separation of adult and juvenile courts by prohibiting the use of incriminating statements made by a juvenile while clearly under the jurisdiction of the juvenile court from being used in adult criminal proceedings subsequent to the juvenile's transfer to adult criminal court jurisdiction.

The court based its ruling on the principle of fundamental fairness as it applies to juvenile court processing, which is more flexible and less governed by procedural rules and regulations than processing in adult criminal court. The court further distinguished between the punitive nature of adult criminal proceedings and the non-criminal *parens patriae* philosophy that governs the juvenile court by emphasizing that the need for information such as that given by the juvenile served a different and potentially rehabilitative purpose in juvenile court, while the same information could be used to enhance the state's criminal case against the juvenile in adult criminal court.

United States v. Miller
453 F.2d 634 (4th Cir. 1972)

Handwriting samples and fingerprints obtained without coercion in a non-custodial setting are admissible in court.

FACTS: Miller, age 14, was charged with possession of stolen mail, forgery, and uttering U.S. Treasury checks. A postal inspector went to Miller's home, in search of the juvenile. Upon being informed that Miller was not at home, he asked Miller's mother to bring him to the Postal Inspector's office the following morning. Miller voluntarily appeared in the Postal Inspector's office without his mother, who was unable to attend. He was informed of his *Miranda* rights, which he waived. Miller then made incriminating statements, gave a handwriting exemplar, and permitted the postal inspector to fingerprint him. He was adjudicated delinquent and committed to the custody of the Attorney General for a period of four years.

ISSUE: Is the use of handwriting exemplars and fingerprints, obtained after a waiver of his rights with no adult guidance or legal advice, valid in the prosecution of a 14-year-old charged with delinquency? YES.

DECISION: If, after having been informed of his constitutional rights and intelligently waiving them, a juvenile submits fingerprints and handwriting exemplars, they may be used in delinquency proceedings in juvenile court because they were obtained without coercion.

REASON: "While we are mindful, and indeed would emphasize, that the Government bears a heavy burden in establishing that an accused has intelligently waived his constitutional rights, it is our conclusion that this burden has been met in the present case and that the statements were properly admitted. We are not prepared to hold that a boy of fourteen is never capable of making an intelligent waiver of his rights. Although the age of the individual is a factor to be taken into account in ascertaining if the waiver was voluntary, no court has held that age alone is determinative.

"There is nothing to indicate that the appellant did not understand his rights and the record supports the observation and conclusion of the District Judge. The appellant had completed the seventh grade of school and was able to read, write, and understand the English language. There is no indication or assertion whatever that any promises or threats were made to the juvenile to induce him to give the statements in question. While a government interrogator should take more care than the Postal Inspector did to insure that the youngster did in fact intelligently waive his rights, in the circumstances of this case we are unable to conclude that the waiver was not voluntary."

CASE SIGNIFICANCE: This case addresses the issue of age as the sole indicator of competence to waive constitutional rights. The juvenile in this case was 14 years old at the time of the alleged offenses and was asked to give a handwriting sample and his fingerprints after having waived his *Miranda* rights. The court found that age alone is insufficient to negate a waiver nor does it invalidate incriminating statements made, as long as the record clearly showed that coercion was not a factor in the waiver decision. The court found that the juvenile in question was fully capable of understanding his *Miranda* rights and the consequences of waiving those rights. Therefore any evidence gathered after such a waiver was admissible in juvenile court.

The court however, did not intend this case to be a categorical ruling on the competence of juveniles within certain age groups. The court said that each case should be considered on individual merits, allowing for other factors besides age to be considered when determining coercion. The court also clearly stated that, had any evidence of coercion been present in this case, its ruling would have been different.

This case reinforces the rule in most states that there are no barriers to a juvenile's intelligent waiver of his *Miranda* rights and that such decisions regarding waivers should be made on a case-by-case basis. The admissibility of juvenile confessions and admissions is governed by the same rules as those for adults in that they are admissible if the *Miranda* warnings are given and there was an intelligent and voluntary waiver. The only exception is if state law provides otherwise—as in states where any waiver of rights is valid only if made in the presence of an attorney.

United States v. Ramsey
367 F. Supp. 1307 (W.D. Mo. 1973)

Statements obtained by state officers in violation of state statutes are admissible if they do not violate the Constitution.

FACTS: Ramsey, 16 years old, was accused of auto theft and auto transportation across state lines. He and several other youths were arrested. At the police station, Ramsey was advised of his *Miranda* rights, after which he made incriminating statements. The Youth Bureau of the Kansas City, Missouri Police Department was contacted, along with Ramsey's mother. The officer assigned to the Youth Bureau again informed Ramsey of his *Miranda* rights and Ramsey again made incriminating statements. At no time during either of these questionings was Ramsey counseled by a parent, attorney, or other sympathetic adult. In addition, according to state law no questioning should have occurred in the absence of a juvenile officer. Due to the interstate aspect of the auto theft, the local FBI office was contacted. FBI agents sought to interview Ramsey and therefore contacted his mother to accompany them. Ramsey's *Miranda* rights were explained to him whereupon he stated that he did not wish to have an attorney at that time. Ramsey again made incriminating statements.

ISSUE: Are statements obtained by state officers in violation of state statutes admissible if they do not violate the Constitution? YES.

DECISION: Because there was a valid waiver of *Miranda* rights, the statements made to local and federal officials were admissible despite the state officers' failure to comply with state statutes concerning the treatment of arrested juveniles. Nor were the juvenile's statements tainted by the federal officer's failure to comply with federal statutes at the time, since the juvenile was not under federal jurisdiction.

REASON: "In regard to the defendant's first contention, . . . [t]hat there has been no showing the defendant understood his rights as explained to him; that he did not understand his rights; and that consequently the defendant could not and did not make a knowing, intelligent, understanding, and voluntary waiver of his rights: . . . the question before the court now becomes twofold: (1) Whether or not under the facts of this case defendant made a valid waiver of his rights in or before speaking to the officers; and (2) whether or not under the totality of the circumstances in this case the situations in which the defendant made the statements in question comport with due process requirements.

"Defendant's second contention is . . . [t]hat the procedures under which the defendant was questioned by Officers Lauffer and Keys [of the Kansas City Police Department] were violative of Missouri state law, and, in the interests of comity, as these statements could not be used against the defendant in a Missouri state criminal proceeding, the Court should not allow them to be used in a federal proceeding: . . . *Elkins v. United States*, 364 U.S. 206 (1960) was the case in which the Supreme Court overturned the so-called 'silver platter' doctrine, and held that evidence obtained by state officers in violation of the Fourth Amendment prohibition against unreasonable searches and seizures was henceforth inadmissible in federal criminal trials. The essence of the holding in *Elkins* is that if evidence is obtained in violation of the Fourth Amendment to the Federal Constitution, such evidence is not admissible in a federal criminal proceeding regardless of whether the officers who obtained the evidence were federal officers or state officers. . . . *Elkins* does not hold, however, that evidence obtained by state officers in compliance with federal constitutional standards but in violation of state statutory guidelines is likewise inadmissible in federal criminal trials of juvenile proceedings. The test is one of federal constitutional law, not one of state statutory interpretation.

"The fact that these statements were obtained by state officers, even if arguably in violation of a state statute, does not render them inadmissible in this federal proceeding unless those statements were obtained in violation of the federal constitutional standards applying, here the Fifth and Sixth Amendments."

CASE SIGNIFICANCE: In this case, the court established a distinction between the legal impact of the violation of a state law by state and federal officials and the violation of a federal law and United States constitutional principles by state and federal officials. The facts of this case show that the state officers violated state statutes in their questioning by not immediately contacting a juvenile officer to assist the juvenile. However, the court found that evidence obtained by the state officers in compliance with federal constitutional standards, although in violation of state statutes, is admissible in federal criminal court. Therefore, when states establish standards for the processing of juveniles that exceed the minimum constitutional standard, failure to follow such standards will not make the evidence inadmissible in federal court.

United States v. Barfield
507 F.2d 53 (5th Cir. 1975)

Advice to tell the truth, given in a noncustodial setting, does not amount to coercion.

FACTS: Barfield (age 14) and two others, Rybka (age 16) and Hales, were accused of burglarizing a bank. Substantial circumstantial evidence implicated the three in the burglary. Each suspect was questioned individually.

Rybka was questioned at his home, with his mother present. He was advised of his *Miranda* rights, indicated his understanding of them, and signed a waiver form. During questioning he at first denied involvement and was advised by federal officers that it would be in his "best interest" to tell the "real story" and that telling a lie might result in his being left "holding the bag." Rybka further claims that agents told him "it will be a hell of a lot easier if you own up to it."

Barfield also was questioned at his home in the presence of an adult female who "looked upon Barfield as one of her own children." The *Miranda* warnings were explained and Barfield signed the standard waiver form. After 45 minutes of questioning, Barfield admitted knowledge of and participation in the burglary. Barfield contends that the agents told him that if he "told the truth he would be placed on probation but that if he lied he could get 30 years." Barfield further contends that an agent told him that lying would get him "thrown in jail for the night."

ISSUE: Did the advice by federal agents create a climate of coercion such that statements made by a 14-year-old juvenile and a 16-year-old juvenile could be deemed involuntary? NO.

DECISION: The advice given by federal agents to tell the truth did not amount to coercion, hence the confessions were admissible.

REASON: "Undoubtedly, there may be circumstances when an admonition to the accused to tell the truth may render a subsequent statement inadmissible but it is now clearly the law that ordinarily such an admonition does not furnish sufficient inducement to render objectionable a confession thereby obtained unless threats or promises are brought into play . . .

"While it is true that Rybka was only 16 years of age and the agents did not ascertain that his mother understood his constitutional rights, the District Court was nevertheless entitled to consider that the interview was conducted in the defendant's home and not at the station house, that it was done in the presence of his mother, that Rybka read the *Miranda* warning and said that he understood it, that Rybka signed a waiver form, and neither he nor his mother ever denied at any time that they understood the rights as explained by the FBI agents and the *Miranda* warning. Our independent review of the 'totality of the circumstances' leaves us in no doubt that the findings of the District Court as to the voluntary character of Rybka's confession are strongly supported by the evidence . . .

"As in Rybka's case, Barfield was questioned at his own home, in the presence of a lady who looked upon him as if he were a son. He was read the *Miranda* warning and said he understood it. He signed the customary form, admitting that he understood his constitutional right to silence but agreed to give it up. Moreover, Barfield has had previous experience with the police. The trial judge found him to have a 'maturity beyond his years.'"

CASE SIGNIFICANCE: In this case, the court reviewed the fine line between advice given by federal officials and verbal coercion of juveniles during accusatory questioning. This case dealt with the questioning of two juvenile male suspects in a bank robbery who were both questioned in their homes and who had sympathetic adults present during questioning. Each juvenile was properly Mirandized and each juvenile chose to waive his *Miranda* rights and talk to the federal officials in the absence of legal counsel.

The court, taking into consideration all aspects of the questioning process—the place of questioning, the waiver of *Miranda*, and the presence of sympathetic adults—found that the "totality of circumstances" indicated that statements made by the juveniles were indeed voluntary and there was no coercion during the questioning process.

This ruling views questioning of juveniles from a "totality of circumstances" viewpoint, taking into consideration multiple factors present that have an impact on whether a juvenile knowingly, intelligently, and voluntarily waives his or her *Miranda* rights prior to answering questions during focused accusatory questioning. If the "totality of circumstances" indicate no coercion, the confession or admission can be used against the juvenile.

United States v. Sechrist
640 F.2d 81 (7th Cir. 1981)

Fingerprints may be taken based on less than probable cause if the juvenile is legally detained.

FACTS: The Menominee Tribal Court Clerk's Office was broken into and money was taken. Later that same year, Sechrist was interviewed regarding the burglary. He was then working off restitution from a previous incident by volunteering in the clerk's office. Sechrist denied any knowledge of the burglary and told the federal agent that his fingerprints would not be found on certain items near where the money was kept. Pursuant to a federal magistrate's order, Sechrist's fingerprints were taken while he was incarcerated at the Shawano County Jail awaiting trial on unrelated charges. His fingerprints were compared with those found at the scene and eight latent prints were determined to match those of Sechrist. Sechrist was adjudicated delinquent based on the burglary.

ISSUE: Can fingerprints of a juvenile be taken, based on less than probable cause, if the juvenile is legally detained? YES.

DECISION: No probable cause was needed to take fingerprints because the juvenile was already in lawful custody at the time of the magistrate's order.

REASON: "The analysis of any Fourth Amendment claim involves a potential violation at two different levels: 'the seizure of the person necessary to bring him into contact with government agents' . . . and the subsequent search for and seizure of the evidence.

"Because he was in lawful custody at the time, there could be no Fourth Amendment violation with respect to the first level of analysis: the 'seizure' of the person.

"The Fourth Amendment tests a search or seizure under a standard of reasonableness, in which the need to search and seize is balanced against the invasion into one's privacy that the search or seizure entails. Although the Government in this case could not establish probable cause, it did have grounds to suspect that Sechrist was the thief. Latent fingerprints had been found on several items left thrown in the clerk's office, and the clerk suspected Sechrist because the youth had recently learned the location of the cash box. In fact, Sechrist was working in the clerk's office to make restitution for a previous theft.

"The degree of invasion of one's privacy is measured by a person's 'reasonable expectation of privacy' and the process of the search or seizure. 'What the Constitution forbids is not all searches and seizures but unreasonable searches and seizures.'

"The taking of a person's fingerprints simply does not entail a significant invasion of one's privacy. . . . The procedure involves only passive participation by the individual and very little inconvenience, particularly in this case where Sechrist was already in legal custody. Fingerprinting is such an unobtrusive process that it is even used in many non-criminal contexts."

CASE SIGNIFICANCE: This case addresses the issue of the degree of certainty needed so fingerprints can be taken from a juvenile who is in custody. The court found that, unlike some other investigative procedures, the taking of fingerprints is quick, painless, and requires no special considerations related to privacy issues. It acknowledged that the use of fingerprints as a means of identification is widespread and extends to non-criminal situations as well.

The court also ruled that the fact that the juvenile was in jail at the time of the request for fingerprints did not create an additional burden on the government to ensure privacy and in fact simplified the process because incarcerated individuals do not enjoy extensive privacy rights.

The issue in this case focuses on whether constitutional protections, such as due process, need to be in place for juveniles who are subject to such non-intrusive searches, such as the taking of fingerprints. The court held that such searches are not intrusive enough to prohibit their application to juveniles.

United States v. Bernard S.
795 F.2d 749 (9th Cir. 1986)

Despite language barriers, incriminating statements made by a juvenile are admissible in court as long as the juvenile understands his rights and waives them voluntarily.

FACTS: Bernard S., age 17, was involved in an altercation in which the other party received head injuries. On May 14, 1985, an FBI agent and a local police officer questioned Bernard S. in the presence of his mother. The local police officer and Bernard S.'s mother both spoke Apache in addition to English. Bernard S. received his *Miranda* warnings in English, with a detailed explanation of each right to Bernard S. and his mother. Bernard S. indicated understanding of his rights and signed the standard waiver form. He responded to questions throughout the interrogation in English. Bernard S. made incriminating statements regarding the altercation of May 3. He was charged and was found delinquent.

ISSUE: Were statements made by the juvenile admissible in court? YES.

DECISION: Language difficulties in this case did not preclude a finding that the minor understood his *Miranda* rights and voluntarily waived them. He stated that he understood his rights and spoke primarily in English during the questioning by government agents. Although he occasionally spoke Apache with his mother and the local police officer to clarify some items of uncertainty, he displayed no evidence of being unable or unwilling to communicate in English.

REASON: "To be valid, a waiver of *Miranda* rights must be voluntarily, knowingly, and intelligently made. . . . Whether there has been a valid waiver depends on the totality of the circumstances, including the background, experience, and conduct of the defendant. . . . The age of the defendant is one factor in applying the totality test. . . . Similarly, any language difficulties encountered by the defendant are considered to determine if there has been a valid waiver.

"It is clear from the record that appellant does have some difficulty with English. He testified that he neither reads nor writes English, he occasionally spoke Apache with his mother and Lt. Stevens [the local police officer] during the questioning to clarify some items, and he was assisted in his testimony at trial by an interpreter. On the other hand, he admitted that he studied English through the seventh grade and that he answered Agent Bedford's [the FBI agent] questions in English.

"Despite the language difficulties encountered by appellant, the evidence seems to indicate that he understood his rights and voluntarily, knowingly, and intelligently waived them.

"In sum, the evidence tends to indicate that appellant made a voluntary, knowing, and intelligent waiver of his *Miranda* rights. At appellant's request, and in the presence of his mother, Agent Bedford read his rights to him and explained each right to him individually. After he was explained each of his rights, appellant stated that he understood that right. He answered Agent Bedford's questions in English and at no time indicated that he did not understand what was being said to him. Finally, appellant signed a written waiver of his *Miranda* rights. Accordingly, the district court's finding that the appellant voluntarily, knowingly, and intelligently waived his *Miranda* rights is not clearly erroneous."

CASE SIGNIFICANCE: This case deals with the issue of language barrier in the understanding of the *Miranda* warning and the intelligent waiver of such rights. The juvenile's primary language was Apache, although he also spoke English and, in fact, answered all questions in English. The court acknowledged that inadequate language skills is a factor that must be considered in determining whether an intelligent waiver of *Miranda* has been made. In this case, however, the juvenile's knowledge of English, coupled with the careful explanation of each *Miranda* right and the presence of adults who were bilingual in English and Apache, created an environment in which full understanding of the rights in the *Miranda* warning was probable and the intelligent waiving of those rights was possible.

The significance of this case is in its discussion of the impact of language barrier on a the waiver of *Miranda*. In prior court cases (*United States v. Gonzales*, 749 F.2d 1329 [9th Cir. 1984], and *United States v. Martinez*, 588 F.2d 1227 [9th Cir. 1978]), the court held that the fact that a juvenile speaks a language other than English as his primary language does not negate his capacity to comprehend and understand the English language and respond to questioning intelligently.

Cason v. Cook
810 F.2d 188 (8th Cir. 1987)

"Reasonable grounds" instead of "probable cause" is the standard used in searches made by public school officials. This is the same standard used even if the search was conducted with the assistance of a police officer.

FACTS: A student approached Vice Principal Connie Cook to report to her that the student's locker had been broken into and a pair of sweat pants and a duffel bag were missing. She also informed Cook that a friend of hers was missing a pair of sweat pants. At 12:40 P.M. a second student approached Cook to report that her wallet and coin purse, containing $65.00 and several credit cards, had been taken from her gym locker. Standing with Vice Principal Cook was a Des Moines police officer who was assigned to the school through a police liaison program. The female police liaison officer wore plain clothes and drove an unmarked car. Her instructions were to "cooperate with school officials." After receiving the reports, Vice Principal Cook initiated an investigation and identified four female students whose presence in the area of the thefts was suspicious. One of the four was Shy Cason. Three of the four were removed from their classrooms and questioned by Vice Principal Cook. Cason was questioned and escorted by Cook and the police liaison officer into a restroom, where her purse was searched. In the purse was found a coin purse that matched the description of the coin purse reported stolen. The female police liaison officer conducted a pat-down search of Cason. Cason was also asked by Cook to open her school locker for the search. The police liaison officer issued each student a juvenile appearance card requiring the student and her parents to report to the police station on a specific date. Cason's mother was not notified at the time of questioning or search, nor was Cason advised of her *Miranda* rights. Each female student and her parents met with the police liaison officer and was suspended from school.

ISSUE: Does the "reasonable grounds" standard for search and seizure by public school officials apply when such searches are conducted with the help of police liaison officers? YES.

DECISION: The "reasonable ground" standard was the appropriate standard in this case because the investigation was initiated by school officials and any involvement of the police liaison officer was in support of school efforts.

REASON: "There is no evidence to support the proposition that the activities were at the behest of a law enforcement agency. The uncontradicted evidence showed that Ms. Cook, the school official, conducted the investigation of the thefts that had been reported to her. Ms. Jones' (the school liaison officer) involvement was limited to a pat-down search conducted after a coin purse matching the description of the one stolen was found and to briefly interviewing Shy and Jerri and presenting juvenile appearance cards to the girls. At most, then, this case represents a police officer working in conjunction with school officials.

"The imposition of a probable cause warrant requirement based on the limited involvement of Ms. Jones would not serve the interest of preserving swift and informal disciplinary procedures in schools.

"It is clear that the correct standard to apply under the circumstances presented in this case is the standard enunciated by the Court in *T.L.O.*: Whether the search was reasonable under the circumstances."

CASE SIGNIFICANCE: This case expanded the principle of "reasonable grounds" established in *New Jersey v. T.L.O.*, 469 U.S. 325 (1985) for public school searches by public school officials to include searches initiated by school officials in which certified law enforcement officers participate.

The distinctions made in this case, which allowed law enforcement participation in the search with less than probable cause, rested on the school's initiation of the search and the officer's official assignment to the school as a liaison officer. The school officials were the primary parties in the investigation and search, with the law enforcement officer playing a secondary support role that consisted of a pat-down search in the presence of school officials, a short interview, and the issuance of appearance cards to the girls determined to be involved in the theft.

The law enforcement officer involved was assigned to the school through a joint police department/school program that allowed law enforcement officers to serve as "liaisons" in the schools as their official assignment with the police department. The assignment was predicated on the officer being of assistance to school officials in any way possible. In sum, all that is needed in school searches is "reasonable grounds," not probable cause, whether the search is conducted by school authorities or in cooperation with police officers.

Smith v. State
623 So. 2d 369 (Ala. Cr. App. 1992)

A juvenile's request during questioning that his grandmother be called invoked his right to remain silent.

FACTS: Three black males, in a stolen car, drove by a house where two of them fired shots at a group of people sitting on the front porch of the dwelling, killing one and injuring another. After the shooting, officers stopped a car occupied by three black males on a routine traffic offense. In the car they found a sawed-off shotgun, a .22 caliber rifle, and latent fingerprints. Smith was arrested and brought to the police station. He was read his *Miranda* rights, and indicated that he understood them. When asked whether he wished to speak to anyone, he said that he wanted to talk to his grandmother. Before calling Smith's grandmother, officers asked Smith about the stolen car in a series of interrogation sessions that extended over the next few hours.

ISSUE: Was the juvenile's request for his grandmother during questioning the same as a request for legal counsel? YES.

DECISION: Statements regarding the shootings and the automobile theft were illegally obtained from the juvenile who had invoked his right to remain silent with his request to see his grandmother.

REASON: [Under Alabama law] . . . "a child who is taken into custody must not only be informed of his *Miranda* rights but he must also be informed that he has the right to communicate with his parents or guardian and that 'if necessary, reasonable means will be provided for him to do so.'

"The appellant was questioned after he exercised his right and requested to speak to his grandmother before answering questions, a right that this court has recently determined to be the equivalent of an adult's requesting to speak to his attorney. . . . This right was violated by the authorities when they continued to question the juvenile. The statement made to the police was therefore due to be suppressed. While a juvenile may waive the right to talk to a parent or guardian . . . there is no indication that the appellant made such a waiver in this case.

"In some limited instances, receipt into evidence of an illegally obtained confession may be considered harmless error. The United States Supreme Court has applied the harmless error doctrine to confessions obtained in violation of *Miranda* and to coerced confessions. . . . Receipt of an illegally obtained confession is harmless if the court can find, based on the circumstances of the case, that admittance of the confession was harmless 'beyond a reasonable doubt.' . . . In this case, the only evidence connecting the appellant to the crime was a fingerprint on the car and his co-defendant's testimony. The fingerprint did not directly connect the appellant to the shooting and the co-defendant was an individual who had a personal interest. We have no other eyewitness testimony here and very little direct evidence."

CASE SIGNIFICANCE: In this case, the court affirmed a juvenile's right to have a sympathetic adult present during accusatory questioning. The sympathetic adult here was the juvenile's grandmother, whom the juvenile had asked to see early in his interaction with police but who was not called by the police until after they had questioned the juvenile for several hours. This delay denied the juvenile his right under Alabama law to have someone other than legal counsel present during accusatory questioning.

The facts in this case show that the juvenile provided police with sufficient information not only to locate his grandmother but also to contact her immediately. The police intentionally delayed making such contact. Failure on the part of the police to comply with the wishes of the juvenile obviously violated the constitutional standards governing accusatory questioning. Questions arose as to whether the police would have acted in the same manner had the juvenile requested legal counsel instead of asking for his grandmother. The court found that the thinking of police that anyone, other than the legal counsel, is to be called only at the discretion of the police is completely unacceptable, and therefore any statements made by the juvenile during this period were illegally acquired and inadmissible in court.

In the Interest of J.L., A Child
623 So. 2d 860 (Fla. App. 1993)

Police must have a reason to stop and frisk a juvenile; a juvenile's mere presence in an area does not justify an investigatory search.

FACTS: J.L. was charged under a petition for delinquency with carrying a concealed firearm. Police observed J.L. walking at a normal pace toward the area where a burglary had recently been reported. J.L. wore a large coat, which police stated they thought was odd because it was a warm night. When approached by police, J.L. answered questions truthfully and provided a reasonable explanation for being in the area. After questioning, the officer conducted a pat-down search when he noticed what he thought was a pistol grip in the area of J.L.'s waistband. Further searching revealed a pistol in his waistband.

ISSUE: Does the mere presence of a minor in the area of a reported crime warrant a police investigatory stop and pat-down search? NO.

DECISION: A minor's presence in an area in which a burglary had recently been reported, without other factors, does not warrant an investigatory stop and pat-down search of the minor by police.

REASON: "The facts in the present record do not justify a stop and search. An officer may briefly detain and question an individual when that individual's behavior creates a reasonable suspicion of criminal activity.

"The officer may further conduct a pat-down of the suspect's outer clothing only where the officer has a reasonable belief that the suspect may be armed.

"It is well settled that stopping an individual simply for being present in a particular location, such as a high crime area, is not permitted.

"Appellant's appearance in the area, without more, did not warrant an investigatory stop."

CASE SIGNIFICANCE: This case is an example of the extension of the rule regulating "stop and frisk" searches as defined in *Terry v. Ohio*, 392 U.S. 1 (1968), to juvenile/police encounters on the street. *Terry* requires "reasonable suspicion" of illegal behavior before a stop and frisk can be conducted by the officer. In this case, the court applies these same standards to juveniles, saying that the mere presence of a juvenile in an area in which a crime has been committed is not sufficient to go beyond the general questioning phase. Police officers must be able to articulate reasons for suspecting that a juvenile is somehow involved in illegal behavior before moving beyond the minimally intrusive questioning for identification purposes to the search process allowed in *Terry*, which is categorized as stop and frisk.

In the Interest of S.A.W.
499 N.W.2d 739 (Iowa App. 1993)

Reasonable suspicion justifies a stop in an area where a crime is alleged to have happened.

FACTS: Police were dispatched to investigate a possible fight in progress. As officers approached within two blocks of the scene, the dispatcher indicated that shots had been fired. As officers entered a narrow road that led to the scene, a car was exiting the scene. Officers stopped the car for investigatory purposes. Because of the reports of gun fire, the officers took precautionary cover, crouching behind the car doors with their weapons drawn. They asked the two occupants to exit the vehicle and to place their hands on the hood of the car. After patting down the driver and S.A.W., the passenger, one of the officers noted S.A.W.'s purse under her jacket. One of the officers asked S.A.W what was in the purse and received no response from her. He then asked if it contained a weapon, again receiving no response from S.A.W. He then felt the purse and discovered a "heavy, semi-large, medium-style object," which he suspected was a gun. Upon a search of the purse, a gun was retrieved. S.A.W. was charged as a juvenile for carrying a weapon, found delinquent, and placed on probation.

ISSUE: Based upon reasonable suspicion, are officers justified in stopping a vehicle and searching its occupants and their possessions in an area where a crime is alleged to have happened? YES.

DECISION: Police officers had reasonable suspicion that criminal activity may be afoot, and therefore, had reasonable cause to stop the juvenile.

REASON: "The Fourth Amendment is not 'a guarantee against all searches and seizures, but only against unreasonable searches and seizures.' . . . While probable cause is often thought of as the hallmark of a reasonable search, 'this starting point is riddled with exceptions.' . . . Police officers may, consistent with the Fourth Amendment, briefly detain and 'frisk' a person on less than probable cause. . . . However, reasonable cause is required to permit a stop for investigating purposes. . . . When a stop is challenged on the basis that reasonable cause did not exist, the State must show the stopping officer had specific and articulable cause to support a reasonable belief that criminal activity may be afoot.

"We are inclined to follow the . . . expansive view recently enunciated by our supreme court: 'Seemingly innocent activities may, however, combine with other factors to give an experienced law enforcement officer reason to suspect wrongdoing. . . . When considering whether evidence is sufficient to justify a stop, we examine all the evidence available to an officer regardless of whether each component would furnish reasonable cause by itself.' *State v. Rosenstiel*, 473 N.W.2d 59, at 62 (Iowa 1991).

"When an officer is justified in believing that the individual whose suspicious behavior [the officer] is investigating at close range is armed and presently dangerous to the officer, it would appear to be clearly unreasonable to deny the officer the power to take necessary measures to determine whether the person is in fact carrying a weapon and to neutralize the threat of physical harm. . . . The overriding concern inherent in a *Terry* stop is officer safety. In this case, the officers were told gunshots had been fired only ten seconds prior to encountering S.A.W. fleeing the location where the gunshots were allegedly fired. Drawing their weapons and using the car doors as shield is entirely reasonable under the circumstances and, absent more, does not constitute an arrest. We find the officers' conduct permissible as part of and consistent with the purpose of a *Terry* stop."

CASE SIGNIFICANCE: In contrast to previous cases, this case justified a "stop and frisk" search based on "reasonable suspicion" because of the "totality of the circumstances" present at the time of the encounter between juveniles and police. The fact that police were responding to a report that shots had been fired a very short time before their arrival and that upon arrival on the scene the police encountered a vehicle exiting the area of activity at a high speed presented at least a superficial level of suspicion that justified the temporary detention of juveniles in the vehicle for the purpose of identification and general questioning.

The significance of this case is in its expansion of the authority of law enforcement to detain juveniles for short periods in situations in which the police suspect an act of violence or a crime has occurred, even if the police have no initial indication that the juveniles in question are in any way connected to the illegal activity.

In re Starvon J.
29 Cal. Rptr. 2d 471 (Cal. App. 1994)

Detention of a juvenile for purposes other than an investigation does not affect the voluntariness of statements made should that juvenile become a suspect.

FACTS: A 15-year-old female was a participant in a two and one-half hour crime spree that resulted in the murder of one man, the robbery of 12 people, and the assault with a handgun of one person. The minor in question drew attention to herself at the scene of the final crime in the spree when she repeatedly approached the sealed crime scene and tried to acquire information about who was hurt and attempted to enter a cordoned-off area to supposedly retrieve her I.D. card. Meanwhile, a witness to one of the robberies provided a description of a female that matched Starvon J. Although still not a suspect, the female and a friend returned to the crime scene twice. The minor and her female companion were transported to police headquarters to be interviewed not as suspects, but as potential witnesses, based on their suspicious behavior. Upon further investigation, it was learned that one of the male suspects was the boyfriend of Starvon J.'s companion. Based on that and other information, police went to the companion's house and impounded a car identified by witnesses as involved in the robberies. Suspicion then spread to include Starvon J., who in the meantime had remained in an interview room where she either napped or watched TV. She had made no request to leave nor had she asked for a relative, asserting that her companion was her aunt. She was never placed in a cell nor was she processed as a suspect. Once attention shifted to her, she was advised of her *Miranda* rights, which she indicated that she understood and waived, before making incriminating statements. After questioning Starvon J., officers proceeded to her home where evidence from the crime spree was seized. Starvon J. was in police custody from a period beginning at about 2:50 A.M. until she was driven home around midday the following day.

ISSUE: Was the incriminating statement made by the minor voluntarily given? YES.

DECISION: The minor's statements were made voluntarily; there was nothing illegal about the circumstances and length of the minor's detention.

REASON: ". . . [T]he officers acted reasonably in detaining the minor and removing her from the area while investigating the crime scene. . . . They gave the minor every opportunity to substantiate her story for her reason for trying to penetrate the cordoned-off area, so that she could be released as soon as the officers' suspicions were allayed. . . . Such detention enables police to quickly determine whether the person detained is innocent of any wrongdoing and if so, to allow him to leave. Placement in the police car did not ipso facto convert the detention into an arrest . . . nor, under the circumstances and the ongoing investigation at the crime scene, did the minor's transportation to the station.

"We have found that the initial detention was legal and the arrest was supported by probable cause . . . Even had there been a showing here that the initial detention was unlawful and the arrest was not supported by probable cause, appellant has failed to establish that her Fourth Amendment claim would have resulted in the suppression of her statement. A voluntary statement obtained following an illegal detention is not automatically suppressed, but is admissible if it is shown that the connection between the illegality and the evidence subsequently obtained is so attenuated as to dissipate the taint.

"The minor was advised of her constitutional rights and waived them; she told police [that] Humphries [her companion] was her aunt, giving them the right to believe a relative was there; no coercion was used, no softening tactics; her confession was free and voluntary and the trial court so found. We conclude that the minor's statement was sufficiently an act of free will and that other circumstances were such as to purge any primary taint."

CASE SIGNIFICANCE: This case defines the boundaries between detention of a juvenile as a possible witness and detention of a juvenile as a suspect in a criminal case. The circumstances presented here were unique but have the potential to be widely applied as the nature of juvenile involvement in crimes changes.

The key factors in this case that allowed incriminating statements made by the juvenile to be admitted into evidence were: the nature of the detention was never punitive in any way throughout the questioning, the fact that the juvenile drew attention to herself through repeated interference in and around the crime scene, and the fact that the juvenile led police to believe that her companion (another juvenile female) was not only an adult who could serve as her advisor but was also a relative, thus strengthening her role as a sympathetic adult.

The facts show that the police initially viewed the juvenile as a mere possible witness and had no hidden agenda in detaining her until she could be interviewed about what she might have seen in connection with the ongoing criminal investigation. If there were other motives on the part of the police, the detention would have been viewed by the court as inappropriate and any statement or evidence acquired in connection with subsequent questioning would have been deemed illegally acquired and therefore inadmissible in court.

In re Gilbert E.
38 Cal. Rptr. 2d 866 (Cal. App. 1995)

A police officer's continued questioning of a juvenile after the juvenile unequivocally refuses to waive his or her *Miranda* rights is a violation of the right to remain silent.

FACTS: Police detained Gilbert E., age 15, and four other minors. After field interview cards were completed, the minors were released. Later that morning, the officers discovered several properties vandalized by graffiti. Gilbert E.'s gang nickname, "Turtle," was included within the graffiti. He was arrested, transported to the local police station, and placed in an interview room where a tape recorder, which was in plain sight, was activated. The record shows that Gilbert E. "unequivocally" refused to waive his *Miranda* rights. Regardless of his invocation of his constitutional rights, the officer continued to ask questions related to the vandalism. After several minutes, an officer noticed that Gilbert E. repeatedly looked at the tape recorder as if he would be more comfortable if the tape recorder was turned off. He asked that question, to which Gilbert E. responded "yes." After the tape recorder was deactivated, the officer reported that Gilbert E. stated that he now wished to answer questions. The officer also reported that he reminded Gilbert E. of his earlier invocation of his *Miranda* rights, to which Gilbert E. reportedly said he "didn't care." He then made incriminating statements to the police.

ISSUE: Does an officer's continued attempt to question a juvenile who has indicated his unwillingness to answer questions violate the juvenile's Fifth Amendment right to remain silent under *Miranda*? YES.

DECISION: The police officer's continued questioning of the juvenile, after the juvenile unequivocally refused to waive his *Miranda* rights, was a violation of the juvenile's right to remain silent.

REASON: "We exercise independent review of the uncontradicted evidence and . . . conclude that under these circumstances, appellant's statements were coerced and involuntary. . . . [C]ontinued questioning of appellant after he had refused to waive his rights was a deliberate violation of *Miranda*. 'Disrespect of the right [to remain silent] is indicative of coercion.'

"The admissibility of statements obtained after the person in custody has decided to remain silent depends under *Miranda* on whether his right to cut off questioning was 'scrupulously honored.' . . . Here the continued questioning was the antithesis of scrupulously honoring appellant's right to terminate the interrogation.

"An accused, . . . having expressed his desire to deal with the police only through counsel, is not subject to further interrogation by the authorities until counsel has been made available to him, unless the accused himself initiates further communication, exchanges, or conversations with the police. . . . An accused 'initiates' such dialogue when he speaks words or engages in conduct that can be 'fairly said to represent a desire on his part to open up a more generalized discussion relating directly or indirectly to the investigation.' . . . Simply looking at a tape recorder is not conduct which is tantamount to the initiation of further communication.

"When the police deliberately step over the line and disobey Supreme Court pronouncements, respect for the rule of law diminishes."

CASE SIGNIFICANCE: This case provides another example of coercion in violation of the Fifth Amendment. When a juvenile clearly states his or her desire to remain silent, no further contact should be made by police officers to induce cooperation. The facts of the case indicate that the juvenile had no desire to participate in the questioning process, as indicated by both his refusal and silence thereafter. Continued attempts by police to initiate conversation and thus continue accusatory questioning can therefore only be construed as coercive and violative of constitutional rights. The fact that the juvenile looked at the tape recorder and replied that he would be more comfortable if it were turned off did not constitute any type of waiver. The rule is clear: when a juvenile invokes the right to remain silent, interrogation must cease. The rule is the same in cases involving adults.

State v. Sugg
456 S.E.2d 469 (W. Va. 1995)

A juvenile may waive *Miranda* rights even in the absence of his or her parents, as long as the juvenile knowingly, voluntarily, and intelligently waives such rights.

FACTS: Sugg, a 14-year-old black male, was accused of robbing a service station. He was observed in the general vicinity of the robbery immediately thereafter, fled when approached by police, and when apprehended was found to have on his person a .22 caliber handgun that matched the one used in the robbery. He was arrested, advised of his *Miranda* rights and transported to the police station, where Sugg waived his *Miranda* rights. When asked if he wanted to call his parents or an attorney, he declined. He made incriminating statements shortly thereafter regarding his involvement in the robbery. After obtaining the statement, the police called Sugg's parents and Sugg was presented to a Magistrate. He was transferred from juvenile court to circuit court to be tried as a adult, was found guilty of aggravated robbery with the use of a firearm and sentenced to 45 years in prison.

ISSUE: Was the juvenile's waiver of his *Miranda* rights valid in the absence of his parents? YES.

DECISION: A juvenile may waive his *Miranda* rights even in the absence of parents, as long as the juvenile knowingly, voluntarily, and intelligently waives such rights, viewed in the totality of circumstances.

REASON: "We know of no law which provides that a minor over the age of sixteen is conclusively presumed to be incapable of waiving his constitutional and statutory rights without the consent of his parents. Thus, we must determine whether the statement in this case was freely and voluntarily given under the totality of the circumstances analysis.

"We adopt the rationale expressed by the majority of jurisdictions and hold that the validity of a juvenile's waiver of his or her rights should be evaluated in light of the totality of the circumstances surrounding the waiver, and the presence or absence of the parents is but one factor to be considered in reaching this determination. In adopting the totality of the circumstances standard, we do so in the belief that circuit courts are equipped with the expertise and experience to make competent evaluations of the special circumstances involved in a juvenile's waiver of rights and should be allowed the discretion to do so. Requiring the presence of parents in every case in which a juvenile is in custody and informed of his rights 'would be overly protective; would exclude from evidence juvenile statements that are, in fact, knowingly and voluntarily given; and would restrict law enforcement unnecessarily.'"

CASE SIGNIFICANCE: The court ruled in this case that the statements made were constitutionally admissible in court based on what it called the "factors of will." In determining that the "factors of will" overcame the flaws in this questioning process, the court considered the fact that the juvenile had had prior experience with the police, had been convicted of a misdemeanor; the waiver of *Miranda* rights form indicated that the juvenile understood his rights because he initialed each right on the form; and the fact that police encouraged the juvenile to call his parents prior to questioning and the juvenile refused to do so.

The absence of parents in this case did not, in and of itself, make the confession involuntary. It must be noted, however, that there are states that require the presence of parents or lawyers for a waiver to be considered valid. In these states, the evidence obtained in this case would most likely have been inadmissible.

Curfew Ordinances and Juveniles 3

I. No United States Supreme Court Cases

II. Lower Court Cases

Bykosky v. Borough of Middletown (1975)
Illinois v. Chambers (1976)
Johnson v. City of Opelousas (1981)
Waters v. Barry (1989)
Panora v. Simmons (1989)
People in Interest of J.M. (1989)
Brown v. Ashton (1992)
City of Maquoketa v. Russell (1992)
Qutb v. Strauss (1993)
State v. Bean (1994)
Matter of Appeal in Maricopa County (1994)

Introduction

A curfew is a social control mechanism. The common assumptions underlying it and other such mechanisms are: (1) human beings must be controlled if society is to be orderly and safe; (2) society has reached a consensus on a set of appropriate values and behaviors; and (3) absent internally motivated voluntary compliance, people can be forced to comply through external control mechanisms.[1] Officials who support curfew ordinances believe that they have a compelling interest to reduce juvenile crime and victimization while promoting juvenile safety and well-being.

Proponents of curfews argue that they serve as a tool for both the police and parents. In high-crime neighborhoods, curfews are a means to protect non-delinquent juveniles from crime and to deny delinquent juveniles the opportunity to engage in criminal activity. In low-crime communities, they provide the police with the means to disperse late-night crowds of juveniles, to stop and question juveniles during curfew hours and, if necessary, to keep juveniles off the streets. For parents, curfews provide support and legitimization for restrictions on the late-night activities of their children. Without curfews, it can be more difficult for parents to place such restrictions on their children when other juveniles in the neighborhood are out late at night.[2]

Opponents' primary objections to curfews are that they violate the equal protection clause by setting up a suspect classification based on age, and that they result in selective enforcement of the law to the detriment of minority juveniles. Curfews are also challenged on the grounds that they infringe on the fundamental rights of free movement and free association, and of family privacy in childrearing. Another argument against curfews is that they violate due process rights through seizure of persons by police without probable cause and through forced confessions in answering police questions. However, when curfew laws have been declared unconstitutional by the court, it has been because of their vagueness and overreach, not because of any violation of equal protection guarantees, fundamental rights, or procedural due process.[3]

There are two distinct types of curfews used in society today—the emergency curfew, which is invoked as a result of a catastrophic situation in a specific location and is of a limited duration, usually until the crisis has passed, and the non-emergency curfew, otherwise known as the blanket curfew, which is invoked in reaction to either a perceived or real threat to the community, is targeted toward the control of a specific group, and is in effect for an indefinite period of time. Whereas emergency curfews have survived constitutional attacks because they are a narrowly tailored means of addressing a specific emergency situation, blanket curfews have not fared so well and rulings on their constitutionality have been mixed.[4]

Juvenile curfew ordinances present the court with a fundamental constitutional dilemma. At the core of the debate is the conflict between state interests in protecting a child and upholding democratic ideals and juvenile constitutional rights, and parents' rights to raise their children.[5]

This chapter focuses on the issues surrounding the use of curfew ordinances. *Bykosky v. Borough of Middletown, Illinois v. Chambers, Panora v. Simmons, People in Interest of J.M., Qutb v.* Strauss, and *Matter of Appeal in Maricopa County* are all examples of curfew ordinances that have been ruled constitutional by the courts. In contrast, *Johnson v. City of Opelousas, Waters v. Barry, Brown v. Ashton*, and *City of Maquoketa v. Russell* represent curfew laws that were too broad, unrelated to articulated governmental interests, and were unclear, thereby rendering them unconstitutional.

It is evident that the debate about juvenile curfew ordinances is far from over; however, differences between constitutional and unconstitutional ordinances have been clearly drawn by the courts, allowing new cases and challenges to emerge. The constitutionality of a curfew ordinance is ultimately decided by the court, based on specific provisions. Overbreadth and vagueness are always a problem in any curfew ordinance, hence the need for careful drafting. A review of the cases in this chapter should shed light on the limits when drafting curfew ordinances.

Curfew ordinances are proof that juveniles are one of the few remaining groups that can be legally singled out and dealt with differently based solely on age. Society's focus on school violence, youths and drugs, gangs, and increasing victimization of juveniles indicates a continuing interest in isolating juveniles through laws that deal with them as a class more restrictively and punitively. Within limits, courts have said that these efforts are constitutional.

Notes

[1]   John E. Holman and James F. Quinn, *Criminology: Applying Theory* (1992).

[2]   William Ruefle and Kenneth Mike Reynolds, "Curfews and Delinquency in Major American Cities," *Crime and Delinquency* Vol 41 no. 3, 347-363 (July 1995).

[3]   William Ruefle and Kenneth Mike Reynolds, "Curfews and Delinquency in Major American Cities," *Crime and Delinquency* Vol 41 no. 3, 347-363 (July 1995).

[4] Susan L. Freitas, "After Midnight: The Constitutional Status of Juvenile Ordinances in California," *Hastings Constitutional Law Quarterly* Vol. 24 no. 1, 219-246 (Fall 1996).

[5] Scott A. Kizer, "Juvenile Curfew Laws: Is There a Standard?" *Drake Law Review* Vol. 45 no. 3, 749-765 (1997).

I. NO UNITED STATES SUPREME COURT CASES

II. LOWER COURT CASES

Bykosky v. Borough of Middletown
401 F. Supp. 1242 (M.D. Pa. 1975)

Curfew ordinances that provide a wide range of exceptions are nonetheless constitutional.

FACTS: Plaintiff, on behalf of her son, a 12-year-old minor, sought declaratory, preliminary, and permanent injunctions alleging that the Borough of Middletown and various officials violated her son's constitutional rights through the enactment of a juvenile curfew. The curfew ordinance specifically prohibited any minor from being on or remaining in or upon the streets within the Borough of Middletown at various hours for various age groups. The ordinance contained 11 exceptions to the general curfew ordinance, specifically:

1. a minor accompanied by a parent;
2. a minor authorized by a parent and accompanied by an adult;
3. a minor exercising a First Amendment right;
4. a case of non-emergency reasonable necessity as determined by and communicated to officials by the juvenile's parents;
5. a minor on a sidewalk of his residence or the residence of a consenting next-door neighbor;
6. a minor returning home by a direct route from a school, religious, or voluntary activity or meeting;
7. a minor with a special permit authorized by the Mayor;
8. a minor who is a member of a group exempted from the curfew by the Mayor;
9. a minor with a certified card of employment going to or from work;
10. a minor in a motor vehicle with parents' consent in intrastate travel and all interstate travel;
11. a minor 17 years of age exempted by the Mayor by formal rule based on level of maturity.

The plaintiff contended that the curfew ordinance:
1. was unconstitutionally vague;
2. violated the substantive due process rights of juveniles (especially movement and the use of public streets);
3. violated the First Amendment's guarantee of free speech, assembly, and association;
4. violated the fundamental right to interstate travel;
5. violated the constitutional right to intrastate travel;
6. encroached on the constitutional rights of parents to direct the upbringing of their children;
7. violated the equal protection clause of the Fourteenth Amendment.

ISSUES: Was the curfew ordinance constitutional? YES.

DECISION: The curfew ordinance was valid. The conduct of minors may be constitutionally regulated more closely than that of adults. The ordinance was a reasonable exercise of governmental power and was not impermissibly vague.

REASON: "The Supreme Court has not yet articulated the special factors that determine how existing frameworks for analyzing the rights of adults are to be applied to minors. . . . Thus, the question is whether the curfew ordinance is reasonable, with reasonableness being determined by weighing the legitimate interests of the state which the ordinance actually furthers, against the competing liberty interests of the minor. This interest balancing-means test requires the court to weigh the governmental interests against the burden upon the minor's rights of freedom of movement and use of the public streets, and to examine the ordinance to insure that it in fact furthers the asserted governmental interests. The ordinance was enacted to further the following Borough interests: (1) the protection of younger children in Middletown from each other and from other persons on the street during the nighttime hours; (2) the enforcement of parental control of and responsibility for their children; (3) the protection of the public from nocturnal mischief by minors; and (4) reduction in the incidence of juvenile criminal activity. . . . the court concludes that the ordinance does in fact further the purposes for which it was enacted. Therefore, there is a rational relation between the end sought and the means chosen. . . . The court holds that the minor's interest in freedom of movement upon the streets during the nighttime curfew hours under circumstances other than those provided for in the numerous curfew exceptions is clearly outweighed by the governmental interests which the ordinance furthers. Hence the ordinance is a reasonable exercise by the Borough of its police power to advance and protect the safety and welfare of the general community and the minors who reside therein. The ordinance is a constitutionally permissible regulation of the minor's right to freedom of movement upon and use of the streets as guaranteed by the due process clause of the Fourteenth Amendment."

CASE SIGNIFICANCE: This case deals with the constitutionality of a juvenile curfew ordinance imposed in varying degrees on anyone under the age of 18 years. The exceptions in the ordinance allowed a wide range of activities to continue while simultaneously attempting to curb illegitimate nighttime activities of juveniles. The curfew ordinance was challenged on several grounds centering around the issue of equity of treatment between juveniles and adults, adults being unregulated in their nighttime activities.

The court ruled that without specific guidance from the Supreme Court on how to measure equity between adults and juveniles, the appropriate framework for analysis was "reasonableness," determined by weighing the legitimate interests of the government against the burden placed on the affected group—in this case juveniles—and to determine whether the interests bear a rational relationship to the methods imposed to achieve them. In this case, the court found that the interests were indeed rationally related to the curfew and that government interests in advancing public safety and community welfare clearly outweighed the limited burden placed on juveniles through the enactment of the curfew.

The court also found that juveniles could in fact be separated from and treated differently from adults. The court, however, did not allow blatant discriminatory actions, nor did it support the enactment of a highly restrictive curfew ordinance that severely limited all movement and activities of juveniles. Those options would have been seen by the court as excessively burdensome to juveniles.

The significance of this case rests in its being one of the first well-drawn curfew ordinances and therefore passed constitutional challenge. This ordinance has become a model for government entities to follow. Its strength lays in the balance between restrictiveness on nighttime juvenile activities and promotion of the legitimate concerns of government. This case is also significant in that the court extensively addresses the constitutional issues raised in juvenile curfew ordinances and indicates limits on what the government can do.

Illinois v. Chambers
360 N.E.2d 55 (Ill. 1976)

Curfew laws imposed statewide for the welfare of juveniles within the boundaries of the state are constitutional.

FACTS: Cynthia Chambers, a 17-year-old, her sister Patricia, a 15-year-old, and a third person were observed by a police officer in a car driven by Cynthia. The car was parked on a one-lane bridge with its lights turned off. As the officer approached in his vehicle, the car lights came on and the car proceeded across the bridge. When stopped by the officer, Cynthia got out of the car, was asked several questions by the officer, who determined that the sisters were within "curfew age," and that no adult accompanied them. He arrested them for violation of the statewide curfew. Both were found guilty and assessed a fine of $10.00 and court costs. The curfew in question was passed by the Illinois Legislature and read in part as follows:

> "(a) It is unlawful for a person less than 18 years of age to be present at or upon any public assembly, building, place, street, or highway at the following times unless accompanied and supervised by a parent . . . or other responsible companion at least 21 years of age approved by a parent . . . or unless engaged in a business or occupation which the laws of this State authorize a person less than 18 years of age to perform:
> 1. between 12:01 A.M. and 6:00 A.M. Saturday;
> 2. between 12:01 A.M. and 6:00 A.M. Sunday;
> 3. between 11:00 P.M. on Sunday to Thursday (inclusive) and 6:00 A.M. on the following day.
>
> (b) It is unlawful for a parent, legal guardian, or other person to knowingly permit a person in his custody or control to violate [the above];
>
> (c) A person convicted of a violation of any provision of this Act shall be guilty of a petty offense and shall be fined not less than $10.00 nor more than $100.00."

The defendants contended that the statute unconstitutionally restricted the rights of minors to move about and to exercise their First Amendment rights of freedom of speech, assembly, and association. They further asserted that the statute was invalid because there was no governmental interest that justified such a broad prohibition of a special groups' rights.

ISSUE: Did this curfew statute violate the constitutional rights of minors, specifically the right to free movement and First Amendment rights? NO.

DECISION: The curfew statute was a constitutional exercise of the state's right to legislate for the welfare of its children. In legislating for the welfare of children, the State is not required to assume that children have an unlimited right to choose the association and the time and place of assembly. The curfew statute was not invalid despite its statewide coverage because it was not confined to any geographical areas of the State, hence was not discriminatory.

REASON: "The primary interest advanced by the State to justify the restrictions of the statute as to time, place and circumstance is the traditional right of the State to protect its children. The statute proceeds upon the basic assumption that when a child is at home during the late night and early morning hours, it is protected from physical as well as moral dangers. Although there are instances, unfortunately, in which this assumption is untrue, we are satisfied that the State is justified in acting upon it. In legislating for the welfare of children, the State is not required, in our opinion, to proceed upon the assumption that minor children have an absolutely unlimited right not only to choose their own associates, but also to decide when and where they will associate with them. Recognition of such a right would require wholesale revision of the large body of law that relates to guardian and ward, parent and child, and minors generally. Compulsory school attendance would be prohibited. A child is carefully safeguarded against errors of choice and judgment in most of the ordinary affairs of life, and we see no constitutional impairment in the limited restriction upon the child's judgment that is involved in this statute. It is only during the very late night and early morning hours that the State has interfered, and then only by requiring that the child be accompanied by an adult."

CASE SIGNIFICANCE: This case deals with a state-wide curfew statute, limiting the movement of juveniles from late night to early morning throughout the state of Illinois. This curfew statute was written very broadly both in terms of coverage and the discretionary decisions allowed by law enforcement officials in enforcing the curfew.

The court ruled that the statute was constitutional based on the state's right to legislate for the welfare of children. The court stated that curfews enacted at the state level were more justifiable under the welfare of the state child provision than local government curfew ordinances because the statute had a well-defined role in protecting juveniles and is charged with the enactment of restrictive laws governing the citizens as a whole.

The court also found that ordinances covering broad geographic areas are acceptable and in fact may be more acceptable than those targeting areas of high crime or areas in which issues of discrimination could arise about enforcement of the curfew ordinance. It concluded that geographical area coverage of a statute, except when discrimination may be an issue, is a matter of legislative determination.

This case is significant because it addresses the constitutionality of broad juvenile curfew ordinances. Decisions like this give states broad authority to enact curfew laws limiting the movement of juveniles.

Johnson v. City of Opelousas
658 F.2d 1065 (5th Cir. 1981)

Curfew ordinances that restrict all movement of juveniles during the specified hours are unconstitutional.

FACTS: Appellant's son, James, then 14 years old, was arrested at 2:05 A.M. by a police officer of the City of Opelousas, Louisiana. James was subsequently found guilty of curfew violation and was first placed on probation, then in a private juvenile residential facility, and was eventually released to the custody of his mother. The appellant filed suit in federal court challenging the constitutionality of the curfew ordinance which read, in part:

> "(a) It shall be unlawful for any unemancipated minor under the age of seventeen (17) years to travel, loiter, wander, stroll, or play in or upon or traverse any public streets, highways, roads, alleys, parks, places of amusement and entertainment, places and buildings, vacant lots or other unsupervised places in the City of Opelousas, Louisiana, between the hours of 11:00 P.M. on any Sunday, Monday, Tuesday, Wednesday, or Thursday night and 4:00 A.M. of the following day, or 1:00 A.M. Friday and Saturday night and 4:00 A.M. the following day, all official time of the City of Opelousas, Louisiana, unless said minor is accompanied by his parents, tutor, or other responsible adult or unless the said minor is upon an emergency errand.
>
> (b) Any minor violating any provision of this section shall be deemed a neglected child . . . "

The appellant challenged the curfew ordinance, asserting that it was unconstitutional.

ISSUE: Does this curfew ordinance violate the constitutional rights of juveniles? YES.

DECISION: The above ordinance violates the First and Fourteenth Amendment rights of juveniles.

REASON: "Although juvenile curfew ordinances are fairly common, only three federal cases to our knowledge have considered the constitutionality of such ordinances. . . . None of the ordinances involved in [those] cases, however, encompassed nearly the breadth of the Opelousas ordinances. A review of the Opelousas juvenile curfew ordinance and pertinent legal authority convinces us that this curfew ordinance is constitutionally infirm in its breadth. . . . It is clear that [the] rights of minors in Opelousas currently are being burdened by that city's juvenile curfew ordinance. The curfew ordinance prohibits unemancipated minors generally from being on public streets between certain hours without their parents, with exception for minors on 'emergency errands.' We express no opinion on validity of curfew ordinances narrowly drawn to accomplish proper social objectives. . . . But, under this curfew ordinance minors are prohibited from attending associational activities such as religious or school meetings, organized dances, and theater and sporting events, when reasonable and direct travel to or from these activities has to be made during the curfew period. The same inhibition prohibits parents from urging and consenting to such protected associational activity by their minor children. The curfew ordinance also prohibits a minor during the curfew period from, for example, being on the sidewalk in front of his house, engaging in legitimate employment, or traveling through Opelousas even on an interstate trip. These implicit prohibitions of the curfew ordinance overtly and manifestly infringe upon the constitutional rights of minors in Opelousas.

". . . [T]his curfew ordinance, however valid might be a narrowly drawn curfew to protect society's valid interests, sweeps within its ambit a number of innocent activities which are constitutionally protected. The stifling effect upon these legitimate activities is overt and is both real and substantial. Regardless of the legitimacy of Opelousas' stated purposes of protecting youths, reducing nocturnal juvenile crimes, and promoting parental control over their children, less drastic means are available for achieving these goals. Since the absence of exceptions in the curfew ordinance precludes a narrowing construction, we are compelled to rule that the ordinance is constitutionally overbroad."

CASE SIGNIFICANCE: This case involves the first juvenile curfew ordinance to be declared unconstitutional based on broadness that placed an undue burden on juveniles by restricting all external activities during certain hours, with no exceptions.

The court said that in weighing the governmental interest against the individual burden to juveniles this curfew ordinance did not serve a legitimate governmental interest. The balance was burdensome to juveniles as a group. The court was further disturbed because the curfew ordinance made no attempt to distinguish legitimate activities from illegitimate activities, banning both with no thought given to activities that may be of benefit to the juvenile.

The court also found that the curfew ordinance, rather than helping parents raise, educate, and supervise their children, interfered with parental rights. The ordinance was seen as so intrusive that parents lost control of their children, leaving that control to the government.

This case is an example of a juvenile curfew ordinance that intruded into parents' rights in raising their children. The city attempted to create a "police state" for juveniles. In doing so, the state overreached its authority.

Waters v. Barry
711 F. Supp. 1121 (D.D.C. 1989)

Overly restrictive curfew ordinances violate the fundamental rights of juveniles and are unconstitutional. However, a properly crafted curfew ordinance does not restrict the government's right to search and seize material from juveniles who violate such curfews.

FACTS: Plaintiffs challenged a curfew ordinance imposed in the District of Columbia. The "old ordinance," which was general and quite vague with regard to exceptions to curfew violations, was originally challenged. While under challenge, the District repealed the "old ordinance" and substituted the "new ordinance," which included a number of exemptions to the curfew restraints. The court allowed the "new ordinance" to be substituted for the "old ordinance" in the original challenge, believing that the issues raised by the plaintiffs, even though no one had yet suffered harm from the "new ordinance," allowed such substitution. The court further allowed the plaintiffs to claim class status to avoid the issue being declared moot, even though not all party types were in agreement on the issues. The elements of the curfew ordinance were as follows:

1. It was designed as a blanket curfew for all minors under the age of 18 years.
2. It prohibited movement, with some exceptions, of minors between 11:00 P.M. and 6:00 A.M. on weekdays and 11:59 P.M. and 6:00 A.M. on weekends.
3. It allowed the following exceptions:
   a. minors traveling in a motor vehicle accompanied by a parent;
   b. minors returning by a direct route from mayoral approved organized activities within 60 minutes of the activity's termination;
   c. minors with proof of legitimate employment during the hours of curfew; and
   d. minors moving as a result of an emergency errand.

The court reviewed the "new curfew ordinance" based on the plaintiff's First, Fourth, and Fifth Amendment challenges.

ISSUES:
1. Is the above curfew ordinance an infringement of First (freedom of asso-
    ciation) and Fifth (due process and equal protection) Amendment rights?
    YES.

2. Does the curfew ordinance violate a juvenile's Fourth Amendment right to
    be protected from unreasonable search and seizure as a result of a curfew
    stop? NO.

DECISIONS:
1. The curfew ordinance unconstitutionally burdens the First and Fifth
    Amendment rights to equal protection and due process by drawing imper-
    missible distinctions between juveniles and non-juveniles.

2. A properly crafted ordinance does not violate a juvenile's Fourth Amend-
    ment right against unreasonable searches and seizures.

REASON: "A brief review of the record indicates the extent to which the Act
tramples upon the associational and liberty interests of the named plaintiffs.
These plaintiffs have been, and hope in the future to be, involved with high
school social activities, political activities, scientific discoveries, and religious
pursuits which often require their presence on the District's streets during the
curfew period. Absent registration, these activities would disappear were the
Act enforced. Moreover, the specific examples contained in the record say
nothing of the countless legitimate but undocumented pursuits which would be
denied juvenile members of the plaintiff class if the Act were enforced. The
right to a late-night game of basketball, to sit in the open air on a muggy summer night, or to walk home at one's leisure from an unregistered church or
synagogue, or from a party at a friend's home, would all be denied. . . . The Act
casts these rights aside like so much straw. The Act subjects the District's juveniles to virtual house arrest each night without differentiating either among
those juveniles likely to embroil themselves in mischief, or among those activities most likely to produce them. The Act is a bull in a china shop of constitutional rights . . .

. . . "The plaintiffs' argument reflects, in essence, an attempt to find in the
Fourth Amendment an absolute right to be free from searches and seizures, a
right that cannot be limited by the government's power to criminalize certain
forms of behavior. The Court finds no such absolute right in the Fourth
Amendment. Instead, as the very language of the Fourth Amendment provides,
a right to be free from such intrusions exists *only* so long as there is not probable
cause to believe that an offense had been committed. Here, the District has at-

tempted to criminalize the public presence of juveniles during the curfew hours. Were they not otherwise unconstitutional, the proscriptions of the Act would provide, in fact, valid substantive references for determining the presence or absence of probable cause in a given case. Although the proposed crime is utterly simple—nocturnal, public youth—that simplicity causes the type of proof required to justify a search or seizure to be similarly uncomplex. Thus, were a police officer to reasonably conclude that an individual looked 'young'—that he or she looked like a minor—the officer would have 'probable cause' to believe that the individual was engaged in an illegal act, i.e., being on the streets during the curfew period. If the individual could not prove that he or she was over 18, or that he or she fell within one of the Act's other exceptions, the officer could reasonably have believed that the individual looked 'young,' the search, seizure and arrest would take place on the basis of probable cause and no Fourth Amendment violation would occur."

CASE SIGNIFICANCE: This case, decided in 1989, is an example of the evolution of the constitutionality of juvenile curfew ordinances. The curfew ordinance challenged included all juveniles under the age of 18 years, standardized time restraints, and allowed only a limited number of exceptions to the general nighttime prohibitions against juvenile movement.

The court found that the broad reach of this ordinance barred all juvenile activities after dark, making no distinction between positive and legitimate activities and those that led to juvenile mischief and crime. In addition, the court saw such a restrictive curfew as resulting in virtual house arrest for juveniles. The court observed that the governmental intent was unrelated to the type of activity it sought to prohibit.

Labeling a class of individuals (juveniles) in this manner was clearly overly broad and therefore unconstitutional. A curfew ordinance must be clearly related to the reason for its enactment and must not be unduly broad, otherwise it violates the Constitution.

Panora v. Simmons
445 N.W.2d 363 (Iowa 1989)

Curfew ordinances that provide for parentally approved exceptions do not infringe on the autonomy of the family or parental rights in general.

FACTS: Simmons, 15 years of age, and a friend were skateboarding in a shopping center parking lot. A police officer issued them citations based on the city's juvenile curfew ordinance, which prohibited juveniles under the age of 18 from being in public places between the hours of 10:00 P.M. and 5:00 A.M. Simmons was found guilty and, although no criminal penalty was attached to the ordinance, was fined $1.00. The juvenile curfew was similar to others around the country, and included the following provisions:

1.   It applied to any juvenile under the age of 18.

2.   It prohibited movement between 10:00 P.M. and 5:00 A.M.

3.   Exceptions were made for juveniles accompanied by parents, guardians, or custodians, or minors traveling between home or public residence and any approved public function.

4.   It included an admonition to parents to assume responsibility for the whereabouts of their children.

5.   It included an admonition to businesses that cater to minors to adjust their hours of operation to conform to the curfew time frame.

6.   It instructed police officers to arrest any juvenile in violation of the curfew and to return the juvenile to the custody of the appropriate parent, guardian, or custodian.

Simmons appealed based on the constitutional issues of vagueness, unconstitutional interference with parenting rights, and unconstitutional interference with gathering, walking, or loitering.

ISSUE: Was this juvenile curfew ordinance constitutional? YES.

DECISION: A municipal ordinance imposing a curfew on juveniles' movement on public streets between the hours of 10:00 P.M. and 5:00 A.M. is not unconstitutionally vague when it allows for exceptions and provides for a mechanism by which juveniles can be returned to parents. The ordinance does not unconstitutionally restrict a juvenile's right to intracity travel when balanced against the municipality's interest in providing a solution to perceived problems. It does not infringe upon a parent's right to raise a juvenile or intrude on a family's autonomy and in fact may promote family life by encouraging children to stay home.

REASON: "Regardless of the nature of the right to travel about town, the Supreme Court has made it clear that minors' activities and conduct on the street may be regulated and restricted to a greater extent than those of adults.

". . . [A] minor's right of intracity travel is not a fundamental right for due process purposes, and the ordinance need not meet a strict scrutiny test. Rather, we need to determine only whether there is a rational relationship between the goals of the ordinance and the means chosen. We believe there is. In weighing the minor's interest in intracity travel against the City's interest in providing a prophylactic solution to the perceived problems inherent in unrestricted minor travel, we believe that the ordinance is a reasonable exercise of the City's power to legislate for the good of its citizens.

"In the present case, the City has a strong interest in protecting minors from the national epidemic of drugs, and the curfew ordinance is a minimal infringement upon a parent's right to bring up his or her child. In effect, the Panora curfew ordinance acts to make parents the primary agent of enforcement. In addition, it could be said to 'promote family life by encouraging children to be at home.' . . . It is difficult, when judging Panora's ordinance, to determine if it forces parents to *abdicate* their authority over their children, or to *accept* such authority. In either case, the City's interference is minimal and its interest is significant. In summary, we conclude that the ordinance is not unconstitutional on any of the grounds urged . . . ."

CASE SIGNIFICANCE: The court ruled in this case that the juvenile curfew ordinance violated no constitutional rights of juveniles or parents and in fact promoted family life by encouraging juveniles to stay home when they would have otherwise been out on the streets. The court felt that although the curfew language was standard, the provision that allowed juvenile travel to and from parentally approved public functions was even more lenient than other curfew ordinances in place across the United States. By providing the parental option to allow unaccompanied juvenile travel, the court found that the ordinance could clearly place the responsibility for the juveniles' actions on their parents.

The significance of this case is twofold. First, the language of the curfew ordinance provides a model for an ordinance that will likely withstand the scrutiny of the courts. Second, the provision allowing parental exceptions to juvenile movement during curfew hours and requiring that parents be responsible for the actions of their children gives the primary responsibility of the control of juveniles to their parents, where the responsibility properly belongs. The ordinance is carefully worded in that it provides no penalties for parental failure to properly supervise. This avoids the issue of penalizing parents who do not take care of their children properly, an issue that raises questions of constitutionality and can invalidate an ordinance.

People in Interest of J.M.
768 P.2d 219 (Colo. 1989)

Curfew ordinances for juveniles enacted for order maintenance are constitutional as long as they do not unduly infringe on liberty interests.

FACTS: At 11:45 P.M. an officer was dispatched to investigate a reported vandalism at a public park. Upon searching the park on foot, the officer found J.M. and a female companion hiding behind some bushes near the site of the alleged vandalism. Although the officer determined that J.M. had not committed the vandalism, he noted that J.M. appeared to be intoxicated and was under the age of 18. J.M. was taken into custody, tried in juvenile court, and was adjudicated delinquent based on his violation of the curfew ordinance and was fined $25.00. The ordinance in place at the time of J.M.'s arrest defined loitering and made it unlawful for an individual under the age of 18 years to loiter on or about any street, sidewalk, gutter, curb, parking lot, alley, vacant lot, park, playground, or yard, whether public or private, without consent of the owner or occupant thereof, during the hours of 10:00 P.M. and 6:00 A.M., unless accompanied by a parent, guardian, or other adult person over the age of 21. J.M. appealed, alleging that the curfew ordinance was unconstitutional based on both the Colorado Constitution and the United States Constitution.

ISSUE: Does the above curfew ordinance infringe on a minor's rights under either the state or federal constitutions? NO.

DECISION: The ordinance prohibiting loitering by minors after curfew did not infringe on a juvenile's rights under either the Colorado Constitution or the United States Constitution, as long as it was carefully crafted so as to further societal goals without unduly infringing on the limited liberty interests of juveniles.

REASON: "The People assert four state interests to justify this juvenile curfew: (1) the protection of children from each other and from other persons on the street during night-time hours; (2) the protection of the public from nocturnal mischief by minors; (3) the reduction of juvenile criminal activity; and (4) the enforcement of parental control of and responsibility for their children. We believe that each of these interests qualifies as a 'legitimate state interest.'

"Furthermore, we note that the Pueblo ordinance is carefully drawn so as to further its goals without unduly infringing upon the liberty interest of minors. Juvenile curfews can be divided into two categories: those proscribing 'presence' and those proscribing 'loitering.' Curfews which prohibit the presence of a minor on the streets after a certain hour have been held unconstitutional as an overly broad restriction on minors' liberty interests and First Amendment activities. . . . In contrast, curfews which simply prohibit undirected or aimless activity of minors during the curfew hours, but which allow the minor to participate fully in employment, religious, civic, and social activities, have been upheld. . . . We believe that the Pueblo ordinance, which restricts minors for only a limited period of time in certain public places, is drawn as narrowly as practicable. A minor is free to participate in any activity, whether it be social, religious, or civic, so long as he travels directly to or from that activity. The ordinance simply prevents youths from aimlessly roaming the streets during the nighttime hours. In light of the state's legitimate interests, and the state's special role in the control and supervision of minors, we do not believe that this ordinance unconstitutionally infringes upon J.M.'s liberty interests."

CASE SIGNIFICANCE: The court in this case upheld the constitutionality of the curfew ordinance, saying that the balance created between the best interests of the general public and any burdens placed on juveniles as a consequence of the ordinance were acceptable and rationally related to the specific state interests articulated by the community, which are:

1. protection of juveniles from others on the streets at night;

2. protection of the public from juvenile mischief at night;

3. reduction in juvenile crime; and

4. the enforcement of parental responsibility.

The court concluded that a clear relationship existed between the ordinance and its purposes without unduly infringing on juvenile rights, hence the ordinance was constitutional. This is the balance that must be achieved when drafting juvenile curfew ordinances.

Brown v. Ashton
611 A.2d 599 (Md. App. 1992)

Curfew ordinances that do not match their specified intent in law are unconstitutional on their face; however, officials who enforce previously unchallenged curfew ordinances are immune from civil liability.

FACTS: In 1978, the Board of Aldermen of the City of Frederick enacted an ordinance restricting the nighttime activities of persons under 18 years of age. The ordinance exempted children accompanied by a parent or guardian, children on an errand directed by a parent or guardian, children attending a cultural, scholastic, athletic, or recreational activity supervised by a bona fide organization, and children engaged in lawful, gainful employment during the curfew hours. In addition, the ordinance made it illegal for parents and owners and operators of establishments to allow a juvenile not otherwise exempted from the curfew ordinance to remain in a public place during the restricted hours.

In October 1990, the Mayor announced, and it was widely reported that police would begin enforcing the 1978 juvenile curfew ordinance. The police established three curfew checkpoints, concentrating on the downtown restaurant area. Approximately 30 minutes into the curfew period, officers entered an establishment that catered to juveniles and detained 28 juveniles until their ages could be determined. Among those detained was a 16-year-old female who was restrained by plastic handcuffs and photographed as part of the detention process. Upon complaint by her that the handcuffs were too tight they were removed and she was placed in a transport vehicle to be taken to police headquarters where she was to be picked up by her parents. None of the juveniles was formally arrested or placed in any cell or detention area.

A second female juvenile was also detained in this sweep of the targeted area when she was stopped on the street and could provide no proof of her age or identity. She also was handcuffed and escorted to a transport vehicle for transfer to police headquarters where she was photographed. Her mother arrived soon after the juvenile's arrival at the police station and provided proper identification with age information. The second juvenile female was promptly released to her mother.

The juveniles involved and their parents filed complaints alleging negligence, assault and battery, false imprisonment, invasion of privacy, and intentional infliction of emotional distress. They also asserted that the curfew ordinance itself violated the due process clause, the equal protection clause, and the First Amendment to the U.S. Constitution and the Maryland declaration of citizen rights.

ISSUES:

1. Was the juvenile curfew ordinance violative of due process, equal protection, and the First Amendment? YES.

2. If yes, should the government entity and its agents be held civilly liable for their actions in enforcing the curfew? NO.

DECISIONS:

1. In the absence of a compelling governmental interest, the juvenile curfew ordinance restricting nighttime activities of persons under 18 years of age within the city limits violated fundamental rights of juveniles and was unconstitutional.

2. The officials who implemented the curfew were acting within the role and scope of their authority and therefore were not civilly liable for any reasonable actions taken in the course of the carrying out their duties in enforcing the curfew ordinance.

REASON: "In light of [the] now established principles, i.e., (1) curfew statutes like that at issue here unconstitutionally burden fundamental constitutional rights of adults; and (2) minors do not lose constitutional rights because of their age, it would seem to follow as a matter of logic that the Frederick ordinance and all similar juvenile curfew ordinances are unconstitutional. This 'logic,' however, ignores a critical factor, which was recognized by the *Thistlewood* court in *Thistlewood v. Trial Magistrate for Ocean City*, 236 Md. 548 (1964), i.e., 'the activities and conduct of those under twenty-one may be regulated and restricted to a far greater extent than those of adults.' . . . The Supreme Court has recognized three factors that will generally be found to justify differential treatment of the constitutional rights of minors: 'the peculiar vulnerability of children; their inability to make critical decisions in an informed, mature manner; and the importance of the parental role in child rearing.' *Bellotti v. Baird*, 443 U.S. 622, 634 (1979).

"In sum, we conclude that the Frederick ordinance burdens the fundamental rights of minors and is not justified by any compelling governmental interest. This is, we note, the same conclusion that has been reached by the vast majority of courts . . .

"We do not here hold that the appellees acted in good faith and so enjoy some sort of immunity from state constitutional claims. . . . All that we hold here is that if a police officer has probable cause to arrest a person (like Bowens or Brown here), there is no basis upon which that person can assert that a search and seizure pursuant to that lawful arrest is unconstitutional. . . . This is so because, when a police officer acts within the scope of his or her law enforcement function, the officer is a 'public official,' and, as such, is protected by a qualified immunity against civil liability for nonmalicious acts performed within the scope of employment. . . . When a police office has probable cause to detain someone, and does so without malice or evil intent, the officer is, therefore, immune from civil liability, even if he or she is incorrect in the decision to act."

CASE SIGNIFICANCE: This case dealt with the enforcement of a juvenile curfew ordinance enacted twelve years prior to its implementation in a set of circumstances that did not match the intent of the curfew ordinance. The curfew ordinance was enacted in 1978 for use in emergency circumstances, and was used sparingly until 1990 when it was applied to a common problem in nightclub/restaurant areas—loitering, noise, and harassment.

The court ruled that application of the ordinance to such a set of "nonemergency" circumstances was unconstitutional because it was: (1) not compelled by an emergency, (2) not imposed for the minimum amount of time possible, and (3) not confined to a specific geographical area which, due to problems therein, justified its imposition.

However, the court ruled that the actions of government officials in enforcing the juvenile curfew ordinance were within the scope of their authority and therefore they could not be held liable for their actions as long as those actions were supported by probable cause. The officers in this case had no way of determining the constitutionality of the juvenile curfew ordinance and therefore assumed it to be legal and enforceable.

This case is significant in that it illustrates how an ordinance enacted for a set of circumstances could not be applied to circumstances of a different sort, particularly when it involves a deprivation of basic juvenile rights. In general, restrictions of basic rights must be justified by a compelling governmental interest. This case also reiterates the principle that government officials are not liable for their actions if those actions are based on a law or ordinance that is later found to be unconstitutional.

City of Maquoketa v. Russell
484 N.W.2d 179 (Iowa 1992)

Curfew ordinances that restrict all movement of juveniles, with no exceptions, are too broad and are unconstitutional.

FACTS: In 1990, two female juveniles attended a teen dance with the permission of their parents, one of whom dropped them off at the event. At 10:30 P.M. the two left the dance and walked to a parking lot within the city limits that was a frequent hangout for their friends. When asked to leave the lot by local police, the two proceeded to another parking lot on the outskirts of the city where they joined a third juvenile male who had a car. At approximately 12:30 A.M. the three left that parking lot and drew the attention of a police officer patrolling the area who suspected that they were speeding. The officer followed the car to a private driveway and proceeded to question the three. During questioning the officer determined that all three were minors in violation of the juvenile curfew ordinance in place at the time. No speeding citations were issued, no alcohol or drugs were found in the car nor were any other illegal substances found in the car. The only basis for detention of the juveniles was the curfew violation. All three were taken to police headquarters, where their parents were called; unable to reach either of the females' parents the police escorted both females to their homes at approximately 1:15 A.M. They were found delinquent of a curfew violation in juvenile court based on the provisions of the following ordinance, which:

> prohibited any person under 18 years of age to be upon the streets, sidewalks, or public places of the city between the hours of 11:00 P.M. and 6:00 A.M. the following day, unless accompanied by a parent, guardian, or adult having care and custody of the juvenile, or unless the juvenile was traveling in a direct route between his place of employment or a parentally approved supervised activity and home.

The two juveniles appealed their delinquency adjudications, alleging that the curfew ordinance was unconstitutionally overbroad, violated their First Amendment rights and their due process rights as guaranteed in the Fourteenth Amendment.

ISSUE: Was the juvenile curfew ordinance constitutional? NO.

DECISION: City curfew ordinances of this type, which include a total restriction on the movement of juveniles with no recognition of emancipated juveniles or exception for matters of emergency or other circumstances, are overbroad and violate a juvenile's First Amendment right to freedom of religion, speech, assembly, and association.

REASON: "The fundamental rights allegedly implicated by the ordinance here are freedom of religion, speech, assembly, and association. All but association are expressly mentioned in the First Amendment. All are within the term 'liberty' as protected by the due process clause of the Fourteenth Amendment against infringement by the states. . . . [W]e begin our analysis to determine whether the ordinance substantially chills First Amendment rights. As we view the ordinance it would prohibit older minors from attending alone any church services beyond 11:00 P.M. . . . Unlike the city, we do not think the exception 'a parentally approved supervised activity' in the ordinance protects minors from arrest when returning home from these services past 11:00 P.M. At best, we think this exception contemplates those events in which adults are physically present for the specific purpose of overseeing or chaperoning minors. School dances with parents present supervising these activities are a good example. Church services, though, can hardly be said to fit in this category.

"We recognize that an ordinance which restricts minors' rights to an extent greater than it restricts adults' rights may be sustained if the State or municipality demonstrates that it protects minors' peculiar vulnerability, accounts for their lesser ability to make sound judgments, and reflects society's deference to the guiding role of parents. . . . Though minors possess fundamental constitutional rights, their rights are not 'automatically coextensive with the rights of adults.' . . . the ordinance here is not drawn narrowly to provide exceptions for emancipated minors and fundamental rights under the First Amendment. For those reasons we think the ordinance is unconstitutionally vague."

CASE SIGNIFICANCE: This case deals with a highly restrictive juvenile curfew ordinance that attempted to control all movements of juveniles. The intent was to keep all juveniles off the streets and in their homes unless accompanied by an adult having care and custody of the juvenile, or unless the juvenile was engaged in direct travel from his place of work or from a parentally approved supervised activity. No exceptions were made for emergency situations, levels of maturity, proximity to home, and other circumstances.

The court ruled that the intent and language of the juvenile curfew ordinance was too narrow and unconstitutionally infringed on juveniles' constitutional rights. The infringement on the movement of citizens, even minor citizens, was considered by the court to be unnecessarily harsh and unjustified.

The court found that the ordinance violated a juvenile's First Amendment rights to freedom of religion, speech, assembly, and association, saying that, as read, the ordinance contemplated the presence of adults with juveniles during the times of curfew and that such restrictions hamper an individual's right to fully exercise his or her religion and other First Amendment rights. In addition, the court had problems with issues of enforcement of the ordinance and determined that various aspects of the ordinance were vague and open to a wide range of interpretation in excess of that commonly allowed in discretionary decisionmaking.

This case demonstrates once again that overly broad and vague ordinances will not be allowed by the courts. Careful drafting is essential in the creation of a constitutional curfew ordinance.

Qutb v. Strauss
11 F.3d 488 (5th Cir. 1993)

Carefully crafted juvenile curfew ordinances do not violate the equal protection clause, nor do they unconstitutionally infringe on parental rights of privacy.

FACTS: On June 12, 1991, in response to citizens' demands for protection of the city's juveniles, the Dallas City Council enacted a juvenile curfew ordinance. The ordinance prohibited persons under 17 years of age from remaining in a public place or establishment from 11:00 P.M. to 6:00 A.M. on weeknights and 12:00 A.M. and 6:00 A.M. on weekends. Public places were defined as "any place to which the public or a substantial group of the public has access, including streets, highways, common areas of schools, hospitals, apartment houses, office buildings, transport facilities, and shops." Establishment was defined as "any privately owned place of business operated for a profit to which the public is invited, including but not limited to any place of amusement or entertainment."

The juvenile curfew ordinance included a number of exemptions or defenses, including:

1. a juvenile accompanied by a parent or guardian;

2. a juvenile on an errand for a parent or guardian;

3. a juvenile traveling in a motor vehicle to or from a place of employment;

4. a juvenile traveling in a motor vehicle to or from an employment-related activity;

5. a juvenile attending a school, religious, or civic organization function;

6. a juvenile exercising his or her First Amendment rights of speech or association;

7. a juvenile engaged in interstate travel;

8.   a juvenile on the sidewalk in front of his or her own house or the house of an immediate neighbor;

9.   a juvenile responding to an emergency.

If a juvenile was suspected of being in violation of the curfew ordinance, an officer was required to ask the age of the juvenile and inquire into the reason for being in a public place during curfew hours. The officer could then issue a citation or arrest the apparent offender only if the officer reasonably believed that the juvenile was in violation of the ordinance and had no defense for such violation. If convicted, the juvenile was subject to a fine of no more than $500.00 for each offense.

Parents of the juvenile and owners, operators, and employees of business establishments were also subject to a fine of no more than $500.00 for each offense. Parents violated the curfew ordinance if they knowingly permitted or had insufficient control that allowed a juvenile to remain in a public place or on the premises of an establishment during curfew hours. Owners, operators, and employees of business establishments violated the ordinance by knowingly allowing a juvenile to remain on the premises of the establishment during curfew hours.

Two weeks after enactment of the ordinance, a group of juveniles and their parents filed suit, alleging that the curfew ordinance was unconstitutional based on the First, Fourth, Fifth, and Fourteenth Amendments and that the ordinance was vague and overly broad.

ISSUES:
1.   Did the Dallas juvenile curfew ordinance violate the equal protection clause? NO.

2.   Did the curfew ordinance violate the fundamental right of parents to determine the manner in which their children are raised? NO.

DECISIONS:
1.   The nighttime juvenile curfew ordinance that made it a misdemeanor for juveniles under the age of 17 years to use city streets or to be present at other public places within the city between certain hours did not violate the Constitution because it was justified by the compelling government interest of reducing juvenile crime and victimization while promoting juvenile safety and well-being.

2. The curfew ordinance did not violate parents' fundamental right of privacy by dictating the manner in which children should be raised because it had broad exemptions that allowed parents to retain the role of decisionmaker regarding their children.

REASON: "In the light of the state's compelling interest in increasing juvenile safety and decreasing juvenile crime, we must now determine whether the curfew ordinance is narrowly tailored to achieve that interest. The district court held that the city 'totally failed to establish that the Ordinance's classification between minors and non-minors is narrowly tailored to achieve the stated goals of the curfew.' We disagree. To be narrowly tailored, there must be a nexus between the stated government interest and the classification created by the ordinance. . . . This test 'ensures that the means chosen 'fit' this compelling goal so closely that there is little or no possibility that the motive for the classification was illegitimate.' . . . The articulated purpose of the curfew ordinance enacted by the city of Dallas is to protect juveniles from harm, and to reduce juvenile crime and violence occurring in the city.

"It is true, of course, that the curfew ordinance would restrict some late-night activities of juveniles; if indeed it did not, then there would be no purpose in enacting it. But when balanced with the compelling interest sought to be addressed—protecting juveniles and preventing juvenile crime—the impositions are minor. . . . Although it is true that in some situations unaccompanied juveniles may be forced to attend early evening features of a movie or leave a play or concert before its conclusion, this imposition is ameliorated by several of the ordinance's defenses so that the juvenile is not deprived of actually attending such cultural and entertainment opportunities. . . . Thus, after carefully examining the juvenile curfew ordinance enacted by the city of Dallas, we conclude that it is narrowly tailored to address the city's compelling interest and any burden this ordinance places upon minors' constitutional rights will be minimal.

"In addition to the claims presented by the minor plaintiffs, the parental plaintiffs argue that the curfew ordinance violates their fundamental right of privacy because it dictates the manner in which their children must be raised. Although we recognize that a parent's right to rear their children without undue governmental interference is a fundamental component of due process, . . . we are convinced that this ordinance presents only a minimal intrusion into the parents' rights. In fact, the only aspect of parenting that this ordinance bears upon is the parents' right to allow the minor to remain in public places, unaccompanied by a parent or guardian or other authorized person, during the hours restricted by the curfew ordinance. Because of the broad exemptions included in the curfew ordinance, the parent retains the right to make decisions regarding his or her child in all other areas . . ."

CASE SIGNIFICANCE: In this case, juveniles and their parents protested the enactment of a juvenile curfew ordinance that limited juveniles under the age of 17 from activities after certain hours, alleging that such government-imposed restrictions violated the equal protection clause of the Fourteenth Amendment and the fundamental right of parents to determine the manner in which their children were to be raised.

The court ruled that the city had developed a comprehensive curfew ordinance that was narrowly tailored to address the city's articulated compelling interest of protecting juveniles from harm while reducing juvenile crime and violence. Furthermore, the court found that the city had used the least restrictive means possible in achieving the goals by including the exemptions that allowed affected juveniles to remain in public areas during curfew hours for a variety of reasons. Thus, the curfew did not violate the equal protection clause because although it did designate a group of targeted juveniles any intrusions imposed by the curfew on that group were minimal when balanced with the compelling interests presented by the city.

The court also ruled that any intrusion by the curfew into the privacy of parents to dictate the manner in which their children are to be raised is minimal, affecting only the right of parents to allow their children to remain outside the home during very late hours of the night engaged in no productive activity included as a legal exemption to the curfew.

The ordinance challenged in this case should serve and has served as a model for numerous city and state curfew ordinances and laws. Similarly worded and structured curfew ordinances have sprung from this model and likewise have, with few exceptions, withstood judicial scrutiny. This case was decided by a Federal Court of Appeals and therefore carries more authority than cases decided by Federal District Courts.

State v. Bean
869 P.2d 984 (Utah App. 1994)

Reasonable suspicion of curfew violation and the fact that a minor might be in possession of alcohol allows officials a limited period of time to question the suspect without infringement of constitutional rights.

FACTS: Early one morning, a Utah deputy was patrolling in a one-person unit when he heard a radio transmission that area city police were looking for two male suspects close to his location. Less than 10 minutes later he encountered Bean and his companion walking slowly in front of a strip mall in which all the businesses were closed. The deputy pulled into the driveway of the mall, in front of the two individuals, who then walked in the direction of his car. The deputy observed that Bean appeared to be very young and was on the streets in violation of the local curfew ordinance. The officer also observed that Bean appeared to be intoxicated. When asked, Bean produced proper identification and indicated that he and his friend were going to a nearby convenience store. A computer check on both individuals indicated that there was an outstanding warrant for Bean's arrest. By this time a second deputy had arrived and after a short time Bean admitted to consuming alcohol, which was also illegal for minors. He was arrested for consumption of alcohol by a minor and on the outstanding warrant and was taken to jail. The entire interaction between Bean and the officers lasted less than 10 minutes. During the required search as part of processing at the police station, a controlled substance and drug paraphernalia were found on Bean and those charges were added to the two previously recorded. At trial, Bean attempted to suppress all evidence gathered as part of the questioning and arrest process, claiming that the officer's stop violated his Fourth Amendment right to be free from unreasonable searches and seizures. Upon denial by the trial court, Bean entered a conditional guilty plea to two of the charges—possession or consumption of alcohol by a minor and possession of drug paraphernalia. He appealed those two convictions.

ISSUE: Did reasonable suspicion on the part of the officer that the juvenile had consumed alcohol and that the minor might be in violation of curfew justify the detention of the juvenile, for a limited time, primarily for identification and warrant check purposes? YES.

DECISION: The state of Utah classifies police encounters with citizens in one of three ways: (1) a level one stop, in which an officer may approach a citizen at any time and pose questions as long as the citizen is not detained against his will; (2) a level two stop, in which an officer may seize a person if the officer has an "articulable suspicion" that the person has committed or is about to commit a crime; however, the detention must be temporary and last no longer than is necessary to effectuate the purpose of the stop; (3) a level three stop, in which an officer may arrest a suspect if the officer has probable cause to believe an offense has been or is being committed.

In this case, the juvenile was clearly interacting with the officer under level one search regulations until such time that the encounter escalated to level two, based on the intoxication of the juvenile and the outstanding warrant for his arrest, which provided the officer with "articulable suspicion" to support the detention and transportation of the juvenile.

REASON: ". . . [W]e hold the trial court was correct in concluding the initial encounter between Deputy Schroeder and the defendant qualifies as a level one stop. In response to an attempt to locate suspects, Deputy Schroeder pulled up alongside the defendant and then stopped approximately ten feet in front of him. At the outset, Deputy Schroeder was the only officer present. He used no lights or sirens, and did not call out to the defendant or tell him he must stay. Deputy Schroeder did not display his weapon, nor did he touch, restrain, or threaten defendant. He merely asked for defendant's identification. Consequently, we conclude that Deputy Schroeder's initial encounter with defendant was a level one stop and the Fourth Amendment was not implicated.

"Deputy Schroeder had a reasonable articulable suspicion that defendant had consumed alcohol and was a minor. After Deputy Schroeder determined from the dispatcher that the defendant had an outstanding warrant, he had probable cause to make the arrest. Thus, the defendant's Fourth Amendment rights were not violated."

CASE SIGNIFICANCE: This case deals with the "field stop" of a juvenile from which a curfew violation charge was filed. Important in this case was that the juvenile was not stopped for a curfew violation; rather, the initial stop was as a result of a call about two male suspects in the area. Only as the two subjects approached the officer did he notice that they were juveniles. The other key to this case is that the officer never used force or the threat of force and the interaction itself lasted for a short period and was for identification purposes only.

The court ruled that the general questioning of a juvenile, who may be in violation of a juvenile curfew ordinance, for identification purposes is a valid use of field interrogation techniques. Furthermore, if as a result of that questioning, probable cause develops for an arrest, any evidence gathered is legally admissible in court. The court found that the conduct of the officer in not using coercive or threatening techniques and the limited time involved in the interaction implied that the juvenile's constitutional rights were not violated even though he was generally questioned by the police.

This case clarifies the issues related to the proper role of police in handling a juvenile, even those suspected of curfew violation. The conduct of the police need be no different than in the handling of an adult in similar circumstances. Had the suspects in this case been adults instead of juveniles, the court decision would likely have been the same.

Matter of Appeal in Maricopa County
887 P.2d 599 (Ariz. App. 1994)

A juvenile's walk in the park in violation of a curfew ordinance is not protected as a First Amendment activity. The ordinance itself did not violate the fundamental rights of juveniles and could be enforced.

FACTS: A 15-year-old high school junior obtained her father's permission to go out with a group of her friends on a Saturday night. She went to a male friend's house to watch television but, deciding not to disturb his sleeping parents, walked to a park that was 50 to 100 yards from her friend's house. The police department received an anonymous report of a juvenile disturbance in that same park and upon arrival found the 15-year-old and two older males laughing and talking loudly. The officer asked all present their ages and upon discovering the female juvenile's age, took her into custody for violating the curfew ordinance, transported her to a detention center where she was fingerprinted, photographed, and eventually released to her mother. At her adjudication hearing, her father testified that he gave his daughter permission to go to her friend's house and to the park, but on cross-examination he acknowledged that he did not give specific permission for his daughter to be in a public park after curfew hours. However, he stated that he would not have forbidden her from such conduct had he been asked.

The juvenile court later found the 15-year-old delinquent for violating the curfew ordinance and fined her $56.00. The juvenile appealed her adjudication, alleging that the curfew ordinance was unconstitutional, primarily based on its being overbroad and vague.

ISSUES:
1. Was the curfew ordinance constitutional? YES.

2. Was the ordinance unconstitutionally broad or vague as to be impossible to equitably enforce? NO.

DECISIONS:
1. The juvenile's walk in the park in violation of the curfew ordinance was not protected as a First Amendment activity.

2. The ordinance itself did not violate the fundamental rights of juveniles and was not impossible to enforce equitably.

REASON: "Walks in the park have been characterized as among historical 'amenities of life' . . . However, we do not believe that the juvenile's walk in the park was protected First Amendment activity.

"Whenever the exercise of a minor's rights to freedom of speech, religion, assembly and association require the minor to move about, freedom of movement must also be protected under the First Amendment. Restricting movement so that an individual cannot exercise First Amendment rights without violating the law is equivalent to a denial of those rights. . . . Even apart from the First Amendment, citizens enjoy a fundamental right to freedom of movement. 'The right to walk the streets, or to meet publicly with one's friends for a noble purpose or for no purpose at all—and to do so whenever one pleases—is an integral component of life in a free and ordered society.' . . . This right is rooted in our federal and state constitutional protections of fundamental liberty interests under the doctrine of substantive due process.

"In determining whether a significant state interest not present in the case of an adult justifies infringing upon minors' fundamental rights, we examine three factors: 'the peculiar vulnerability of children; their inability to make critical decisions in an informed, mature manner; and the importance of the parental role in child rearing.' . . . If the state does not have a significant interest that is unique to children in terms of one of these factors, then the state must treat adults and children the same. . . . [W]e note that the plague of crime and drugs at which the curfew is directed, while not *peculiar* to minors, is more damaging to them because they are more vulnerable. . . . We recognize that certain temptations may arise during curfew hours which could end in serious consequences for a juvenile. Other statutes also offer specific protection against the consequences of such choices . . . The curfew ordinance, however, rests on the implicit assumption that in many cases the traditional family unit, in which two parents exercise control over their children's activities, has dissolved. Courts like this one, given the overview of life seen in their caseloads, know that this is undeniably true for overwhelming numbers of children in this country including Arizona . . ."

CASE SIGNIFICANCE: The ordinance in this case involved typical boilerplate language including the exceptions of juveniles whose activities have been parentally approved. In this case the juvenile exceeded the range of activity approved by her father, even though if asked he would have had no objection to the juvenile's conduct.

The court ruled that the juvenile curfew ordinance was constitutional and that it included refinements imposed by the courts in previous cases. It covered as many areas of contingency as possible, was well-drafted, clear, and fully implementable.

The court acknowledged that it was possible that enforcing the ordinance would result in the violation of some juveniles' constitutional rights, but that the protection of society as a whole and the insignificant level of such intrusion combine to achieve a balance between the juvenile's rights and society's interests. This case once again demonstrates that a well-drafted curfew ordinance can be and is legally valid.

Detention of Juveniles 4

I. United States Supreme Court Cases

Schall v. Martin (1984)

II. Lower Court Cases

Baldwin v. Lewis (1969)
Martarella v. Kelley (1972)
Cox v. Turley (1974)
Martin v. Strasburg (1982)
D.B. v. Tewksbury (1982)
Horn by Parks v. Madison County Fiscal Court (1994)

Introduction

In some cases, juvenile offenders accused of delinquent acts are not allowed to return to the custody of their parents. One of the alternative placements for juveniles is a secure juvenile detention center. Juvenile detention is defined as "the temporary confinement of children within a physically restricting facility pending adjudication, disposition, or implementation of disposition."[1] Recent studies show that the use of detention in the juvenile justice system is increasing. In 1985, delinquency admissions to juvenile detention centers numbered 224,500. By 1994, the number of annual admissions rose to 321,200, more than a 43 percent increase.[2]

Most of the juveniles that come through the juvenile system do not spend time in detention centers. Recent research suggests that in 1994, of all delinquency cases referred to juvenile court, only 22 percent of the referred males and 16 percent of the referred females were detained.[3]

Juveniles are entitled to a detention hearing to determine whether detention is required. Usually there is a requirement that detention hearings be held within a certain period after the juvenile is detained. In general, that time frame falls between 48 to 72 working hours after the child is placed in detention.[4] The criteria that must be met for a child to be held in detention are usually stated in a state's juvenile code. The legal criteria to hold juveniles in detention appear similar across the states. Research suggests that the most often cited legal criteria for the detention of juveniles are: the protection of self or others, or others' belongings; the nature of the current offense or the depth of the juvenile's record; the child lacks adequate parental supervision; and ensuring that the child does not abscond from the jurisdiction of the juvenile court.[5] However, according to Ellen Schall:

> Children are held in detention for a variety of reasons: the nature of the charge, their previous record, a history of not appearing in court, lack of an adult to whom they can be released, a judge unavailable on nights or weekends, or even for an extra-legal reason—to teach the kid a lesson.[6]

One of the concerns about putting juveniles into secure facilities is that bail is generally not an option for juveniles. The Supreme Court has not addressed the issue of whether bail is a constitutional right for juveniles. Lower courts that have heard cases regarding bail for juveniles are not consistent in their holdings.[7]

> Decisions have found that juveniles have a constitutional right to bail; that juvenile act procedures, when applied in a manner consistent with due process, provide an adequate substitute for bail; or that juveniles do not have a consti-

tutional right to bail. Nine states . . . have enacted laws granting juveniles the right to bail .[8]

There have been many legal and constitutional issues regarding the housing of juveniles in detention facilities. The cases in this chapter were chosen to illustrate some of the most controversial legal areas.

The 1984 *Schall v. Martin* case is the landmark Supreme Court case concerning the detention of juvenile offenders. The Court held that it was constitutional for juveniles to be held in preventive detention. Preventive detention allows the youth to be detained if there is a serious risk that the child will commit more delinquent acts if released. *Martin v. Strasburg* addressed the same question and illustrates a much different conclusion reached by the lower courts.

The process of detention is an issue addressed by numerous courts. This is demonstrated in the 1969 case of *Baldwin v. Lewis*. The 1972 case *Martarella v. Kelley* demonstrates the concern of the federal courts regarding the question of the housing of delinquent youth and youth considered *persons in need of supervision* (PINS) in the same facility. It also dealt with the conditions of confinement found in juvenile detention facilities. The 1974 case, *Cox v. Turley*, again demonstrates the concern of the courts with the   constitutional rights of juveniles who are detained.

D.B. v. Tewksbury (1982), and   the 1994 *Horn by Parks v. Madison County Fiscal Court* are included to illustrate concerns of the courts when addressing the issues of housing juveniles in adult jails rather than in juvenile detention centers. Given the increased reliance on detention in juvenile justice, the issues that these cases address—the processes, conditions, and placement of youth who need to be held in secure detention—will continue to come to the attention of the courts. In addition, if juvenile courts continue to take on the trappings of the adult court, cases regarding the right to bail for juveniles may increase.

Notes

[1]   Robert M. Regoli and John D. Hewitt, *Delinquency in Society*, Third Edition (1997) at 528.

[2]   Jeffrey A. Butts, Howard N. Snyder, Terrence A. Finnegan, Anne L. Aughenbaugh, and Rowen S. Poole, *Juvenile Court Statistics 1994*. Washington, DC: National Center for Juvenile Justice. Office of Juvenile Justice and Delinquency Prevention. U.S. Department of Justice, Office of Justice Programs. (1996).

[3]   Jeffrey A. Butts, Howard N. Snyder, Terrence A. Finnegan, Anne L. Aughenbaugh, and Rowen S. Poole, *Juvenile Court Statistics 1994*. Washington, DC: National

Center for Juvenile Justice. Office of Juvenile Justice and Delinquency Prevention. U.S. Department of Justice, Office of Justice Programs. (1996).

[4]   Clemens Bartollas, *Juvenile Delinquency*, Fourth Edition (1997).

[5]   Barry Krisberg and James F. Austin, *Reinventing Juvenile Justice* (1993).

[6]   Ellen Schall, "Principles for Juvenile Detention." In *From Children to Citizens. Volume II: The Role of the Juvenile Court.* (Frances X. Hartmann, ed. 1989) at 351.

[7]   Clemens Bartollas, *Juvenile Delinquency*, Fourth Edition (1997).

[8]   Clemens Bartollas, *Juvenile Delinquency*, Fourth Edition (1997) at 436.

I.   UNITED STATES SUPREME COURT CASES

✓ Schall v. Martin
104 S. Ct. 2403 (1984)

Preventive detention of juveniles is constitutional.

FACTS: Martin was arrested and charged with first degree robbery, second degree assault, and criminal possession of a weapon. Martin was 14 years old at the time of arrest and therefore came under the jurisdiction of New York's Family Court. At the delinquency proceedings, the Family Court judge ordered Martin detained under New York statute. Five days later, a probable cause hearing was held and probable cause was found to exist for all charges against Martin. At the fact-finding hearing, Martin was found guilty of robbery and criminal possession of a weapon. He was adjudicated delinquent and placed on two years' probation. Martin was detained a total of 15 days.

The New York law challenged by Martin contained the following provisions: it authorized the pretrial detention of an accused juvenile delinquent on the basis of a finding, preceded by notice and a hearing and supported by a statement of reasons and fact, of a "serious risk" that the child "may before the return date commit an act which if committed by an adult would constitute a crime," and provided for a more formal hearing within at least 17 days if detention is ordered.

ISSUE: Is the preventive detention of juveniles charged with a delinquent act constitutional? YES.

DECISION: Preventive detention is constitutional because it protects both the juvenile and society from the hazards of pretrial crime. This objective is compatible with the "fundamental fairness" requirement of the due process clause in juvenile proceedings.

REASON: "There is no doubt that the Due Process Clause of the Fourteenth Amendment is applicable to juvenile proceedings. . . .We have held that certain basic constitutional protections enjoyed by adults accused of crimes also apply to juveniles. But the Constitution does not mandate elimination of all differences in the treatment of juveniles. *See*, e.g., *McKeiver v. Pennsylvania,* 403 U.S. 528 (1971) (no right to a jury trial). The state has a 'parens patriae' interest in preserving and protecting the welfare of the child. *Santosky v. Kramer*, 455 U.S. 745, 766 (1982) which makes a juvenile proceeding fundamentally different from an adult criminal trial. We have tried to strike a balance—to respect the 'informality' and 'flexibility' that characterize juvenile proceedings and yet to ensure that such proceedings comport with the 'fundamental fairness' demanded by the Due Process Clause.

"The juvenile's countervailing interest in freedom from institutional restraints, even for a brief time involved here, is undoubtedly substantial as well. But that interest must be qualified by the recognition that juveniles, unlike adults, are always in some form of custody. Children, by definition, are not assumed to have the capacity to take care of themselves. They are assumed to be subject to the control of their parents, and if parental control falters, the State must play its part as *parens patriae*. In this respect, the juvenile's liberty interest may, in appropriate circumstances, be subordinated to the State's '*parens patriae* interest in preserving and promoting the welfare of the child.' *Santosky v. Kramer, supra*, at 766."

CASE SIGNIFICANCE: This case is important because, for the first time, the Supreme Court recognized the constitutionality of pretrial detention of juveniles, an issue previously unresolved. The Court held that while a juvenile's constitutional interests must be protected, the interests of the state and society must also be considered. When these interests appear to conflict, it is the Court's duty to weigh and balance these interests and rule in favor of the more compelling interest. The type of pretrial detention used in New York had the best interests of both the child and the community in mind. Under New York law, the juvenile is held only as long as necessary to process the case and these proceedings are bound by time requirements. What little harm might be done to the juvenile while being detained does not outweigh the harm that conceivably could be inflicted on community members by an unsupervised juvenile.

The decision does not say that unlimited preventive detention is constitutional. The New York law that was upheld in this case provided for preventive detention on the basis of a finding, preceded by notice and a hearing, and supported by a statement of reasons and facts of a serious risk that the child "may before the next return date commit an act which if committed by an adult would constitute a crime." The law also provided for a more formal hearing within at least 17 days if detention was ordered. These provisions of the New York law were deemed constitutional. What this means is that any state statute with provisions for preventive detention similar to New York's would also be upheld as constitutional. Those with different provisions, particularly if they are more arbitrary, might not be constitutional. State juvenile detention laws will be decided by the Court on a case-by-case basis. The closer the provisions of these laws are to the New York statute, the greater are their chances of being held constitutional.

II. LOWER COURT CASES

✓Baldwin v. Lewis
300 F. Supp. 1220 (E.D. Wis. 1969)

Juveniles are entitled to a hearing on the existence of probable cause for continued detention subsequent to arrest.

FACTS: Baldwin was taken into custody for arson. At the Court Detention Center, a "Detention Authorization" form was filed with no reason for detaining the youth cited. The following day, before the child's mother arrived, the child was ordered detained because "[I]t is reasonably believed that the child has committed an act which if committed by an adult could be a felony" and "The child is almost certain to commit an offense dangerous to himself or the community before the court disposition or transfer to an institution or another jurisdiction." Two days later, at a detention "rehearing," a juvenile judge ordered the juvenile held without bail.

The child's attorney objected to certain facts of the arrest, stating that because one month had elapsed between the arson and the arrest, there should have been some "judicial determination of probable cause prior to the petitioner's arrest." The counsel stated that he was requesting "a discharge of the petitioner due to the failure of the Milwaukee Police Department to obtain any judicial determination of probable cause prior to petitioner's arrest." The court told the attorney to file a motion, and to return to the matter of the hearing—the child's detention.

The attorney argued for release of the child to the custody of the mother without bail, or with bail if the court felt it necessary. The probation department representative recommended further detention. The state argued for continued detention without bail. The court stated that "it would be in the best interests of the juvenile and the community that the boy be detained pending further proceedings in this matter" as "the child is almost certain to commit an offense dangerous to himself or the community before the court disposition or transfer to an institution or another jurisdiction."

The next day a writ of habeas corpus was filed. The Circuit Court held that the detention hearing in the Children's Court was not proper and that the child should be given a new detention hearing. That court then assumed plenary powers and a detention hearing was conducted. The state was asked to produce evidence of why the petitioner had been detained, and the state produced the three "Detention Authorization" forms and testified that all procedures were followed in the youth's detention. The Circuit Court held that the actions of the State in not showing probable cause that the juvenile committed the act were within statutory requirements. The court further found the actions of the Milwaukee Police Department in the initial arrest, and the Children's Court in the initial detention of the juvenile to be in compliance with the children's code. The court held that the juvenile be held in detention with no right to bail.

ISSUES:
1. Must probable cause exist before a juvenile must be taken into custody on suspicion of having committed a violation of law which would constitute a crime if committed by an adult? YES.

2. Must the determination of probable cause be made by a judicial officer prior to arrest? NO.

3. Was the petitioner entitled to a hearing on the existence of probable cause for his continued detention subsequent to his arrest? YES.

4. Does the petitioner have a constitutional right to bail? DOES NOT REQUIRE COURT DECISION.

DECISION: The child was "denied due process of law, in violation of the Fourteenth Amendment during his detention hearings before both the Children's Court and the Circuit Court." The writ of habeas corpus was justifiably granted.

REASON:
ISSUE ONE: "As the United States Supreme Court has interpreted this amendment, it requires that a person may be validly arrested only if there is probable cause to believe that a crime has been committed and that the person to be arrested has committed such crime. While the Fourth Amendment is a limitation upon the powers of the Federal Government only, it is well settled that the prohibition of the Fourth Amendment against unreasonable arrest is enforceable against the states through the due process clause of the Fourteenth Amendment; hence, a state has no power to sanction arrests prohibited by the Fourth Amendment."

ISSUE TWO: "The Fourth Amendment requirement of probable cause for arrest does not necessarily require that an arrest warrant be obtained. An arrest can be validly effected without an arrest warrant or any other prior judicial determination of probable cause if the officer making the arrest, at the time of the arrest, had knowledge of facts sufficient to establish probable cause."

ISSUE THREE: "The Circuit Court interpreted Sec. 48.29 as not requiring the State to show probable cause that the petitioner committed an act which would have been a crime had he been an adult, or even that such a crime was in fact committed. It is my opinion that such an interpretation is not consistent with the requirements of due process as guaranteed to the defendant by the Fourteenth Amendment. Any person, regardless of age, who is detained on suspicion of criminal conduct, and thus deprived of his liberty, without a judicial determination of probable cause to believe that a crime has been committed and that he committed that crime, at any time prior to trial of the charges against him, is denied the very fundamental fairness which the Fourteenth Amendment is designed to protect."

ISSUE FOUR: "I find it unnecessary to reach the question of whether there is a 'constitutional right to bail' in juvenile proceedings, because I believe that the Wisconsin Children's Code, when applied consistent with the aforementioned requirements of due process, provides an adequate substitute for bail."

CASE SIGNIFICANCE: The significant issues in this case are Issue Three and Issue Four—the probable cause hearing for continued detention; and the constitutional right to bail for juveniles. The juvenile was detained without any indication of why he was detained and what evidence or documents were used to make the detention decision. The court in its detention decision showed no evidence that the child was beyond parental control, that his home was not an appropriate placement for him, or that he would be likely to abscond from the jurisdiction of the court. In addition, his lawyer was not allowed to examine the evidence that warranted further detention. Thus, the due process rights of the juvenile were denied.

Also noteworthy is the refusal of the court to address the issue of the right to bail for juveniles, an issue that remains unresolved in the Supreme Court today. The right to bail has not been given juveniles to date by any U.S. Supreme Court decision. It only is given by state statute or state constitution.

Martarella v. Kelley
349 F. Supp. 575 (S.D.N.Y. 1972)

Punitive, hazardous, and unhealthy conditions of confinement violate juveniles' constitutional rights.

FACTS: Robert Martarella was declared a Person in Need of Supervision (PINS) pursuant to New York law. The suit, filed on behalf of alleged and adjudicated PINS (Persons in Need of Supervision), alleges that the temporary detention in three of the maximum-security juvenile facilities operated by New York City deprives the children of due process and equal protection because treatment is not provided. The suit also declared that the treatment within the facilities constituted cruel and unusual punishment and because the children were held with juvenile delinquents their constitutional rights were further violated.

ISSUES:

1. Does the detention of a PINS in maximum-security facilities under conditions described as "punitive, hazardous, and unhealthy" and lacking treatment violate due process under the Eighth and Fourteenth Amendments? YES, in one facility.

2. Does the detention of PINS with juvenile delinquents violate the equal protection clause? NO.

DECISION: Conditions that existed in the Manida maximum-security juvenile facility violated the Eighth Amendment and did not furnish adequate treatment for the children who were not merely temporary detainees. The housing of PINS and delinquents together did not violate the PINS constitutional rights.

REASON:

ISSUE ONE: "The rapid urbanization of the United States in this century and the heavy influx of the poor to the cities in the last two decades have produced a numerous class of children whose conduct, although not criminal in character or legal designation, results in their incarceration.

"Generally speaking, children who have been adjudicated as PINS are truants, or runaways, or have been ungovernable at home. The acts for which they may be brought before a court, detained at the centers and thereafter held in custody for a term would not constitute crimes if committed by an adult.

"What we have said, although the record would justify more, is sufficient to establish that, however benign the purposes for which members of the plaintiff class are held in custody, and whatever the sad necessities which prompt their detention, they are held in penal condition. Where the state, as *parens patriae*, imposes such detention, it can meet the Constitution's requirement of due process and prohibition of cruel and unusual punishment, if, and only if, it furnished adequate treatment to the detainee."

ISSUE TWO: ". . . [E]ven though we may find more persuasive the view of the experts who strongly favor separation of PINS and JDs, we are bound by the rule, most recently explicated in *Sostre v. McGinnis*, 442 F. 2d 178, 191 (2d Cir. 1971), that:

> Even a lifetime of study in prison administration and several advanced degrees in the field would not qualify us *as a federal court* to command state officials to shun a policy that they have decided is suitable because to us the choice may seem unsound or *personally* repugnant. As judges we are obliged

to school ourselves in such objective sources as historical usage, *see Wilkerson v. Utah*, 99 U.S. 130, 25 L. Ed. 345 (1870), practices in other jurisdictions, *see Weems v. United States*, 217 U.S. 349, 30 S. Ct. 544, 54 L. Ed. 793 (1910), and public opinion, *see Robinson v. California*, 370 U.S. 660, 666, 82 S. Ct. 1417, 8 L. Ed. 2d 758 (1962), before we may responsibly exercise the power of judicial review to declare a punishment unconstitutional under the Eighth Amendment." (Emphasis in original.)

CASE SIGNIFICANCE: This case examined the detention practices of the New York Family Court. The suit alleged that juveniles declared as Persons in Need of Supervision (PINS) were deprived of their due process rights by their temporary detention in three maximum-security juvenile facilities. It was alleged that the treatment of the juveniles held in the three facilities constituted cruel and unusual punishment as treatment for the juveniles was not provided and that it also violated the constitutional rights of PINS to be held in the same facility with children adjudicated delinquent.

Whether the treatment of juveniles constitutes cruel and unusual punishment is addressed on a case-by-case basis, taking into account the circumstances in a particular facility. Placing PINS and juvenile delinquents together in the same facility is not in itself unconstitutional.

Cox v. Turley
506 F.2d 1347 (6th Cir. 1974)

Denial of statutory provisions in juvenile arrest and detention processes is unconstitutional.

FACTS: Duane Cox was 16 years old when he was arrested for violation of the curfew law in Madison County, Kentucky. Cox lived in the next county, and was apparently visiting relatives in Madison County. He was taken to the Madison County jail and ordered to be held there by Robert Turley, the non-lawyer judge who handled juvenile matters. When Cox was taken to the jail, he asked to call his father; the request was refused. Cox was placed under the custody of the jailer, and there was no hearing before he was jailed. The arresting officer did not notify Cox's parents, nor did he choose to release the child with a specified return date, as was permissible under the Kentucky statutes. Five days after the arrest, the child was brought before Turley, ordered to have his hair cut, his beard shaved, and to come back before the judge one week later. The child was released to the custody of his father, who promised to return his son the following week. When the child returned a week later, he was again released to the custody of his father "pending juvenile court proceedings." The complaint was brought by Duane's father, Thomas, for his son and "on behalf of all other juveniles residing within the confines of Madison County, Kentucky."

ISSUE: Were the child's constitutional rights violated when he was denied a telephone call to his parents, his parents were not notified by the arresting police officer (as required in the Kentucky statute), and he was detained in the general jail population for five days without any probable cause hearing? YES.

DECISION: The United States Court of Appeals for the Sixth Circuit held that the actions of the officials involved in the case violated the Fourth, Fifth, and Eighth Amendments to the Constitution.

REASON: "No notice was given him or his parents of the cause of his arrest. There was no probable cause hearing. The due process clause requires that notice of the charges must be given to the accused *at the earliest practical time and, in any event, sufficiently in advance of scheduled court proceedings so that reasonable opportunity to prepare will be afforded, and it must 'set forth the alleged misconduct with particularity.'*

"A boy 16 years old is not to be slighted and his rights bandied about because of his youth by a lay judge who knows nothing of the treatment to be accorded citizens, due to his lack of experience and training in the rigorous discipline of the law. There is something rather offensive to moral decency in considering the police officer telephoning the judge that he had arrested the boy, and the judge's immediate consent that the boy be forthwith locked up in the jail, without the right to call his father—all in violation of the law. It is difficult to define the relationship between the judge, the police officer, and the turnkey, as anything else but a well-understood collusion and connivance, and avoidance of the law.

"A boy 16 years old is not to be slighted and ignored by a court because of his youth, and he is not to be arrested, denied the right to call his father or counsel, imprisoned without a charge placed against him, and without even being arraigned, any more than a judge of this court is to be so treated for a trivial misdemeanor . . .

"We are of the opinion that the constitutional rights of plaintiff's son were violated, as heretofore set forth. By failing to arraign the boy and by keeping him in custody, denying him any rights to communicate with his parents, and without releasing the boy to his parents in accordance with the Kentucky statutes, and by failing to give notice of the cause of his arrest within the earliest practicable time, he was deprived of his liberty in violation of the Fourth and Fifth Amendments of the Federal Constitution. *See United States v. Hegstrom,* 178 F. Supp. 17, 20 (2d Cir.)."

CASE SIGNIFICANCE: In this case, the question of rights violations centered around certain practices of the courts when dealing with juveniles during arrest and detention. In this case, the child was denied a telephone call to his parents and was subsequently detained for five days in the general population of the adult jail.

The Federal Court of Appeals held what happened in this case to be a denial of the juvenile's constitutional rights. This case was decided in 1974 and reflected the practices in many juvenile courts at that time. Juvenile courts today have become much more conscious of the constitutional rights of juveniles because of court decisions and state laws, and therefore violations of this nature at present are less likely to occur.

Martin v. Strasburg
689 F.2d 365 (2d Cir. 1982)

Preventive detention of a juvenile is unconstitutional.

FACTS: The case was filed in the District Court as a habeas corpus class action on behalf of Martin and all other youths who were being held or would be held in juvenile detention under the provision of the New York Family Court Act, which authorized preventive detention for youths accused of juvenile delinquency. The section of the New York Family Court Act under challenge was FCA Sec. 739, which states:

> Sec. 739. *Release or detention after filing of petition and prior to order of disposition.*
> (a) After the filing of a petition under section seven hundred thirty-one or seven hundred thirty-two, the court in its discretion may release the respondent or direct his detention. In exercising its discretion under this section, the court shall not direct detention unless it finds and states the facts and reasons for so finding that unless the respondent is detained: (i) there is a substantial probability that he will not appear in court on the return date; or (ii) there is a serious risk that he may before the return date do an act which if committed by an adult would constitute a crime.

ISSUE: Did the preventive detention of juveniles under the New York Family Court Act violate the due process rights of juveniles detained? YES.

DECISION: The provision for preventive detention violates the due process clause of the Fourteenth Amendment.

REASON: "The statutory scheme can be summarized as follows. The challenged provision is Section 739 (a)(ii). It authorizes detention of a juvenile after filing of a petition, but before fact-finding, when a Family Court Judge determines 'there is a serious risk that [the juvenile] may before the return date do an act which if committed by an adult would constitute a crime.' Juveniles detained under 739 (a)(ii) are entitled to a probable cause hearing within three to six days and an expedited fact-finding hearing . . .

"The result in practice is that the vast majority of juveniles considered sufficiently dangerous by the Family Court to justify pre-trial incarceration under 739 (a)(ii) are in fact released by prosecutors or by the Family Court within days or weeks . . . Detention decisions under 739 (a)(ii) emphasize crime prevention and are made on the basis of limited information presented in summary fashion. Dispositional determinations, on the other hand, take the juvenile's welfare and potential for treatment into account and are based on more detailed and extensive information.

"The presumption of innocence and the requirement that guilt be proven beyond a reasonable doubt are important elements of due process itself, *In re Winship*, 397 U.S. 358, 90 S. Ct. 1068, 25 L. Ed. 2d 368 (1970), which would be gravely diminished in the protection they afford if individuals can be routinely incarcerated pending trial. Even the most persuasive demonstration of innocence cannot prevent the deprivation of liberty if incarceration precedes, rather than follows, the adjudication of criminal liability."

CASE SIGNIFICANCE: This case examined the Family Court Act of New York's pretrial detention provision. The court held that holding juveniles in detention under the Act was primarily done for punishment purposes and not for anticrime reasons. If pretrial detention was imposed for punishment, it violated the rights of children presumed innocent during their pretrial detention. The finding of the court was based on the fact that most of the children who were detained under the Act were not confined in any institution as part of their disposition. If there was no need for confinement at their disposition, there was, presumably, no need for confinement at the pretrial stage. In the 1984 case of *Schall v. Martin*, however, the Supreme Court reached a different conclusion, hence this case, decided by a court of appeals, may no longer be authoritative. Its significance is more historical than current.

D.B. v. Tewksbury
545 F. Supp. 896 (D. Or. 1982)

It is a violation of constitutional rights to hold juveniles in adult jails if they are status offenders, pending adjudication or held in circumstances that constitute punishment.

FACTS: All of the plaintiffs were children who were detained "or subject to confinement" in the Columbia County Correctional Facility (CCCF). CCCF is an adult jail in St. Helens, Oregon. They all claimed that their confinement was unconstitutional.

ISSUES:
1.   Does detaining juvenile pretrial detainees in jail under certain circumstances constitute punishment and violate the due process clause? YES.

2.   Does the confinement of runaways and children beyond parental control in jails violate the due process clause because it constitutes punishment? YES.

3.   Does holding a child pending adjudication of criminal charges in an adult jail violate due process rights? YES.

DECISION: Children held in adult jails in circumstances that constitute punishment, juveniles who are status offenders, and juveniles who are held in jail pending adjudication of criminal charges are all being held in violation of their constitutional rights.

REASON:
ISSUE ONE: "CCCF is designed for the purpose of confinement, without regard for human dignity or need. Nothing over and above the basic minimum necessary for maintenance of bodily functions is provided to children at CCCF. Nothing at CCCF is responsive to the emotional and physical needs of children in conflict with the law and their families. CCCF is a maximum security lockup facility.

"The requirement that children wear jail 'uniforms' and the lack of privacy for the use of showers and bathrooms contribute to feelings of anxiety and loss of self-esteem which are counterproductive to the goals of the juvenile justice system. The failure to provide counseling or psychiatric care for children in CCCF is also counterproductive to these goals.

"Confinement in CCCF is clearly and fundamentally intended to punish children. Punishment is the treatment of choice of Columbia County's Juvenile

Department for its detained children. This 'treatment' has little or nothing to do with simple detention, rehabilitation, or even the protection of society.

"Defendants have violated plaintiffs' due process rights under the Fourteenth Amendment to be free from pre-trial punishments by confining plaintiffs in CCCF. Those extraordinary conditions which alone and in combination constitute punishment are:

1. Failure to provide *any* form of work, exercise, education, recreation, or recreational materials.
2. Failure to provide minimal privacy when showering, using toilets, or maintaining feminine hygiene.
3. Placement of intoxicated or drugged children in isolation cells without supervision or medical attention.
4. Placement of younger children in isolation cells as a means of protecting them from older children.
5. Failure to provide adequate staff supervision to protect children from harming themselves and/or other children.
6. Failure to allow contact between children and their families.
7. Failure to provide an adequate diet.
8. Failure to train staff to be able to meet the psychological needs of confined children.
9. Failure to provide written institutional rules, sanctions for violation of those rules, and a grievance procedure.
10. Failure to provide adequate medical care."

ISSUE TWO: "A child who has run away from home or is out of parental control is clearly a child in distress, a child in conflict with his family and his society. But nobody contends he is a criminal. A runaway child or a child out of control, as an addict or an insane person, may be confined for treatment or for the protection of society, but to put such a child in jail—any jail—with its criminal stigma—constitutes punishment and is a violation of that child's due process rights under the Fourteenth Amendment to the United States Constitution. No child who is a *status* offender may be lodged constitutionally in an adult jail."

ISSUE THREE: "Juvenile proceedings, in the State of Oregon as elsewhere, are in the nature of a guardianship imposed by the state as *parens patriae* to provide the care and guidance that under normal circumstances would be furnished by the natural parents. It is, then, fundamentally fair—constitutional—to deny children charged with crimes rights available to adults charged with crimes if that denial is offset by a special solicitude designed for children.

"But when the denial of constitutional rights for children is not offset by a 'special solicitude' but by lodging them in adult jails, it is fundamentally unfair. When children who are found *guilty* of committing criminal acts cannot be placed in adult jails, it is fundamentally unfair to lodge children *accused* of committing criminal acts in adult jails.

"To lodge a child in an adult jail pending adjudication of criminal charges against that child is a violation of that child's due process rights under the Fourteenth Amendment to the United States Constitution."

CASE SIGNIFICANCE: In this case, the Court addressed the issues of confinement of status offenders and the confinement of children being held pending adjudication of delinquent charges in adult jails. The court examined the conditions of confinement in those jails. The court held that holding children prior to trial in adult jails does, under certain circumstances, constitute punishment. In addition, jailing children who were non-delinquent offenders—such as those who ran away from home and disobeyed parents—constituted punishment. The court also held that housing juveniles who were facing their juvenile adjudication hearing in an adult jail was fundamentally unfair and violated the child's due process rights. This exemplifies the movement in the juvenile justice system to classify and regard children as different from adults in the justice system and therefore they should be treated and housed differently.

Horn by Parks v. Madison County Fiscal Court
22 F.3d 653 (6th Cir. 1994)

Detention officials who exercise reasonable caution in protecting juveniles detained in facilities primarily dedicated to the housing of adults are not liable for injuries.

FACTS: In May 1990, Christopher Horn, age 17, pled guilty to a robbery charge in District Court. He was committed to the Cabinet of Human Resources and released to the custody of parents pending placement, with the stipulation that he remain "within an arm's reach of his parents." Toward the end of May, his parents reported him missing and signed a complaint and a pick-up order on him. Soon thereafter, Horn turned himself in to his court caseworker and was transported to the Madison County Detention Center, a newly opened facility designed for intermittent juvenile holding (intermittent being defined in part as for not more than 24 hours). Horn was processed into the facility with his court caseworker accompanying him. Both the detention staff member conducting the processing and the court caseworker testified that Horn appeared coherent and in a good mood. Horn was escorted to his cell in the juvenile detention area at approximately 1:45 P.M. and was visually checked at 1:58 P.M. and again at 2:15 P.M. On none of those occasions did he appear to staff to be upset or agitated, in fact he was watching television and requested bed linens and a face cloth. At approximately 2:20 P.M., Horn was discovered hanging from the bunk in his cell with a bed sheet tied around his neck. He subsequently suffered brain damage and paralysis and was confined to a wheelchair. He and his family contended that the county was negligent in the management of the juvenile detention area and failed to protect and care for the persons contained therein.

ISSUES:
1. Did the actions of county detention facility staff amount to deliberate indifference to the juvenile's medical needs? NO.

2. Are juvenile detainees as a group such a high suicide risk population as to constitute a special class requiring special consideration based strictly on age? NO.

DECISION: The failure of jail officials to take more than ordinary precautions to protect juvenile detainees from suicide did not constitute deliberate indifference to his medical needs. Actions by such employees were consistent with the policies in place within the detention facility. Even though the Juvenile Justice Act discourages the placement of juveniles in facilities primarily dedicated to adult inmate care, the actions of the staff in this case did not amount to negligence. This is true even if juveniles as a class are determined to be prone to suicide.

REASONS: "We assume appellant would have been able to establish that his temporary lodging in the Madison County Detention Center was technically in violation of the Juvenile Justice Act because an acceptable alternative placement was available. However, the record is devoid of proof tending to show that the center's nature, being a secure adult facility as opposed to a secure juvenile facility, contributed in any way to appellant's suicide attempt or resulting injury. In fact, the record unequivocally demonstrates appellant was scrupulously shielded from the deleterious influences associated with adult facilities. The Madison County Detention Center was brand new, approved for use as an intermittent juvenile holding facility. Appellant was received in an area specially designated and labeled 'juvenile intake.' He was accompanied and reassured during the intake procedure by his court designated worker. The intake production was sufficient to enable the attending officers to observe that appellant did not appear to be ill, upset, agitated, depressed, or under the influence of alcohol or drugs. He was segregated from adult offenders and detainees by sight and sound. He was not placed in restraints of any kind. After being escorted to his cell, he was permitted to take a shower and watch television. He was thereafter monitored at intervals of approximately 15 minutes. When appellant was discovered hanging from his bunk, CPR was administered and he was resuscitated after the sheet was removed from his neck. Appellant's claim that the technical violation of the Juvenile Justice Act caused his injury is not articulately asserted. The theory presumably is that if he had been placed in a secure juvenile facility, he would have been less likely to attempt suicide because: (1) he might not have been isolated, and (2) he would have been attended by officers better trained in the handling of juveniles. The theory is a matter of pure speculation, not supported by evidence of record. It amounts to nothing more that a hypothetical argument that his injury would not have occurred but for the violation of the Act.

"Plaintiff alleged that defendants were deliberately indifferent to the special needs of juvenile detainees, in violation of the Eighth Amendment. Where prison officials are so deliberately indifferent to the serious medical needs of prisoners as to unnecessarily and wantonly inflict pain, they impose cruel and unusual punishment in violation of the Eighth Amendment. . . . Officials may be shown to be deliberately indifferent to such serious needs without evidence of conscious intent to inflict pain. . . . However, the conduct for which liability attaches must be more culpable than mere negligence, it must demonstrate deliberateness tantamount to intent to punish."

CASE SIGNIFICANCE: This case dealt with the detention and attempted suicide of a juvenile in an adult detention center. The detention center was newly constructed, designed for intermittent juvenile custody, and as an acceptable placement for juveniles. The juvenile contended that the facility and staff failed to provide for the special needs of juveniles and were not appropriately equipped and trained to recognize the risks attached to the custody of juveniles, such as suicide.

The court found that the juvenile created a speculative argument with no actual basis for asserting liability against either the detention center or the center staff. Although the juvenile assumed that he would have been treated by a better trained staff in an exclusively juvenile detention center, he offered nothing to prove it. Nor did he present any incidents, events, or facility design of the adult detention center that caused him to take the extreme action of attempting suicide.

The court also ruled that contrary to the juvenile's assertion, juveniles are not a class of detainees particularly vulnerable to suicide and thus based solely on their age, entitled to special treatment and care, nor did the court find any fault in the processing of the juvenile, the placement of the juvenile or the monitoring of the juvenile while housed in the detention center.

The significance of this case is in the importance of an agency having a trained staff, updated policies, documentation of events, and having quality facilities in liability lawsuits against the state. When the government and its employees are doing the best job possible with appropriate resources and in an appropriate environment, the chances of a lawsuit succeeding are remote. This case also establishes that not every injury to a juvenile results in state liability. In general, only when gross negligence or a violation of a constitutional right is involved does liability ensue. Note that this case was decided by the federal Sixth Circuit Court of Appeals, thus affecting only states in that circuit, although the ruling may have a persuasive effect on other federal circuit courts.

Intake and Court Process Before Adjudication 5

I. No United States Supreme Court Cases

II. Lower Court Cases

Introduction

One of the most important stages in the juvenile justice process is the time between a juvenile's arrest and the adjudicatory hearing.[1] A juvenile may become involved in the juvenile justice process as a result of having allegedly committed a law violation that would be a criminal offense if committed by an adult, or having committed a violation of law that only applies to juveniles, otherwise known as a *status offense*. Such referrals may come from the police, parents, social service agencies, schools, or the general public.

Depending on the seriousness of the alleged law violation, the juvenile may be removed from the system or processed into the system through a unique feature of the juvenile justice system—intake. Intake is the first stage in processing a juvenile in the juvenile justice system. By bringing the juvenile to intake, the complaining party is asking the juvenile court to take jurisdiction of the case. Intake involves the screening of referrals to determine which cases can be handled judicially and which can be handled less formally. Intake officers have a substantial discretionary range of resolutions which include dismissal due to lack of evidence or the minor nature of the offense, warning and release, filing a formal petition of delinquency with the court, or diverting the juvenile out of the system.[2]

Diversion from the juvenile justice system is more than simply screening out cases that are trivial or unimportant for which no further attention is needed. Diversion encourages and even requires the juvenile to participate in a specific program or activity determined to be for the betterment of the juvenile. The threat of future prosecution generally prompts juvenile compliance with the provisions of diversion agreements.[3]

If diversion is not granted, a referral is made to the juvenile court in the form of a petition requiring the juvenile to appear before a juvenile judge. The process from this point on mirrors the adult criminal trial process with one exception—the entire proceeding is considered confidential and is closed to the public.

If the charges against a juvenile are serious enough or if he or she is a repeat offender, the juvenile may face a transfer of certification hearing to determine whether the juvenile should be processed under the adult system. Such hearings involve issues of age, maturity, mental competence, and understanding of the nature and consequences of the alleged act, among others. Even though a case may qualify for certification as an adult, the juvenile judge retains discretion to determine the appropriate avenue for processing.[4]

This chapter features cases that focus on post-police, pre-adjudication processes involving juveniles. Some of the stages, such as intake and transfer of certification to adult criminal court hearings, are unique to the juvenile justice systems of each state. Other stages involve broader processing issues such as detention, diversion, and competency procedures commonly used throughout the criminal justice system.

The case law on pre-adjudication processing is limited, but the importance of processes such as the ones discussed in this chapter is enormous because many of them involve the most basic of jurisdictional issues—whether a juvenile is tried in juvenile or adult criminal court and whether a juvenile is competent to stand trial in either court system.

Cases in this chapter deal with such issues as the Sixth Amendment right to counsel at intake, the need for probable cause at intake, and the appropriate use of information gathered at intake. Other cases deal with a juvenile's right to diversion, the constitutional basis for pre-adjudication detention of a juvenile, and the appropriate time frame for a juvenile to be presented to a judge for an initial hearing.

Two cases, *Christopher P. v. New Mexico* and *United States v. A.R.*, deal with issues involved in psychiatric or psychological evaluations of juveniles as part of the determination of appropriate jurisdiction. *Christopher P.* extended the Fifth Amendment right to remain silent to psychiatric or psychological evaluations to determine amenability to treatment in the juvenile justice system. The court in *United States v. A.R.* found that the same procedure, a psychiatric evaluation, was not a critical stage in juvenile justice processing and therefore was not protected by the United States Constitution, effectively denying juveniles such basic rights as the right to remain silent and the right to have counsel present during such evaluations. Other cases in this chapter deal with the relevance of local court rules and the use of technology in the pre-adjudication processing of juveniles.

Even though the cases included in this chapter are primarily from lower federal courts, as a whole they represent the diversity of early court processes of importance to juveniles charged with criminal behavior. No U.S. Supreme Court decision has addressed the issues raised by the cases in this chapter.

Notes

[1] Larry J. Siegel and Joseph J. Senna, *Juvenile Delinquency: Theory, Practice & Law* (1991).

[2] Peter C. Kratcoski and Lucille D. Kratcoski, *Juvenile Delinquency* (1996).

[3] Mary Clement, *The Juvenile Justice System: Law and Process* (1997).

[4] Peter C. Kratcoski and Lucille D. Kratcoski, *Juvenile Delinquency* (1996).

I. NO UNITED STATES SUPREME COURT CASES

II. LOWER COURT CASES

In re Frank H.
337 N.Y.S.2d 118 (1972)

Juveniles do not have a right to counsel at intake.

FACTS: Frank H., a minor, was apprehended by the police for auto theft. A delinquency petition was filed, alleging unauthorized use of an automobile. Counsel for the minor moved to vacate the petition, on the grounds that Frank H. was not afforded counsel at the intake stage of the Family Court proceeding.

ISSUE: Does a juvenile have a constitutional right to counsel at intake? NO.

DECISION: The intake conference is not a critical stage in the juvenile justice proceeding; therefore, a juvenile does not enjoy the constitutional right to counsel during intake.

REASON: "Intake is not a legal term and with the exception of juvenile and family courts, is foreign to the court field. Its use in juvenile and family courts has no doubt been adopted from the field of social welfare. In the welfare field, the client has complete freedom of choice. He comes to the agency and he may or may not decide to accept the service if offered. At the same time, the agency also has freedom of choice. It may or may not accept the client for service, particularly in the private welfare field. The same is not true with court intake. The 'client,' defined as the person complained about or alleged to be in a situation necessitating action, has no freedom of choice. Here the request for action is initiated by someone other than the client. Whatever freedom of choice exists as to whether action will be taken rests in the court, not in the client.

"To require counsel at intake would be an intolerable burden on an already overburdened court. The lack of manpower is both frightful and appalling."

CASE SIGNIFICANCE: This case focused on a juvenile's right to legal counsel during intake interviews. The court found that, based on protections in place in the system—such as the fact that information acquired from a juvenile during intake cannot be used in any guilt-finding phase, whether juvenile or adult, and the intent of intake, which is to provide relevant and valuable information for use by the court to better help the juvenile—the protection of legal counsel during the intake conference was unnecessary.

The court made note of the burden that would attach to the juvenile justice system if legal counsel was required at intake. It acknowledged that the system was already seriously overburdened and to add this requirement would only make a crisis imminent.

This case draws the line between critical and non-critical phases of juvenile justice processing. The line drawn is in accordance with the constitutional requirements in adult criminal cases in which counsel is required only in "critical phases" of the criminal justice process.

Wansley v. Slayton
487 F.2d 90 (4th Cir. 1973)

Spontaneous statements made by a juvenile while under the exclusive jurisdiction of the juvenile court can be used in adult criminal proceedings.

FACTS: Wansley filed a writ of habeas corpus while serving time in prison for the rape and robbery of a woman and several other crimes when he was 16 years old. Upon arrest, he was interrogated for five hours without the assistance of counsel or parent. His mother was called. Upon her arrival at the police station she was met by Wansley's juvenile probation officer. He informed her of the charges against her son and escorted her to his cell, whereupon she asked Wansley, "Buddy, did you do it?" to which Wansley replied "Yes." Because of his age, Wansley was under the jurisdiction of the juvenile and domestic relations court at the time he made the statement in the presence of his probation officer. Upon transfer to adult court, the juvenile probation officer testified at Wansley's trial as to the contents of the conversation at his cell. After numerous trials, Wansley was convicted of the rape and robbery and received sentences of life in prison and 20 years. He appealed.

ISSUE: Can spontaneous statements made by a juvenile in the presence of his juvenile probation officer, while under the exclusive jurisdiction of the juvenile court, be used against him in a trial as an adult? YES.

DECISION: When a 16-year-old made spontaneous admissions to his mother in the presence of his juvenile probation officer, while subject to the jurisdiction of the juvenile court, the probation officer's testimony with regard to those statements at a criminal trial of the juvenile did not violate the juvenile's constitutional right to due process and is therefore admissible.

REASON: "Suffice it to say, in rejecting this contention that counsel overlook or brush aside the fact that Wansley's spontaneous admission resulted from an unprompted question asked by his mother, not from questioning by Read or police or any other person.

". . . [Lower courts] concluded that the admission of such evidence offended 'fundamental fairness' because it arose out of a violation of the witness' 'role as a juvenile court officer, in *parens patriae*.' It relied for this conclusion on a line of cases from the District of Columbia Circuit, the first of which was *Harling v. United States* (1961) . . . 295 F.2d 161, and the last, *Harrison v. United States* (1965) . . . 359 F.2d 214. In those cases, however, unlike the situation here, the admission or confession, which had been held excludable, had been given in response to police interrogation and decisions did not purport to cover spontaneous statements such as was involved here. That is made clear in *Harrison*, where the Court pointedly remarked that '*Harling* puts to one side, as we do, the case of spontaneous statements. What are involved . . . are statements, secured by police questioning and confrontation.'

Of course, the officer was subjected to sharp cross-examination on this testimony, and it was argued by petitioner's counsel that the statement, if made, related to another offense. But whether the testimony was to be believed was a matter of resolution by the jury and was not a proper basis for denial of admissibility."

CASE SIGNIFICANCE: In this case, it was clear that the juvenile probation officer was acting in his official capacity and would not have been in a position to hear the spontaneous exchange between son and mother had he not been acting as an officer of the juvenile court.

It was also clear that the appearance of a probation officer as a prosecution witness under certain circumstances clearly violates the relationship of trust encouraged by the philosophy of the juvenile justice system and hampers the goals of rehabilitation. However, in this case the probation officer merely testified to a conversation he overheard between the juvenile and his mother. He did not participate in the conversation, neither did he intrude into the dialogue between mother and son. His testimony was purely that of an observer and therefore could not be excluded in a court of law.

Moss v. Weaver
525 F.2d 1258 (5th Cir. 1976)

Pretrial detention of juveniles without a probable cause determination is unconstitutional.

FACTS: The specific facts of the cases included in this class action suit are not important. What is important is the common process through which all these juveniles passed—a process established by the juvenile court judges in which accused juvenile delinquents were held in pretrial detention without a determination of probable cause that they had committed the offenses.

ISSUE: Does pretrial detention of a juvenile without a determination of probable cause violate the Fourth Amendment? YES.

DECISION: Pretrial detention without a probable cause determination violates the Fourth Amendment requirements of due process.

REASON: "Under Florida law a juvenile taken into custody on a charge of violating the criminal law is brought within 48 hours to a 'pre-detention hearing,' where the court decides whether to release or detain him [or her] pending a formal 'adjudicatory hearing.' The applicable statute specifies three factors for the judge to consider: whether detention is necessary to protect the person or property of the child or of others; whether a parent or guardian is available and able to provide adequate care and supervision for the child; and whether the parent or guardian convincingly assures the court of the child's future presence at the adjudicatory hearing. . . . The parties agree that in practice the seriousness of the alleged offense is also frequently taken into consideration. If a decision is made to detain the child, money bail is not available. . . . The District Court concluded that this scheme embodies fatal constitutional infirmities. The court quoted from *Cooley v. Stone*, 414 F.2d 1213 (1969), to the effect that the Fourth Amendment's prohibition on penal custody without a prompt judicial determination of probable cause applies to adults and juveniles alike.

"Upon examining the judgment below in light of *Gerstein v. Pugh*, 420 U.S. 103 (1975), our proper course is clear. First, we affirm the District Court's opinion insofar as it discerned a Fourth Amendment violation in Florida's current juvenile justice system. A finding of probable cause—i.e., of 'facts and circumstances sufficient to warrant a prudent man in believing that the [suspect] had committed or was committing an offense' . . . is central to the amendment's protections against official abuse of power. Pretrial detention is an onerous experience, especially for juveniles, and the Constitution is affronted when this burden is imposed without adequate assurance that the accused has in fact committed the alleged crime."

CASE SIGNIFICANCE: The court found in this case that no juvenile accused of delinquency could be held in custody prior to adjudication without a showing of probable cause made in an adversarial proceeding. Even though a pre-detention hearing is not generally viewed as part of a criminal proceeding, Fourth Amendment principles detailing when a juvenile should and should not be detained pending adjudication must be observed.

Fourth Amendment principles that require a pre-detention hearing do not dictate the structure of such a hearing, therefore the hearing itself may vary considerably from jurisdiction to jurisdiction. The only constitutional requirement is that the juvenile be granted a hearing. There is no constitutional right to hear or cross-examine adverse witnesses, nor is there a limitation as to the quality of testimony, hence allowing for the use of testimony of lesser reliability than that allowed during adjudication.

The significance of this case rests in its mandate that probable cause be established for pre-adjudication detention through an adversary hearing process, but that the hearing process itself is not bound by the strict requirements of an adjudicatory hearing. Such flexibility affords the juvenile an avenue for detention review without burdening the juvenile justice system with another full-blown proceeding.

In re Wayne H.
596 P.2d 1 (Cal. 1979)

Information gathered at intake cannot be used in any guilt-finding process, be it juvenile or adult.

FACTS: Wayne H., a 16-year-old male, was the passenger in a vehicle observed by police speeding away from the scene of a gas station robbery. The vehicle in which Wayne H. was found was pursued after its driver ran a stop sign. During the pursuit, Wayne H. threw a pistol out the car window. Upon arrest, Wayne H. was wearing clothes similar to those identified as worn by the robber, had a dark skin cap as identified by witnesses, and there was $54 in $20s, $5s, and $1s found on the passenger side floorboard of the car—exactly the amount stolen from the gas station in the exact denominations taken in the robbery. Wayne H. was taken into custody at 9:10 P.M. and held overnight. When questioned the following morning by police, he denied any involvement in the robbery and offered an alibi. At 8:10 P.M., he was taken to Juvenile Hall and was interviewed by a probation officer to determine whether he should be detained and whether transfer proceedings were warranted. Wayne H. was given his *Miranda* rights, but again denied any involvement. At the end of the interview, upon hearing that the probation officer intended to recommend detention and a transfer hearing to adult court, Wayne H. said, "I did this one." At the transfer hearing, in which Wayne H. was found amenable to treatment in the juvenile system, the probation officer testified as to Wayne H.'s admission. Wayne H. objected, but was adjudicated delinquent and appealed.

ISSUE: Is information acquired by a probation officer at intake admissible in a subsequent adjudication or criminal trial? NO.

DECISION: The purpose of an intake interview between a minor suspect and his or her probation officer is not to gather evidence of guilt, but to assemble all available information relevant to an informed disposition of the case, if guilt is established, and to assist in evaluating the need for detention and the minor's fitness for treatment as a juvenile. Therefore, it was an error to admit as evidence of guilt an incriminating statement that the minor made to the probation officer.

REASON: . . . "Admissions by a juvenile to a probation officer for use in the preparation of the social study, and to the juvenile court itself in the course of a . . . jurisdictional hearing, have both been excluded from subsequent adult criminal proceedings.

"The minor who is subject to the possibility of a transfer order should not be put to the unfair choice of being considered uncooperative by the juvenile probation officer and juvenile court because of his refusal to discuss his case with the probation officer, or of having his statements to that officer used against him in subsequent criminal proceedings. . . . Such a result would frustrate the rehabilitative purposes of the Juvenile Court Law.

"We conclude that the subsequent use of statements made by a juvenile to a probation officer in an [initial interview] would frustrate important purposes of that statute, and of the Juvenile Court Law generally. We therefore hold that such statements are not admissible as substantive evidence, or for impeachment, in any subsequent proceeding to determine criminal guilt, whether juvenile or adult. Such statements may, of course, be admitted and considered in hearings on the issues of detention and fitness for juvenile treatment."

CASE SIGNIFICANCE: This case dealt with the issue of whether information acquired by an officer of the court during an intake conference was admissible in any guilt-finding phase of judicial processing. The court found that the potential use of information acquired during intake in a guilt-finding phase of judicial processing would frustrate the intent and purpose of intake—to assemble all information relevant to an informed disposition of a case so that the juvenile justice system can treat juveniles individually, based on the particular dynamics of their environment.

The court saw the use of information acquired during the intake process as tainted primarily because of the nature of intake interviews, which encourage juveniles to be truthful and cooperative and which penalize juveniles who refuse to cooperate by deeming them as unamenable to treatment and possibly contributing to the decision to transfer them to adult criminal court. Although the court acknowledged that information acquired during intake could be used in determining detention status and in transfer hearings, it clearly distinguished those processes as preliminary to guilt-finding phases with few long-term ramifications for the juvenile.

The significance of this case rests in its protection of the juvenile during intake by prohibiting the admission of incriminating information acquired by officers of the court during an intake conference from being used in any subsequent adjudication or criminal trial. Note, however, that this decision was based primarily on state law. The United States Supreme Court has not ruled on the issue of whether exclusion of such evidence is required by the Constitution.

Washington v. Chatham
624 P.2d 1180 (Wash. App. 1981)

Juveniles do not have a constitutional right to diversion.

FACTS: Chatham, a minor, was among a group of juveniles who were part of an altercation with several adult golfers at a golf club. During the altercation, one of the adult golfers sustained serious and permanent eye injuries caused by blows struck by Chatham. Testimony further revealed that at least one of the juveniles was armed with a club. Because the juvenile was eligible for diversion consideration, the prosecutor contacted the chairperson of the local diversionary agency by telephone and relayed the facts of the case as they appeared in the police report. Based on that conversation, the chairperson declined acceptance of Chatham into a diversionary program. The denial was based on the seriousness of the offense, which did not fall within the list of acceptable offenses for inclusion in the diversion program. Chatham appealed.

ISSUE: Do juveniles have a constitutional right to diversion? NO.

DECISION: Although a juvenile has a right to be considered for diversion, he or she does not have the constitutional right to be guaranteed admission into a diversion program.

REASON: "The juvenile's statutory right to have his or her case referred to a diversion unit does not guarantee that the unit will enter into a diversion agreement with the juvenile. Diversion is not always an appropriate disposition, even in first offender juvenile cases.

"Although the informal procedures followed in this case are not exemplary, the juvenile's case was referred to a diversionary unit, was considered by that unit through its authorized representative and was rejected for reasons that were neither arbitrary nor capricious.

. . . "Because the rejection of the juvenile's referral was based on standardized safeguards properly adopted and reasonably applied to determine candidates with whom the committee would be likely to enter diversion agreements, it is not violative of due process. On these facts, exercise of some degree of informality in these preliminary proceedings did not deprive the defendant of a fair and reasoned decision or deny him his right to due process."

CASE SIGNIFICANCE: This case dealt with the issue of whether juveniles have a constitutional right to diversion. The court ruled that although juveniles have a constitutional right to be considered for diversion, they do not have a right to be placed in a diversion program regardless of program criteria.

The juvenile in this case was informally pre-screened by the diversion program staff and was deemed unfit for placement in diversion programming, based on the nature and seriousness of the alleged offense and the violence involved in the alleged act. Even though the juvenile's legal counsel contended that the juvenile was the perfect candidate for diversion, being a first-time offender and amenable for treatment, the court felt that the juvenile did not fit within the diversion program's criteria for admissions and that the diversion program had the right to refuse admission to the program based on established criteria, as long as they did not act in a discriminatory manner.

The court chastised the system on the laxity of the diversion review process in place at the time, saying that formal consideration is more appropriate in decisions of this magnitude. The court went on to say, however, that even though the review was less than satisfactory, the diversion program was clearly justified in refusing to accept the juvenile in question

This case is significant in that it clearly defined acceptance into a diversion program as a discretionary decision on the part of the agency. Diversion is not a constitutional right given to a juvenile who wants to avoid institutionalization.

United States v. Nash
620 F. Supp 1439 (S.D.N.Y. 1985)

If the requirements of the Federal Juvenile Delinquency Act concerning admonition of legal rights, notification of a responsible adult, and present-ment to a magistrate are not satisfied, any post-arrest statements made prior to presentment before the magistrate must be suppressed.

FACTS: Nash and his co-defendant Negron, both minors, were arrested for attempted armed bank robbery. Nash was arrested first, informed of his consti-tutional rights, and driven to FBI headquarters. Upon his arrival, he was es-corted to an interview room, again advised of his rights, and basic information was obtained. At that time, the FBI agents established his juvenile status and immediately called his mother to advise her of her son's arrest and the charges against him. His mother expressed her unwillingness to come to court for her son. Nash was processed and presented to a magistrate in the early evening. Approximately nine hours passed before his first appearance before a court.

Negron was arrested just after Nash. The arresting officers determined that he was a juvenile at the time of arrest and informed him of his constitutional rights. They then drove him to his mother's home where they intended to search the house and notify his mother of Negron's arrest. She was not at home so the officers informed relatives present of the situation (two of whom were juveniles). The officers then drove Negron to FBI headquarters, where he waived his rights and made a statement. He was processed and taken before a magistrate in the early evening. Approximately eight hours passed before his first appearance before a court.

The Federal Juvenile Delinquency Act provides:

> Whenever a juvenile is taken into custody for an alleged act of juvenile delin-quency, the arresting officer shall immediately advise such juvenile of his le-gal rights, in language comprehensible to the juvenile, and shall immediately notify the Attorney General and the juvenile's parents, guardian, or custodian of such custody. The arresting officer shall also notify the parents, guardian, or custodian of the rights of the juvenile and of the nature of the alleged of-fense.

> The juvenile shall be taken before a magistrate forthwith. In no event shall the juvenile be detained for longer than a reasonable period of time before being brought before a magistrate.

ISSUE: Were the notification procedures and time delay before the first court appearance justifiable, thereby allowing incriminating statements made by the juveniles to be admissible in court? NO.

DECISION: The requirements of the Federal Juvenile Delinquency Act concerning admonition of legal rights, notification of a responsible adult, and presentment to a magistrate were not satisfied, therefore any post-arrest statements made prior to presentment to the magistrate must be suppressed.

REASON: "In looking at the present language of the statute, we are influenced by the order in which its commandments appear. The first statement is that '[t]he juvenile shall be taken before a magistrate forthwith.' It is followed by the statement, '*In no event* shall the juvenile be detained for longer than a reasonable period of time before being brought before a magistrate.' The Government relies on the second statement as modifying and weakening the strength of the first sentence. We do not so interpret it. It is not always possible to take a juvenile before a magistrate. In the middle of the night or on weekends (at least from Saturday afternoon on in this District) it would be impossible to do so. Consequently, we interpret the second statement as covering that situation. When there is a magistrate available, we interpret the first statement as being a literal requirement to take the juvenile there immediately. In so interpreting the statute, we do not infer a constitutional right to such a presentment or suggest that the requirement is necessarily a wise one. We are merely attempting to interpret a congressional commandment in light of its plain language.

. . . "The statute provides for notification of a parent or guardian or custodian, and it seeks to alert a more knowledgeable and responsible adult not only of the arrest and the charges, but also of the juvenile's constitutional rights, in order to protect the defendant from himself. Given the purpose, notification made after a statement has been given, or made without spelling out the juvenile's rights to a 'responsible' adult, cannot satisfy the statutory mandate. We do not imply that a juvenile has a constitutional right to have an adult present during the interviewing process. We do find that the statute requires the notification of such an adult before a waiver of rights occurs. The Government's efforts at notification, although made with good intentions, do not satisfy the statute under the above analysis."

CASE SIGNIFICANCE: The court in this case addressed the required period before first appearance in court and the notification of parents or guardians when juveniles are arrested. The court recognized a substantial difference between the requirements of the Federal Juvenile Delinquency Act and what law enforcement officials did in this case. The Act specifically provides that law enforcement officials were to immediately notify the juvenile's parents of custody and of the juvenile's constitutional rights, and that the juvenile shall be presented to a magistrate as soon as possible. None of these was done in this case.

This court stated that although the judiciary will allow reasonable delays, it will not allow outrageous neglect of procedural rules as normal behavior on the part of law enforcement agencies. Note, however, that this decision is based on the provisions of federal law and does not necessarily apply to proceedings in state juvenile courts.

Washington v. Chavez
761 P.2d 607 (Wash. 1988)

Local court rules establishing time frames for juvenile processing do not violate the separation of powers doctrine.

FACTS: This case involves a consolidation of four fact situations with the common theme of testing a local court rule providing that an action brought against a juvenile may be dismissed if there is more than a 30-day delay between the completion of the police investigation and the filing of an information by the prosecuting attorney. The rule in question read as follows:

> To Dismiss for Delay in Referral of Offense, the Court may dismiss an information if it is established that there has been an unreasonable delay in referral of the offense to the Court. For purposes of this rule, a delay of more than thirty (30) days from the date of completion of the police investigation of the offense to the time of filing of the charge shall be deemed prima facie evidence of an unreasonable delay. Upon a prima facie showing of unreasonable delay, the Court shall then determine whether or not dismissal or other appropriate sanctions will be imposed. Among those factors otherwise considered, the Court shall consider the following: (1) the length of the delay; (2) the reason for the delay; (3) the impact of the delay on ability to defend against the charge; and (4) the seriousness of the alleged offense. Unreasonable delay shall constitute an affirmative defense which must be raised by motion not less than one (1) week before trial. Such motion may be considered by affidavit.

All four cases were dismissed. The state sought review of the four dismissals.

ISSUES:
1. Did the local rule violate the separation of powers doctrine? NO.

2. Was the local rule properly applied when the court dismissed the cases against four juveniles? NO.

DECISIONS:

1. The local rule limiting the time frame between the completion of a police investigation and the filing of an information by the prosecutor to 30 days did not infringe on the prosecutorial functions in violation of the separation of powers doctrine because it is a proper exercise of the court's inherent power of review over the procedural aspects of cases before it.

2. A dismissal pursuant to the local rule is unwarranted unless the court makes a finding of actual prejudice resulting from the filing delays as specified in the rule itself.

REASON: "It is well established that the promulgation of rules governing practice and procedure is part of a court's inherent power. The issue of a court's authority to adopt a rule affecting preinformation or prearrest procedures, however, is one of first impression in this state. The local juvenile court rule in this case, . . . clearly applies before a court has jurisdiction over a juvenile case. Our own juvenile court rule, . . . states that '[j]uvenile court jurisdiction is invoked over a juvenile offense proceeding by filing an information.' In addition, this court has concluded that 'jurisdiction over offenses committed by a juvenile is to be determined at the time proceedings are instituted against the offender.' . . . [T]he local rule here under scrutiny examines the validity of prosecutorial delay *before* proceedings are instituted against a juvenile. The State argues that courts have no authority to make such an examination and that the timing as well as the content of charging decisions should be left totally to the prosecutor's discretion. The juvenile defendants respond that prefiling delays can prejudice a juvenile defendant's ability to obtain a fair trial and that a juvenile ought to be able to bring such delays to a trial court's attention. '[A] preprosecution delay can result in the loss of physical evidence, the unavailability of potential witnesses, and the impairment of the ability of the prospective defendant and his witnesses to remember the events in question . . .' The juvenile defendants contend that a court may review prefiling delays pursuant to state and federal speedy trial provisions. The United States Supreme Court has concluded, however, that either a formal indictment or information, or else the actual restraints imposed by arrest and holding to answer to a criminal charge, are necessary to engage the protection of the Sixth Amendment speedy trial provisions. This court has similarly determined that the right to a speedy trial attaches with the formal filing of an information or indictment under both federal and state constitutions. Thus, constitutional speedy trial provisions provide no support for court rules affecting preprosecution aspects of a case."

CASE SIGNIFICANCE: In this case, the court reviewed the validity of local judicial rules that established a limited period during which charges could be filed by the prosecutor after the police investigation had been completed and submitted for review. The court upheld the rule as not only legal but also entirely appropriate as a proper exercise of the court's inherent power to review procedural aspects of cases being processed and in no way a violation of the separation of powers doctrine.

This case is significant because it states that rules established at local levels to promote efficient judicial processing are valid. As long as those rules are not in direct conflict with the Constitution or other government documents pertaining to judicial processing, a court may promulgate rules to govern juvenile proceedings.

Christopher P. v. New Mexico
816 P.2d 485 (N.M. 1991)

A juvenile has a Fifth Amendment privilege to remain silent that applies during a psychological evaluation to determine amenability to juvenile treatment. Evidence obtained in violation of that right is not admissible in court.

FACTS: Christopher P., a minor, was charged in the children's court division of district court, with two counts of first degree murder and one count of conspiracy to commit first degree murder. At the time the delinquency petition was filed, the state attorney filed a motion to transfer the matter to the adult division of the district court. In New Mexico, transfer proceedings are bifurcated, with Stage I focusing on reasonable grounds to believe that the juvenile committed the alleged acts, and Stage II addressing whether the juvenile is "amenable to treatment and rehabilitation as a child through available facilities." Prior to Stage II, the children's court judge ordered Christopher to submit to a psychological evaluation to aid the court in its amenability determination. Over objections of the juvenile's counsel, the court ordered Christopher to discuss the alleged delinquent acts with the psychologist during the evaluation. The court ordered that any information about the alleged incident discussed during the examination could be used only for the amenability portion of the transfer hearing and for no other purpose. The juvenile's counsel and the state attorneys viewed the evaluation through a one-way mirror. During the evaluation, Christopher described his activities before and during the alleged offenses and the feelings he experienced. The record reflects that the psychologist's testimony during the amenability proceedings included specific references to the juvenile's statements and that, at least in part, the psychologist relied on the child's statements in reaching his conclusion that Christopher was not amenable to treatment in the juvenile justice system. The children's division court granted the transfer motion. The juvenile appealed.

ISSUE: Was the juvenile's Fifth Amendment privilege against self-incrimination violated when the court ordered him to discuss the alleged crimes during a psychological evaluation to determine whether he could benefit from treatment in the juvenile justice system? YES.

DECISION: The juvenile's Fifth Amendment privilege was violated by the court's order compelling him to discuss alleged offenses with a psychologist, without advice of counsel, during a psychological evaluation ordered by the court for the purpose of determining whether he would benefit from treatment in the juvenile justice system.

REASON: "The child does not contest the authority of the children's court to order him to submit to a psychological evaluation for the purpose of aiding the court in its determination of the question of amenability. . . . However, the child challenges the court's order that he discuss the specifics of the alleged criminal behavior as compelling him to testify against himself in violation of the Fifth Amendment. . . . The state argues the transfer proceedings are nonadversarial, determine only the forum in which the child will be tried, and that no penalty or determination of guilt attaches as a result of the proceedings. . . . Consequently the state contends that the Fifth Amendment is not applicable to transfer proceedings and that any potential subsequent violation of the Fifth Amendment is remedied by the court's order limiting the use of the child's statements to those proceedings only. The characterization of the transfer proceedings by the state and the court of appeals diminishes the impact of the proceedings on the child.

"Transfer proceedings exempt the child from the conceptual framework and protections the Children's Code envisions and expose the child to adult criminal liability. [T]he waiver [transfer] decision does more than determine a judicial forum for an accused youth. It invokes a jurisprudential philosophy that governs the nature of the proceedings as well as the purpose and severity of the sanctions. It also raises the important issues of when a child is no longer a child and what factors, other than age, are relevant for removing some youths from juvenile court jurisdiction.

"Having considered the nature and implications of juvenile transfer proceedings, we adopt the position that these proceedings are a critical stage in a child's involvement with the juvenile justice system. The provisions of the Children's Code . . ., read in the light of *Kent, Gault,* . . . compel our holding that the Fifth Amendment privilege against self-incrimination extends to transfer proceedings initiated . . . We do not suggest the privilege excludes a court-ordered evaluation properly limited in scope. We do conclude the child's Fifth

Amendment rights were violated in the proceedings below by the court's order compelling him to discuss the alleged offenses with the psychologist without the advice of counsel."

CASE SIGNIFICANCE: This case established a juvenile's right to remain silent and to seek the advice of counsel at certification hearings, with the court calling such hearings a "critical phase" in juvenile processing. The court further ruled that ancillary processes, in this case psychological evaluations, were subject to Fifth Amendment protections because information acquired therein could have substantial influence over the court in determining appropriate jurisdiction.

The court also ruled that compelling a juvenile to discuss the details of a crime that he had not been convicted of was entirely inappropriate because it was in effect coercing the juvenile into confessing in order to seem cooperative and possibly remain in the juvenile justice system.

In addition, allowing the state's attorney to view the psychological evaluation offers the prosecution an unfair advantage, especially when coupled with the court's denial of counsel to the juvenile during the evaluation process. Even with the restrictions imposed by the court, that the information acquired could only be used to determine amenability, the juvenile was unduly influenced and the state was unduly advantaged.

Finally, and most significantly, the court extended the constitutional protections of "critical phase" components of juvenile justice processing to information-gathering aspects of those processes when the court orders the juvenile to discuss aspects of the alleged offense and in circumstances when counsel for the state is allowed to observe the evaluation. The court created an umbrella of protection that includes the juvenile's time in court and his time during external evaluations ordered by the court.

<hr>

In the Matter of Jason J.
590 N.Y.S.2d 893 (A.D. 1992)

Minor mistakes are allowed in a juvenile delinquency petition as long as they do not jeopardize the integrity of the petition.

FACTS: Jason J., a minor, was charged in family court with assault in the second degree, criminal possession of a weapon in the fourth degree, assault in the third degree (which was a mistake—the charge should have read assault in the second degree), menacing, and unlawful possession of a weapon by a person under 16 years of age. He was adjudicated delinquent on all charges and committed to the Division of Youth for a period not to exceed 18 months. The juvenile appealed, attacking the content and accuracy of the petition filed against him.

ISSUE: Are mistakes in a petition for delinquency constitutionally permissible? YES.

DECISION: The juvenile delinquency petition is legally sufficient even when it incorrectly identifies certain elements, as long as the mistakes in totality are minor and do not jeopardize the overall integrity of the petition.

REASON: "Contrary to the appellant's contention, the juvenile delinquency petition, along with its supporting deposition, was legally sufficient. . . . While it is true that the petition incorrectly alleged that the appellant had committed assault in the second degree by means of a 'deadly weapon, to wit a box-cutter razor,' a juvenile delinquency petition need not set forth facts which are evidentiary in nature. . . . In any event, the complainant's supporting deposition, which contained non-hearsay allegations, clarifies that the 'box-cutter razor' was not used in the assault, but related, instead, to the weapon possession charges.

"Viewing the evidence in the light most favorable to the presentment agency . . ., we find that it was legally sufficient to establish beyond a reasonable doubt, the 'physical injury' element of the crimes of assault in the second degree and assault in the third degree. . . . The complainant's testimony established that he was punched in his head and chest and was thrown to the ground where six assailants, including the appellant, kicked him. As a result of the assault, he sustained 'chest pain for at least three days' and a 'big bump' on his forehead which later developed into a bruise. He requested medical attention after the assault, and subsequently treated his injuries by taking aspirin, rubbing a topical medication on his chest, and putting an icepack on his head. He also felt 'dizzy and weak' for about a day. The evidence was sufficient to support the fact-finder's determination that the complainant had sustained 'physical injury' . . ."

CASE SIGNIFICANCE: This case dealt with what on the surface appears to be a relatively minor issue of how to deal with mistakes in a delinquency petition. Although the issue appears to be minor, the more bothersome question is: How many mistakes will be allowed and how significant can those mistakes be? In this case the mistake dealt with an improper determination of the crime to be charged, using accurate but misapplied information from the case file. The juvenile court had the correct information, even though the petition did not reflect the accurate information. The court held that under those circumstances, minor mistakes on the face of warrants and petitions were allowable as long as such mistakes did not jeopardize the integrity of the petition. The key for future juvenile documentation is the phrase "jeopardize the integrity of the petition." Therefore, in assessing the magnitude of future mistakes courts will have to individually evaluate the impact of the mistake on the petition and determine whether such mistakes are minor or are of such magnitude as to "jeopardize the integrity of the petition."

United States v. A.R.
38 F.3d 699 (3d Cir. 1994)

Psychiatric evaluation for the purpose of determining amenability to juvenile treatment is not a critical stage in the juvenile justice process and therefore the Fifth and Sixth Amendment rights do not apply.

FACTS: A.R., 17 years old, and several companions allegedly spotted a white Pontiac Trans Am in a hotel parking lot and stole it. They were apprehended following a high-speed chase. A.R. was charged with conspiracy to commit carjacking and use of a firearm during the commission of a crime of violence. After he was in custody, the state filed charges against him for a number of automated teller machine armed robberies. Due to his age at the time of arrest, A.R. was taken to a juvenile detention facility, where he was subjected to a psychological evaluation and a psychiatric evaluation within five days of each other. The evaluation reports were designed for the transfer proceeding and were not intended to be used in either prosecution at juvenile delinquency proceedings or in a criminal trial. A.R. contends that he was not informed of his constitutional rights prior to the evaluations and that he did not enjoy the advice of counsel during the evaluations. The government was allowed to try A.R. as an adult. He appealed, contending that his Fifth and Sixth Amendment rights were violated by the evaluation process.

ISSUE: Did the process of psychological/psychiatric evaluations used in this case violate the juvenile's Fifth Amendment right to remain silent and his Sixth Amendment right to have counsel present during questioning? NO.

DECISION: Psychiatric evaluations for the purpose of determining adult transfer status are not critical stages of the proceedings and thus are not subject to the protections of the Fifth and Sixth Amendments to the United States Constitution.

REASON: "The Fifth Amendment provides that '[n]o person . . . shall be compelled in any criminal case to be a witness against himself.' The privilege against self-incrimination is rooted in the notion that ours is an accusatorial, rather than an inquisitorial system. As such, the individual may not be forced, through his own testimony, to assist the state in securing a conviction against him. Toward that end, the privilege 'protects *any disclosures* which the witness may reasonably apprehend *could be used in a criminal prosecution or which could lead to other evidence that might be so used.' In re Gault*, 387 U.S. 1, 47-48 (1967) . . . The focus, then, is not on the type of proceeding in which a statement is made 'but upon the nature of the statement or admission and the exposure which it invites.'

"The Sixth Amendment provided that '[i]n all criminal prosecutions, the accused shall enjoy the right . . . to have the Assistance of Counsel for his defense.' . . . Applied to the instant case, it seems clear that the evaluations of A.R. are not the sort of 'critical stage' to which the right to counsel attaches. . . . No significant rights are at stake in the evaluation itself. At the transfer hearing, where a determination is actually made as to the juvenile's status, a juvenile has the right to counsel as well as the opportunity to attack the methods employed and conclusions reached by the person who conducted the evaluation. Nor is the evaluation a legal confrontation that can only be fully understood after consultation with counsel. . . . Simply stated, counsel would serve no functional purpose at a psychiatric evaluation the results of which are used, as is necessarily the case here, only in making the neutral determination whether a juvenile should stay within the juvenile justice system or be treated as an adult."

CASE SIGNIFICANCE: This case dealt with psychiatric/psychological evaluations conducted in connection with certification hearings from juvenile to adult criminal court. The court ruled that such evaluations were not a "critical phase" in the overall processing of the juvenile and therefore were not protected by the provisions of the Fifth and Sixth Amendments to the United States Constitution.

The court considered psychiatric/psychological evaluations as neutral in nature, where no significant rights of the juvenile were at stake, where no legal confrontations occurred, and where the merits of the case were not at issue. The court equated such hearings to adult competency hearings and asserted that because no legal questions were at issue, the right to remain silent and to have legal counsel present during questioning did not extend to such evaluations as long as the integrity of the evaluation was maintained.

R.R. v. Portsey
629 So. 2d 1059 (Fla. App. 1994)

Conducting detention hearings by electronic means must be formally established either through legislation or by court rules, otherwise it is not an acceptable alternative to physical presence in the courtroom.

FACTS: R.R., a minor, was charged with arson of a dwelling and taken into custody by police. He was placed in a regional detention center and a detention hearing was held in the judge's chambers. Present in chambers with the judge were an assistant public defender representing R.R., an assistant state attorney, and an employee of the state agency that had responsibility for juvenile care and custody in the system. R.R. was not physically present, but was connected to the proceedings through video-telephone from the regional detention center. Both the public defender and R.R. himself objected to the use of the video-telephone in place of physical presence, but were overruled by the judge. The court ordered R.R. held in secure detention until further proceedings were held.

ISSUE: Are technology-assisted distance detention hearings constitutional if the juvenile is not physically present but is allowed to participate via video hookup? NO.

DECISION: Absent rule or statute that allows such proceedings, there is no authority for the court to hold a detention hearing with the juvenile's presence secured only by video-telephone. The juvenile's presence is required in the absence of a waiver or a specific finding that the juvenile's mental or physical condition precludes his presence.

REASON: "We conclude that petitioner's arguments have merit and reject the state's argument on this issue. . . . [T]he accused child is required to be physically present at all hearings held under the juvenile rules, except when there has been a waiver of the right to be present or the court makes specific findings regarding the child's physical or mental condition that precluded physical presence. Since neither of these exceptions occurred in this case, the video-telephone procedure failed to comply with the rule's requirement.

"By this decision we do not intend to offer any view on the feasibility of using such technology to improve the efficiency of the court system. Nor do we intend to discourage the investigation and use of innovative techniques that can enhance the efficiency of court procedure. We only hold that the use of video-telephones for juvenile detention hearings is a substantial change in policy which should not be made *sua sponte* by a trial court, but should be developed and approved through the rule-making authority of the Florida Supreme Court or through the legislative process."

CASE SIGNIFICANCE: This case dealt with the use of technology to improve the efficiency of juvenile court processing. The technology used was a video-telephone hookup between the juvenile judge's chambers and the juvenile detention center. The judge used the video-telephone hookup to conduct detention hearings without having to physically bring the juvenile from the detention center to the courtroom. There was no law or court rule that allowed such processing; neither was there a voluntary consent on the part of the juvenile or his legal counsel to such processing.

This case represents a challenge to attempts by courts to streamline early processing phases of the judicial process through the use of technology. The implementation of such technology will require extensive planning to ensure that its use is not in conflict with existing laws and constitutional restraints and to ensure that it is possible to use such time-saving devices in the early processing phases of juvenile justice processing without running afoul of the Constitution. This case implies that such use of technology in these proceedings would likely be allowed if authorized by state law or court rule.

State v. K.K.H.
878 P.2d 1255 (Wash. App. 1994)

A probable cause hearing generally must be held within 48 hours after arrest.

FACTS: This case involves three fact situations with the common element of early court processing with regard to the manner of probable cause determination and the time required for such determination.

1. K.K.H. was arrested for possession of stolen property and was placed in a Department of Youth Services detention center later the same day. His first appearance in court was approximately 96 hours after his arrest.

2. K.K.G. was arrested for possession of cocaine with intent to deliver. His first appearance in court occurred approximately 60 hours after his arrest.

3. H.J.D. was arrested for theft in the third degree. H.J.D.'s first appearance before a court was approximately 96 hours after her arrest.

ISSUE: Within what time must a juvenile be given a probable cause hearing and what are the appropriate procedures for establishing probable cause when the juvenile is detained?

DECISION: The constitutional time frame for such a determination is generally within 48 hours, not the 60- to 96-hour delay in these cases. Procedures for determining probable cause may vary by jurisdiction as long as they can withstand constitutional scrutiny.

REASON: "In light of the amendments . . ., and Fourth Amendment challenge the subsection on its face must fail. We also reject the juvenile's argument that a 24-hour limit should be imposed on the time between a juvenile's arrest and the probable cause determination. The 48-hour limit . . . was designed to, and does, embody the constitutional safeguards prescribed in *County of Riverside v. McLaughlin*, 500 U.S. 44 (1991). A shorter time limit is not constitutionally mandated.

"Prior to its amendment, [the rule] provided for 'a hearing on the issues of probable cause and detention.' The amended rule no longer requires a hearing on the issue of probable cause, but rather a 'judicial determination' of probable cause. Consequently, under the current version . . . the issue is not whether juveniles are timely granted a preliminary hearing, but rather whether they receive a judicial determination of probable cause within 48 hours of arrest.

"The contention is made that in cases in which the prosecutor files an information before the juvenile receives a probable cause determination, the routine practice is for the probable cause determination to be stricken so that the juvenile is deprived of a probable cause determination within 48 hours of his or her arrest. We agree with the claim that this practice violates [the rule], *Gerstein*, and *Riverside*. . . . We hold that filing an information, even within 48 hours of the juvenile's arrest, cannot be a substitute for a judicial determination of probable cause . . ."

CASE SIGNIFICANCE: This case provides an example of the need to review, clarify, and amend state law or judicial rules to conform to constitutional standards set by the United States Supreme Court. In this case, the procedures in question were the probable cause determination and the detention hearing associated with juvenile justice processing. In accordance with *County of Riverside v. McLaughlin*, 500 U.S. 44 (1991), the juvenile court had to adjust its time frame for these early court processes to within 48 hours, not the 24 hours requested by the juveniles' legal counsel. *McLaughlin* holds that if a probable cause hearing is held within 48 hours after arrest, the presumption is that the detention is valid. The burden of proof is on the suspect to establish that such detention was so unnecessarily long such that it was invalid. On the other hand, if the detention exceeds 48 hours, the presumption is that the detention is invalid. The burden of proof is on the police to establish that such delay was in fact justified. According to this case, the *McLaughlin* rule applies to juveniles as well as adults.

Waiver of Juvenile to Adult Court

6

I. United States Supreme Court Cases

Kent v. United States (1966)
Breed v. Jones (1975)

II. Lower Court Cases

Summers v. State (1967)
United States v. Howard (1971)
People v. Fields (1972)
Fain v. Duff (1973)
United States ex rel. Bombacino v. Bensinger (1974)
In re Mathis (1975)
Russell v. Parratt (1976)
United States v. J.D. (1981)
Matter of Seven Minors (1983)
State v. Muhammad (1985)
R.H. v. State (1989)
People v. P.H. (1991)
People v. R.L. (1994)
C.M. v. State (1994)
Laswell v. Frey (1995)

Introduction

As long as the juvenile court has existed, since 1899, there has been a process in the juvenile court that allows the jurisdiction of the juvenile to be transferred to the adult court.[1] This process still exists today, and is called by different names: transfer, waiver, certification, bindover, and remand to criminal court. All define the process of removing a juvenile from juvenile court jurisdiction and transferring that juvenile to an adult court to be subjected to the adult criminal process.

There are three basic ways in which juveniles can have their case handled in the adult court. These are *judicial waiver, prosecutorial discretion*, and by *statutory exclusion* or *mandatory transfer*.[2] States can employ all three methods in their juvenile codes.[3]

Early juvenile courts used *judicial waiver* to transfer juveniles into the adult system.[4] Today, judicial waiver remains an option in 47 states.[5] In judicial waiver, the juvenile judge decides whether the child will remain in juvenile court or whether the jurisdiction of the case will be transferred to the criminal court.[6] During the transfer hearing, the judge examines numerous criteria, and makes a decision based upon conclusions gleamed from that examination.[7]

You will learn in this chapter that the Supreme Court case of *Kent v. United States* in 1966 shaped the judicial waiver process and afforded children certain rights in the transfer process. In addition, the Supreme Court advised juvenile judges concerning the eight criteria that should be examined during a transfer hearing based on the Appendix of the *Kent* case. These criteria include the seriousness of the crime, the "sophistication and maturity" of the child, and the aggressiveness displayed during the crime.[8]

In *prosecutorial discretion*, the prosecutor holds the decision concerning in which court, juvenile or criminal, to file the charges.[9] The prosecutor has this discretion because concurrent jurisdiction provisions allow jurisdiction to exist simultaneously in both the juvenile court and the criminal court.[10] Many times the age of the offender, and the crimes that can be under concurrent jurisdiction are limited by state statute.[11] For example, some juvenile codes require that the crime be serious or violent or that a repeat pattern of behavior is established for the prosecutor to hold concurrent jurisdiction.[12]

Under *statutory exclusion* or *legislative mandate*, the legislature of a state may define certain delinquent acts as criminal acts that are to be automatically handled in adult court.[13] These provisions "automatically exclude certain juvenile offenders from the juvenile court's original jurisdiction."[14] The statutes that exclude juveniles from juvenile court jurisdiction through statutory exclusion tend to focus on serious, repeat, or violent juvenile crime[15] and are currently in use in some form in the District of Columbia and 36 states.[16]

In 1966, the Supreme Court held in *Kent v. United States* that juveniles have certain constitutional rights in judicial waiver proceedings. The Court granted juveniles the right to a transfer hearing, the right to an attorney, access to records, and a statement of the reason the court decided to transfer the jurisdiction of the case to the adult court. Many cases have examined certain procedural requirements set forth in *Kent*. *Summers v. State* (1967), *People v. Fields* (1972), and *United States v. J.D.* (1981) demonstrate the holding of a lower court in finding a transfer process or application of that process proper or defective. *United States ex rel. Bombacino v. Bensinger* (1974) presents the decision of a lower court, which held that the juvenile judge in this case was not required to give a statement of the reasons for transfer, and *State v. Muhammad* (1985) in which the courts held that a juvenile did not have to be present at a transfer hearing.

In *Kent*, the Supreme Court also noted factors that judges should consider when making the decision to transfer. These include seriousness of the offense, violence demonstrated, maturity and sophistication of the child, and rehabilitative resources available in the juvenile court. Several cases included in this chapter address the decision of the judge to transfer and the factors that the judge considered. These include *United States v. Howard* (1971), *In re Mathis* (1975), *Matter of Seven Minors* (1983), and the 1994 case of *C.M. v. State*.

In 1975, the Supreme Court held in *Breed v. Jones* that the child would be put in double jeopardy if convicted of a crime in adult court after having been adjudicated delinquent for the same offense in juvenile court. *Fain v. Duff* (1973) addresses the same issue in the lower courts.

Other cases are included to demonstrate the courts' reactions to other issues concerning transfer. *Russell v. Parratt* (1976) held that due process was not violated by a County Attorney having unreviewable discretion to charge a juvenile as an adult. *R.H. v. State* (1989) examines the issue of a child participating in pre-transfer psychological evaluation and the privilege against self-incrimination. *People v. P.H.* (1991) represents a very current and controversial topic—the constitutionality of a "gang-transfer" provision. *People v. R.L.* (1994) examines a challenge to mandatory transfer statutes. *Laswell v. Frey* (1995) examines the confusion that still surrounds the juvenile court process.

The issues mentioned above will likely be the same issues that the courts will face in the future. Courts will continue to address the constitutionality of the process, who holds the power to make the decision to transfer, and the constitutionality of defining certain actions as criminal, such as the "gang-transfer" statute.

Notes

[1] Martin Forst, *The New Juvenile Justice* (1995).

[2] Howard N. Snyder and Melissa Sickmund, *Juvenile Offenders and Victims: A National Report*. Washington, DC: National Center for Juvenile Justice. Office of Juvenile Justice and Delinquency Prevention. Office of Justice Programs, U.S. Department of Justice. (1995). Patricia Torbet, Richard Gable, Hunter Hurst IV, Imogene Montgomery, Linda Szymanski, and Douglas Thomas, *State Responses to Serious and Violent Juvenile Crime*. Washington, DC: National Center for Juvenile Justice. Office of Juvenile Justice and Delinquency Prevention. Office of Justice Programs, U.S. Department of Justice. (1996).

[3] Melissa Sickmund, *How Juveniles Get to Criminal Court*. Washington, DC: National Center for Juvenile Justice. Office of Juvenile Justice and Delinquency Prevention. U.S. Department of Justice, Office of Justice Programs (1994)

[4] Howard N. Snyder and Melissa Sickmund, *Juvenile Offenders and Victims: A National Report*. Washington, DC: National Center for Juvenile Justice. Office of Juvenile Justice and Delinquency Prevention. U.S. Department of Justice, Office of Justice Programs (1995).

[5] Jeffrey A. Butts, *Delinquency Cases Waived to Criminal Court, 1985–1994*. Washington, DC: National Center for Juvenile Justice. Office of Juvenile Justice and Delinquency Prevention. U.S. Department of Justice, Office of Justice Programs (1997).

[6] Howard N. Snyder and Melissa Sickmund, *Juvenile Offenders and Victims: A National Report*. Washington, DC: National Center for Juvenile Justice. Office of Juvenile Justice and Delinquency Prevention. U.S. Department of Justice, Office of Justice Programs (1995).

[7] Howard N. Snyder and Melissa Sickmund, *Juvenile Offenders and Victims: A National Report*. Washington, DC: National Center for Juvenile Justice. Office of Juvenile Justice and Delinquency Prevention. U.S. Department of Justice, Office of Justice Programs (1995).

[8] *Kent v. United States* 383 U.S. 541: 566-567.

[9] Howard N. Snyder and Melissa Sickmund, *Juvenile Offenders and Victims: A National Report*. Washington, DC: National Center for Juvenile Justice. Office of Juvenile Justice and Delinquency Prevention. U.S. Department of Justice, Office of Justice Programs (1994)

[10] Patricia Torbet and Richard Gable, Hunter Hurst IV, Imogene Montgomery, Linda Szymanski, and Douglas Thomas, *State Responses to Serious and Violent Juvenile Crime*. Washington, DC: National Center for Juvenile Justice. Office of Juvenile Justice and Delinquency Prevention. U.S. Department of Justice, Office of Justice Programs (1996). Melissa Sickmund, *How Juveniles Get to Criminal Court*. Washington, DC: National Center for Juvenile Justice. Office of Juvenile Justice and Delinquency Prevention. U.S. Department of Justice, Office of Justice Programs (1994).

[11] Patricia Torbet and Richard Gable, Hunter Hurst IV, Imogene Montgomery, Linda Szymanski, and Douglas Thomas, *State Responses to Serious and Violent Juvenile Crime*. Washington, DC: National Center for Juvenile Justice. Office of Juvenile Justice and Delinquency Prevention. U.S. Department of Justice, Office of Justice Programs (1996).

[12] Melissa Sickmund, *How Juveniles Get to Criminal Court*. Washington, DC: National Center for Juvenile Justice. Office of Juvenile Justice and Delinquency Prevention. U.S. Department of Justice, Office of Justice Programs (1994).

[13] Patricia Torbet and Richard Gable, Hunter Hurst IV, Imogene Montgomery, Linda Szymanski, and Douglas Thomas, *State Responses to Serious and Violent Juvenile Crime*. Washington, DC: National Center for Juvenile Justice. Office of Juvenile Justice and Delinquency Prevention. U.S. Department of Justice, Office of Justice Programs (1996).

[14] Patricia Torbet and Richard Gable, Hunter Hurst IV, Imogene Montgomery, Linda Szymanski, and Douglas Thomas, *State Responses to Serious and Violent Juvenile Crime*. Washington, DC: National Center for Juvenile Justice. Office of Juvenile Justice and Delinquency Prevention. U.S. Department of Justice, Office of Justice Programs (1996).

[15] Melissa Sickmund, *How Juveniles Get to Criminal Court*. Washington, DC: National Center for Juvenile Justice. Office of Juvenile Justice and Delinquency Prevention. U.S. Department of Justice, Office of Justice Programs (1994).

[16] Patricia Torbet and Richard Gable, Hunter Hurst IV, Imogene Montgomery, Linda Szymanski, and Douglas Thomas, *State Responses to Serious and Violent Juvenile Crime*. Washington, DC: National Center for Juvenile Justice. Office of Juvenile Justice and Delinquency Prevention. U.S. Department of Justice, Office of Justice Programs (1996).

I.   UNITED STATES SUPREME COURT CASES

Kent v. United States
383 U.S. 541 (1966)

A juvenile must be given due process before being transferred from a juvenile court to an adult court.

FACTS: Kent, at age 16, was arrested and charged with housebreaking, robbery, and rape. Because of his age, he came under the jurisdiction of the District of Columbia Juvenile Court. That court, however, waived jurisdiction after a "full investigation" (in accordance with District of Columbia law) and transferred him to the United States District Court for an adult criminal trial. Kent's attorney filed motions to have a hearing on the waiver. He also recommended that Kent be hospitalized for psychiatric observation and that he be allowed access to the file that the juvenile court had on his client. The juvenile court did not rule on these motions. Instead, the judge ordered that jurisdiction be transferred to the adult criminal court and stated that this finding was made after the required "full investigation." The judge held no hearing before his ruling and gave no reason for the waiver. Kent was convicted in criminal court on six counts of housebreaking and robbery, and was acquitted on two rape counts by reason of insanity.

ISSUE: Do juveniles have any due process rights in cases in which jurisdiction over a juvenile is transferred from a juvenile court to an adult court? YES.

DECISION: A transfer of jurisdiction in a juvenile hearing is a "critically important" stage in the juvenile process. Therefore, the juvenile is entitled to the following due process rights: (1) a hearing; (2) to be represented by counsel at such hearing; (3) to be given access to records considered by the juvenile court; and (4) to a statement of the reasons in support of the waiver order.

REASON: "Because the State is supposed to proceed in respect of the child as *parens patriae* and not as adversary, courts have relied on the premise that the proceedings are 'civil' in nature and not criminal, and have asserted that the child cannot complain of the deprivation of important rights available in criminal cases. It has been asserted that he can claim only the fundamental due process right to fair treatment . . .

   "It is clear beyond dispute that the waiver of jurisdiction is a 'critically important' action determining vitally important statutory rights of the juvenile.
. . . The statutory scheme makes this plain. The Juvenile Court is vested with

'original and exclusive jurisdiction' of the child. This jurisdiction confers special rights and immunities. He is, as specified by the statute, shielded from publicity. He may be confined, but with rare exceptions he may not be jailed along with adults. He may be detained, but only until he is 21 years of age. The court is admonished by the statute to give preference to retaining the child in the custody of the parents 'unless his welfare and the safety and protection of the public can be adequately safeguarded without . . . removal.' The child is protected against consequences of adult conviction such as the loss of civil rights, the use of the adjudication against him in subsequent proceedings, and disqualification for public employment."

CASE SIGNIFICANCE: Although not as significant as *In re Gault*, this case is important because it marks the first time that basic due process rights were extended to juveniles, thus heralding the demise of the pure *parens patriae* approach. The justification for this departure was stated by the Court when it said:

> There is much evidence that some juvenile courts, including that of the District of Columbia, lack the personnel, facilities and techniques to perform adequately as representatives of the State in a *parens patriae* capacity, at least with respect to children charged with law violation. There is evidence, in fact, that there may be grounds for concern that the child receives the worst of both worlds: that he gets neither the protections accorded to adults nor the solicitous care and regenerative treatment postulated for children.

Though limited in scope, these rights infused juvenile proceedings with due process guarantees. The Court said that the *parens patriae* philosophy "is not an invitation to procedural arbitrariness." It then added that "the waiver of jurisdiction is a 'critically important' action determining vitally important statutory rights of the juvenile."

The rights given in *Kent* are limited to waiver of jurisdiction hearings and are not extended to any other phase of the juvenile proceeding. While these rights, as well as others, were extended one year later to juvenile delinquency proceedings in cases in which the juvenile might be institutionalized (*In re Gault*, 387 U.S. 1 [1967]), they still do not apply constitutionally to all phases of juvenile proceedings. The Supreme Court based its decision in this case on the "critically important" nature of the waiver proceeding. Indeed, a waiver of jurisdiction (other terms used in various states are "transfer of jurisdiction" and "certification") carries far-reaching consequences for the juvenile. For example, instead of being kept in a juvenile institution and automatically released upon reaching the age of adulthood, a juvenile tried in an adult criminal court is treated just like any other criminal and can be subjected to incarceration or a period of punishment that extends beyond the age of majority. The consequences of juvenile proceedings are also vastly different from the effects of an adult conviction. In sum, the Court saw the serious consequences to the juvenile with such a transfer, and provided for due process rights before the transfer of jurisdiction could take place.

Breed v. Jones
421 U.S. 517 (1975)

Juveniles are entitled to the constitutional right against double jeopardy.

FACTS: On February 9, 1971, a petition was filed in the Los Angeles County Juvenile Court, alleging that a 17-year-old male committed acts which, if committed by an adult, would constitute the crime of robbery with a deadly weapon. A detention hearing was held the following day and the accused was ordered to be detained pending a hearing on the petition. At the adjudicatory hearing (the equivalent of a trial), the juvenile court found the allegations against the accused to be true and ordered further detention. At the dispositional hearing (the equivalent of sentencing), the juvenile court said that it intended to find the juvenile offender unfit for the programs available through its juvenile facilities. The defense was not prepared for a fitness hearing and the matter was continued for one week. At the conclusion of the court's next hearing, it declared the offender unfit for treatment as a juvenile and ordered that he be prosecuted as an adult. The juvenile was subsequently found guilty of robbery in the first degree by the criminal court and it was ordered that he be committed to the California Youth Authority. The juvenile appealed, claiming a violation of his constitutional right against double jeopardy because he was adjudicated in the juvenile court and then tried by the criminal court.

ISSUE: Does the double jeopardy clause of the Fifth Amendment protect a juvenile from being prosecuted as an adult after undergoing adjudication proceedings in juvenile court? YES.

DECISION: A juvenile who has undergone adjudication proceedings in juvenile court cannot be tried on the same charge as an adult in a criminal court because to do so would constitute double jeopardy.

REASON: "Jeopardy denotes risk. In the Constitutional sense, jeopardy describes the risk that is traditionally associated with a criminal prosecution. . . .

"Although the juvenile-court system has its genesis in the desire to provide a distinctive procedure and setting to deal with the problems of youth, including those manifested by antisocial conduct, our decisions in recent years have recognized that there is a gap between the originally benign conception of the system and its realities. With the exception of *McKeiver v. Pennsylvania*, 403 U.S. 528 (1971), the Court's response to that perception has been to make applicable in juvenile proceedings constitutional guarantees associated with traditional criminal prosecutions. *In re Gault*, 387 U.S. 1 (1967); *In re Winship*, 397 U.S. 358 (1970).

"We believe it is simply too late in the day to conclude, as did the District Court in this case, that a juvenile is not put in jeopardy at a proceeding whose object it is to determine whether he has committed acts that violate a criminal law and whose potential consequences include both the stigma inherent in such a determination and the deprivation of liberty for many years.

"We deal here, not with the formalities of the criminal adjudicative process, *McKeiver v. Pennsylvania*, 403 U.S. at 551, but with an analysis of an aspect of the juvenile-court system in terms of the kind of risk to which jeopardy refers. Under our decisions we can find no persuasive distinction in that regard between the proceeding conducted in this case and a criminal prosecution, each of which is designed 'to vindicate [the] very vital interest in enforcement of criminal laws.' We therefore conclude that respondent was put in jeopardy at the adjudicatory hearing. Jeopardy attached when respondent was 'put to trial before the trier of the facts,' 400 U.S. at 479, that is, when the Juvenile Court, as the trier of the facts, began to hear evidence."

CASE SIGNIFICANCE: This case is significant because: (1) it extended the double jeopardy protection to juvenile proceedings, and (2) it implies that juvenile proceedings, although considered civil proceedings, do in fact have penal consequences and are therefore tantamount to criminal trials. The juvenile in this case had been adjudicated, but the judge transferred jurisdiction to the adult criminal court because he found the juvenile "unfit for the programs available through its juvenile facilities." The juvenile was subsequently tried in adult court and convicted. The Court concluded that there was double jeopardy, saying that "the Double Jeopardy clause . . . is written in terms of potential or risk of trial and conviction, not punishment." The Court added: "Respondent was subjected to the burden of two trials for the same offense; he was twice put to the task of marshaling his resources against those of the State, twice subjected to the 'heavy personal strain' which such an experience represents."

Some scholars maintain that although juvenile proceedings are civil in nature, the Supreme Court in reality considers the substance and effect of the proceedings to be criminal. This case validates that assertion. Double jeopardy is generally defined as successive prosecution for the same offense by the same jurisdiction. By definition, double jeopardy applies only to criminal, not civil, cases. Nonetheless, the Court in this case considered an adjudication as equivalent to a trial, and thus, applied the double jeopardy prohibition. The giving of rights to juveniles in adjudication proceedings, as mandated in the

Gault case (*In re Gault,* 387 U.S. 1, [1967]) further attests to the "criminalization" of juvenile proceedings.

The policy implication of this case is clear: if a juvenile is to be transferred to the adult criminal court for trial in connection with a criminal offense, such transfer (or "waiver" or "certification") must be made prior to the adjudicatory hearing, otherwise double jeopardy attaches.

II. LOWER COURT CASES

Summers v. State
230 N.E.2d 320 (Ind. 1967)

Juveniles cannot be denied the rights guaranteed in the transfer process under *Kent*.

FACTS: A 15-year-old defendant was charged with aggravated assault and waived to the adult court. The waiver order from the court contained nothing but the words of the waiver statute and said that after a full preliminary investigation of alleged delinquent acts, the court did waive the juvenile to the jurisdiction of the adult court. The child was ordered held for trial. The defendant was committed by the criminal court and his counsel filed a motion of appeal stating that it was "error to deny his verified motion for leave to withdraw guilty plea."

ISSUE: Was the transfer procedure defective? YES.

DECISION: Under the Juvenile Act, the juvenile was entitled to a transfer hearing with the assistance of counsel, to confront witnesses, to present evidence, and to a statement of the reasons for transfer. Because the juvenile's rights were violated, the case was "remanded to the criminal court with instructions to vacate and expunge all records and transfer the matter to the juvenile court."

REASON: "It is readily apparent from an examination of the waiver and transfer order before us that it is merely a printed order signed by the judge. It contains nothing but the words of the statute authorizing transfer. Under the rule in the *Kent* case it clearly is pregnant with the same defects as the order considered there and is only *pro forma*.

"Further, we hold in accordance with *Kent* that the appellant Summers should have a right to a full hearing in the Lake Juvenile Court. He should have the right to counsel at such hearing; the right to confrontation of the witnesses against him; and the right to present evidence, if any be available to him, of any circumstances that would entitle him to the benefits that might be afforded to him by the provisions of the Juvenile Act. And it is only after such a hearing that a waiver and order of transfer to the Lake Criminal Court may be lawfully made. Such order and transfer should be accompanied with an appropriate statement of the reasons as herein before indicated. Of course a record of such proceedings should be made for the criminal court and this court in determining the justification for the transfer and waiver."

CASE SIGNIFICANCE: This case examines the process of the waiver of jurisdiction to the adult court. This child was waived to the adult court on an order that contained nothing but the words of the waiver statute. The question was whether this violated the rights that the Supreme Court gave to juveniles in *Kent*, and whether it reflected the intent of the Indiana Juvenile Act. The court held that it violated the intent of both *Kent* and the Indiana Juvenile Act. The court stated that the juvenile facing possible judicial transfer in Indiana should have the right to a hearing, the right to counsel, the right to confront witnesses, and the right to present evidence. In addition, if the juvenile is waived to adult court, he or she is entitled to a full statement of the reasons for the transfer.

This case reflects the continuing court insistence on due process in juvenile justice. Just the previous year, the Supreme Court granted juveniles certain rights during the transfer hearing in the *Kent* case. Those rights included a transfer hearing, representation of counsel during that hearing, and a statement of the reasons for transfer. This court reiterated that ruling and applied it to juvenile proceedings in the state of Indiana.

United States v. Howard
449 F.2d 1086 (D.C. Cir. 1971)

A transfer hearing must involve a full review of all relevant issues in determining fitness for transfer to adult court.

FACTS: Howard, 18 years old, and three others attempted to rob a drug store during operating hours. Howard's delinquency history began at the age of 14, with an adjudication for housebreaking, for which he received probation. During his probation he was arrested for unauthorized use of a vehicle and driving without a permit. The current crime spree, which culminated with the present arrest, began with the robbery of a credit union at gunpoint on March 19, 1968. It included a second robbery of a credit union on March 25, 1968, and a complaint from Howard's mother that he was habitually beyond her control, staying out all night and not explaining his whereabouts. Howard was placed in detention on those charges on April 24, 1968; he escaped five days later. His current offense occurred on May 7, 1968. After his arrest on this charge, two other robberies were attributed to him.

At his transfer hearing, the court heard from numerous experts, most of whom testified that Howard could be adequately treated in the juvenile justice system and that there were facilities and programs in the juvenile justice system to treat someone with Howard's background. The transfer hearing itself coincided with the U.S. Supreme Court's decision in *Kent v. United States*, thus the court recessed to study the *Kent* opinion. The court heard from one psychologist who found no sign of mental illness in Howard. The court determined that Howard was appropriate for transfer to the adult district court. The district court heard from five psychiatrists on appeal of the transfer decision, two of whom found Howard "borderline psychotic" or a "sociopath" and three of whom found that Howard showed no signs of mental illness or condition. The district judge upheld the transfer to adult court based on the fact that available juvenile facilities were not likely to rehabilitate Howard and that he was 18 at the time of the transfer and thus would be subject to juvenile jurisdiction for less than three years.

ISSUE: Must a transfer hearing involve a full review of all relevant issues related to fitness for transfer? YES.

DECISION: As long as the court conducts a full hearing and exercises all relevant options, proper consideration is deemed to have been given before transfer to an adult court.

REASON: "Appellant challenges the validity of his waiver on the grounds that the Juvenile Court did not fully explore the possibilities for his rehabilitation as required by statute and by decisions of this court and the Supreme Court. The provision of the Juvenile Court Act governing waiver provides that jurisdiction may be waived only after 'full investigation.' . . . The 'full investigation' required prior to waiver 'cannot be mere ritual.' The statutory mandate anticipates a thorough exploration of the possible dispositions, short of waiver, by which the welfare of the juvenile and the interest of the District may be secured.

"With due regard for the presumption in favor of treating juvenile defendants in a juvenile setting, and the grave consequences that may follow from waiver to the District Court, we nevertheless conclude that the Juvenile Court did not abuse its discretion in determining, after exhaustive inquiry, that appellant's 'rehabilitation within the presently available juvenile facilities is unlikely.'

"The Court was also entitled to consider, as it did, that appellant had reached the age of 18 at the time of his waiver hearing, and would be subject to juvenile jurisdiction for less than three years. . . . The court could reasonably conclude, on the basis of testimony and appellant's past record, that even assuming a juvenile like appellant could be rehabilitated if provided with rehabilitation programs over a longer period of time, the short span available to the Juvenile Court as to this appellant would be insufficient to ensure success in any rehabilitative endeavor." . . .

CASE SIGNIFICANCE: This case was heard during the period of major change in juvenile justice processing, with the United States Supreme Court deciding *Kent v. United States*, 383 U.S. 541 (1966), while this case was in process. In fact, the court in this case recessed while the juvenile judge studied the opinion in *Kent* to determine its impact on the proceedings. The importance of this case rests in its consideration of all relevant evidence before deciding on transfer eligibility. The court's adherence to the concept of a full hearing, even before it was mandated by *Kent*, is evidence that at least some juvenile courts gave careful consideration to transfer decisions.

People v. Fields
199 N.W.2d 217 (Mich. 1972)

Juvenile transfer statutes must contain standards to be constitutional.

FACTS: On August 16, 1968, the judge ruled on a motion by the prosecution for waiver of jurisdiction in the case of Andrew Fields. Fields was charged with "uttering and publishing of checks and breaking and entering." The judge ruled that a "prime facie case had been made out on both petitions." The probate judge then reviewed the three tests of the transfer statute: the nature of the offense, the court's use of juvenile dispositions, and the child's amenability to treatment and any demonstration of maturity that might make the child unwilling to accept treatment as a child. The judge referred the case to adult court. The child appealed on the issue of whether the probate judge had the authority to waive him to the circuit court to stand trial as an adult.

ISSUE: Does a lack of standards in a transfer statute make the statute unconstitutional? YES.

DECISION: The statute regarding transfer is unconstitutional because of lack of standards.

REASON: "The probate judge, as appears from his quoted opinion, carefully, thoroughly and conscientiously set forth well-considered reasons for taking the action he did. However, the circuit judge was unable to find in the statute any guidelines for the juvenile judge to follow . . .

"It is important to understand the precise issue in this case. It is not whether the constitutional requirements of due process stated in *Kent v. United States*, 383 U.S. 541, 86 S. Ct. 1045, 16 L. Ed. 2d 84 (1966), were met. Rather, it is whether the lack of standards in the statute precludes a waiver proceeding.

"I agree with Justice Black 'that a statute, invalid for want of standards according to the constitutional rule . . . [cannot] be validated by any rule of court which, although in itself well within the constitutional powers of the Court, undertakes to supply what the statute does not.' *Devereaux v. Township Board of Genesee Twp.*, 211 Mich. 38, 177 N.W. 967 (1920), involved a statute providing for the issuing of permits by a township board for the conducting of poolrooms, dance halls, etc. The court said (p. 43, 177 N.W. 969):

> The statute in question provides no method for the application of licenses, contains no qualifications which the applicant must possess, provides no standard of fitness, makes no provisions as to the character of the structure or equipment to be used in the business regulated. It, in fact, attempts to confer upon the township board the arbitrary power to grant or refuse a license, according to its whim or caprice. Under all the authorities, we think this cannot be done.

"If the legislature is to treat some persons under the age of 17 differently from the entire class of such persons, excluding them from the beneficent processes and purposes of our juvenile courts, the legislature must establish suitable and ascertainable standards whereby such persons are to be deemed adults and treated as such subject to the processes and penalties of our criminal law. The statute is unconstitutional because it lacks standards."

CASE SIGNIFICANCE: In this case, the court examined the transfer process and asked whether a lack of standards in the transfer statute renders that statute unconstitutional. The Supreme Court of Michigan held that the transfer law in Michigan was unconstitutional because it lacked standards. The statute is reflective of many state statutes that set an age and offense criteria for transfer. In Michigan, the statute allowed for the judge to be able to transfer juveniles if they were over the age of 15 and charged with a crime that would constitute a felony, if the judge deemed the transfer to be warranted. The court in this case said that this was unconstitutional because the statute lacked standards. What would be the basis of a judicial decision to transfer under this statute? That, stated the court, is what is missing from the process. What the court says is that there must be specific standards in transfer statutes in order for the statute to be constitutional. What these standards specifically should be was not addressed by the court.

Fain v. Duff
488 F.2d 218 (5th Cir. 1973)

It is double jeopardy to adjudicate a juvenile as a delinquent on an offense, and to then transfer him or her to adult court to face criminal charges on the same offense.

FACTS: Roger Fain, age 16, was arrested and charged with breaking into a woman's residence and raping her. Five days later a petition was filed in juvenile court. A hearing was held in which an assistant state attorney asked the judge to waive jurisdiction and to send the case to adult court. The judge did not waive jurisdiction. Instead, Fain was adjudicated delinquent and committed to the Division of Youth Services for an indeterminate period of time not to extend beyond his twenty-first birthday. The state attorney asked the judge not to send Fain to the State Division of Youth Services and to stay his order of commitment. The judge declined. The next day, an indictment was returned against Fain citing the same crimes that had previously resulted in his adjudication. Two weeks later, the state attorney again urged the judge to have the case remanded to the adult court. In the circuit court, the judge dismissed the indictment, citing former jeopardy. The state appealed.

ISSUES:
1. Did the district court have jurisdiction to entertain Fain's application for a writ of habeas corpus? YES.

2. Was the district court correct in determining that the actions of the state of Florida violated the double jeopardy clause of the Fifth Amendment, made applicable to the states by the Fourteenth Amendment? YES.

3. Was the district court correct in determining that the actions of the state of Florida violated the Fourteenth Amendment and notions of fundamental fairness? YES.

DECISION: Fain would be placed in double jeopardy if, after adjudication in a juvenile court, he would again be tried in a criminal court.

REASON: "Fain is not asserting merely a federal defense to a state prosecution. He is asserting a constitutional right not to be twice put in jeopardy for the same offense. Although double jeopardy (if shown) would certainly be a proper defense to assert at trial and in postconviction proceedings, the right consists of more than having the second conviction set aside. It consists of being protected from having to undergo the rigors and dangers of a second—illegal—trial. Double jeopardy is not a mere defense to a criminal charge; it is a right to be free from a second *prosecution,* not merely a second *punishment* for the same offense (though that is obviously included in the right.) The prohibition of the double jeopardy clause is 'not against being twice punished, but against being twice put in jeopardy.'

"The state's argument that the purpose of the commitment is rehabilitative and not punitive does not change its nature. No authority needs to be cited for the proposition that a court should look past the labels to the substance of an action. Regardless of the purposes for which the incarceration is imposed, the fact remains that it is incarceration. The rehabilitative goals of the system are admirable, but they do not change the drastic nature of the action taken. Incarceration of adults is also intended to produce rehabilitation. A court proceeding which may result in incarceration places a person, adult or juvenile, in jeopardy. 'The problem in this case is that Florida failed to indict Fain before the juvenile court judge adjudged him delinquent.' "

CASE SIGNIFICANCE: The question in this case is whether the juvenile was placed in double jeopardy after he was adjudicated delinquent and then indicted for the same offense. The court held that jeopardy attaches at the juvenile adjudication and any subsequent prosecution would constitute double jeopardy. The court held that because the child was adjudicated before the indictment, his rights were violated.

This case was decided prior to the Supreme Court case of *Breed v. Jones,* in which the Court held that a juvenile adjudicated delinquent through the juvenile court could not then be tried in the adult court on the same charges. This would constitute double jeopardy. This case illustrates that two years before the *Breed v. Jones* decision (1975) by the U.S. Supreme Court, some federal courts had already held that this practice constituted double jeopardy.

United States ex rel. Bombacino v. Bensinger
498 F.2d 875 (7th Cir. 1974)

Transfer hearing processes that do not include presentation of evidence and a statement of the reasons for transfer are constitutional.

FACTS: The 16-year-old petitioner and two other young men had petitions filed in juvenile court alleging that they committed aggravated battery. The victim died, and the prosecutor moved to have the cases transferred to the adult court. The attorney for the petitioner objected. The juvenile judge heard oral arguments, but did not receive any evidence. The judge granted the motion of the prosecutor and transferred the juveniles into the jurisdiction of the adult court. The three young men were indicted for murder. Two of the youths were acquitted of the charges of murder, while the defendant was found guilty of voluntary manslaughter. The youth was sentenced to one to five years, and placed in the care of the Department of Corrections. The case was appealed. The Illinois Supreme Court affirmed.

ISSUES:

1.   Was the juvenile judge required to give a statement of the reasons for transfer? NO.

2.   Did evidence need to be presented at the transfer hearing? NO.

DECISION: The Court of Appeals found nothing in the procedure of the transfer that was fundamentally unfair and therefore the transfer of jurisdiction was valid.

REASON: "There is some uncertainty about the impact of the due process clause on the procedure followed by a state in determining whether to transfer a youth from the jurisdiction of a juvenile court to that of a court of ordinary jurisdiction. There is respectable authority for the view that the determination may be committed entirely to the discretion of the prosecutor. Under this view, procedural safeguards would not be constitutionally required unless the state elected to provide for judicial participation in the transfer decision. Since the Illinois procedure under review did not provide that the juvenile judge could object to a decision by the State's Attorney to transfer, for purposes of our decision we may assume that the transfer proceeding is of such critical importance to the juvenile that any fundamental procedural unfairness in that proceeding will require a subsequent conviction to be set aside.

"We find no such unfairness in the record before us. Petitioner made only two objections to the proceedings which resulted in his transfer: First, that no evidence was heard; and second, that the judge gave no statement of reasons for his decision. . . . It is first significant that the court did not refuse to hear any evidence offered on behalf of the petitioner because no such offer was made. . . . "We are also satisfied that there is no flexible requirement that a statement of reasons always be given by a juvenile judge before allowing a transfer to occur. The need for a statement of reasons in any procedural context must be evaluated in the light of the function such a statement would perform . . . "Moreover, a statement of reasons is less necessary when the person affected is represented, as was petitioner in this case, with competent counsel.

"Unlike *Kent,* in which the decision to transfer was for the juvenile judge and the Supreme Court apparently had some doubt as to whether he had had the opportunity to consider it sufficiently, the present case involves a statutory scheme in which the role of the judge was confined to supervising the exercise of prosecutorial discretion and the undisputed fact the judge was given, but the oral argument he heard, sufficient opportunity to consider whether objection was appropriate. In this case the absence of a statement of reasons cannot be termed fundamentally unfair."

CASE SIGNIFICANCE: In this case, the petitioner voiced two concerns. One was that there was no evidence presented in the transfer hearing, and second, that the judge did not supply a statement of the reasons why the petitioner was transferred to the adult court. The court stated that the judge did not refuse to hear any evidence—no evidence was offered by the defense attorney. The court did not find that the introduction of evidence was denied. The petitioner's claim that the prosecutor is required to present evidence to prove probable cause of the crime, was "quite clearly, under the Illinois statutory procedure . . . unnecessary."

The significance of this case is in the two-pronged decision of the United States Court of Appeals. First, the court held that in a transfer hearing the prosecutor is not required to introduce evidence to the court that the juvenile was guilty of the criminal offense before the jurisdiction of the juvenile court could be waived. The court is reaffirming that the purpose of the transfer hearing is to determine where the jurisdiction of the case should lay, not whether the child was guilty.

Second, the court stated that "there is no inflexible requirement that statement of reasons always be given by a juvenile judge before allowing a juvenile to be transferred for prosecution as an adult." The court held that the representation of counsel makes the statement of reasons for the transfer "less necessary." In this case, unlike *Kent*, the Court held that the presiding judge heard sufficient testimony to make a decision in his role, which was "supervising the exercise of prosecutorial discretion."

In re Mathis
537 P.2d 148 (Or. App. 1975)

A decision to transfer based on the strength of the evidence, the child's age, and the need for long-term care is constitutional.

FACTS: A juvenile petition was filed against Mathis, alleging murder and robbery. The juvenile apparently presented a long history of problems with drugs, alcohol, truancy, and running away. Prior to the alleged act of juvenile delinquency, the juvenile had been under psychiatric care for about seven or eight months. Two psychiatrists testified that Mathis would probably require long-term counseling. The trial judge remanded the juvenile to adult court, citing that the evidence strongly supported the offenses that were alleged, and that the juvenile's age and need for long-term care also justified transfer of jurisdiction. The juvenile appealed.

ISSUE: Is a decision to transfer a juvenile to adult court proper if based on the strength of the evidence, the juvenile's age, and the need for long-term care? YES.

DECISION: If based on the strength of evidence, the juvenile's age, and the need for long-term care, a decision to transfer a juvenile to adult court is constitutional.

REASON: "Mathis is at the threshhold [sic] of maturity. He was a juvenile heretofore; he will not be hereafter. He would, if retained in juvenile court, enter the only facility available to him above the average age of other inmates. From the testimony, it is unlikely that he would be retained beyond his nineteenth year, or any more than three years. A longer period for any re-adjustment as well as a subsequent period of continued supervision seems clearly indicated. The public's interest cannot be otherwise reasonably recognized. On the other hand, he would, if convicted and sentenced to incarceration in adult court, enter an institution at the lowest age level. The former consideration outweighs the latter.

"There are other considerations. The factual circumstances which would be relied upon for conviction involve the decedent's reputation. Moreover, the offense chargeable carries lesser included offenses so that mens rea, that is, state of mind, is very significant. *Indeed, one of the possible alternative results of proceedings in adult court is exoneration.* (Emphasis supplied.)

"For all the foregoing reasons, the court is of the opinion that the best interest of Mathis and the public can be most properly served by granting the motion to remand."

"The trial judge thoroughly considered the legal alternatives, the alleged crime and the particulars relating to this juvenile, his welfare and public protection. The trial judge's decision is well buttressed with reason and we agree with it."

CASE SIGNIFICANCE: This case addressed the issue of the transfer process. Specifically, the case asked whether the transfer was the right choice given all the circumstances of the child and his past. The court upheld the decision of the judge to transfer, citing that the transfer of the juvenile appeared to be the best decision for the child and for the public. The court also stated that the judge in the case made a thorough decision based on all the presented issues.

The significance of the case lays in the Court of Appeals' affirmation of the decision of the Circuit Court to transfer the case to the adult system. The decision was based on facts regarding the child's future treatment and not on the process of transfer. The Court of Appeals recognized that the guarantee for a transfer of juvenile cases to adult court was a valid decision held in the trial court. That decision could be made based on factors of amenability to, and options of, treatment and placement.

Russell v. Parratt
543 F.2d 1214 (8th Cir. 1976)

The practice of a prosecutor holding unreviewable discretion to charge a juvenile as an adult without holding an evidentiary hearing is constitutional.

FACTS: A woman spotted 17-year-old Russell attempting to break into her father's automobile. She called a police officer, who located the boy in a nearby store and interrogated him. The owner of the vehicle declined to press charges, but the information about the boy was noted by the police officer, including his address and the perception of the police officer that the boy was in a "deranged mental condition." When the officer returned to the police station, he heard that the body of a missing eight-year-old boy had just been found in a vacant apartment. He had been strangled with a telephone cord and was dead approximately 72 hours before the discovery of the body. The officer noticed that the empty apartment where the body was found was close to the address of Russell. His information led to additional interrogation of Russell. Two police officers went to Russell's apartment, saying they wanted to take Russell to the police station to talk to him about the automobile incident. Subsequently Russell was charged with first degree murder. He was charged as an adult per the unreviewable discretion of the county attorney, who chose to treat the defendant as an adult. Russell appealed, stating that the transfer process was a violation of his due process rights and that the confession was not voluntary and intelligent, and that the waiver of counsel by the defendant was erroneous.

ISSUES:
1. Was due process violated by the county attorney having unreviewable discretion, without applicable standards to charge a juvenile as an adult? NO.

2. Did the juvenile knowingly and intelligently waive his rights to counsel and self-incrimination? YES.

DECISION: The minor's due process rights were not violated by the county attorney's exercise of unreviewable discretion to charge the juvenile as an adult without holding an evidentiary hearing. The finding that the juvenile's confession was voluntary and intelligent, and the juvenile's knowing and voluntary waiver of his right to counsel was not erroneous.

REASON: "The defendant's reliance upon *Kent v. United States* is misplaced. *Kent* involved a decision of the Juvenile Court of the District of Columbia, waiving jurisdiction to the United States District Court for the District of Columbia. It is the holding of *Kent* that when the question is one of waiver of jurisdiction of a Juvenile Court, and it is to be decided by a judge of the Juvenile Court, the juvenile is entitled to a hearing on the question of waiver and to the assistance of counsel in that hearing. The decision is, of course, harmonious with our tradition that juvenile proceedings involving substantial rights of an alleged criminal shall be attended by the full panoply of due process. But we do not here confront judicial proceedings. Rather, we have simply a traditional exercise of discretion within the executive branch, and while we recognize that the prosecutor's decision has a substantial impact on the course of subsequent proceedings, we cannot equate the prosecutorial decision with judicial proceedings absent legislative direction.

"As to the allegations that defendant's confessions were involuntary, gained by trickery, and without knowing and intelligent waiver of his rights to counsel and silence prior to his confessions, we have scrutinized the record with great care. . . . It was the holding of the Nebraska Supreme Court on these issues that the defendant's allegations were without substantial merit.

"The District Court . . . found that 'the confession was intelligent and voluntary and petitioner knowingly and voluntarily waived his right to counsel,' that '[t]he confession was not obtained by lengthy interrogation or coercion,' that '[p]etitioner was capable of understanding his constitutional rights,' and that 'the totality of circumstances supports the state court's conclusion that the confession was voluntary.' "

CASE SIGNIFICANCE: This case examined two issues. The first involved the child's waiver of rights. The court held that the child knowingly and voluntarily waived his rights.

The second issue involved the question of who holds discretion in the decision to transfer jurisdiction of a juvenile case to the adult court. In this case the child was charged as an adult by the prosecutor who held unreviewable discretion to charge the child as an adult. The court held that the juvenile's reliance on the *Kent* case to argue that the county attorney did not have the right to "unbridled discretion to proceed against him" without an evidentiary hearing was faulty. *Kent* did, the court conceded, grant juveniles the right to a transfer hearing and counsel when the waiver of jurisdiction is handled by the Juvenile Court. The decision to "exercise discretion" within the "executive branch" of government, such as the county attorney's discretion to determine where to place jurisdiction—adult or juvenile court—was not a judicial proceeding, and the juvenile's rights were not violated.

This case is significant because it upholds the constitutionality of the practice to put the decision of transfer of jurisdiction in the hands of the prosecutor. When this happens, the procedure for the transfer shifts from consideration by the judge of the elements in *Kent* to a determination by the prosecutor of whether the case should be tried in adult court.

United States v. J.D.
517 F. Supp. 69 (S.D.N.Y. 1981)

Evaluative information to be used in a transfer hearing cannot include information that would violate the privilege against self-incrimination.

FACTS: Three juveniles were taken into custody and charged with attempted robbery. Six days later, a juvenile information was filed, which charged the juveniles with conspiracy, attempted bank robbery, carrying of firearms during the commission of a felony, and possession of an unregistered firearm. The government sought transfer of the cases to adult court. Pursuant to state statute, the government sought an order to commit the defendants to the custody of the Attorney General so that observation and study could be conducted by an "appropriate agency on an outpatient basis." The purpose of the study would be to determine the personal traits, capabilities, backgrounds, previous delinquencies, intellectual development, psychological maturity, and any mental or physical defects, and to report the findings to the court, government, and defense for use in the transfer hearing to help determine the appropriate decision. The lawyer for the three juveniles opposed the study and observation on the grounds that the statute that contains the motion was unconstitutional because such study would force the juvenile to render potentially self-incriminating testimony. The defense also challenged the transfer statute, saying that the statute contained no clear guidelines for the judge to decide whether a transfer is in "the interest of justice," and therefore violated due process.

ISSUES:
1.   Was the statute providing for commitment for study constitutional? YES.

2.   Did the statute, as applied to these juveniles, violate their Fifth Amendment rights? YES.

DECISION: The statute governing the commitments for study is constitutional, but the statute as applied to these juveniles was unconstitutional because it violated the juveniles' Fifth Amendment privileges against self-incrimination.

REASON: "The government contends that ordering the defendants to submit to the proposed study would not violate their Fifth Amendment rights. It argues, first, that a transfer proceeding is not a criminal case but an 'intermediate' step, designed to ascertain how the juvenile should be treated in the interest of justice, *United States v. Rombom*, 421 F. Supp. 1295, 1298 (S.D.N.Y. 1976), and contends therefore the Fifth Amendment does not apply to this stage of a juvenile action. Second, the Government takes the position that even if the Fifth Amendment does apply, it would not be violated by the proposed study because the compulsion involved would not be used to elicit 'incriminatory testimony,' as those terms have been interpreted under authorities claimed to be relevant here. The defense disputes both arguments, claiming, in essence, that they are based on fictions.

"The government's argument that a transfer proceeding is only an 'intermediate step' is besides the point. Its irrelevance to the issue of whether the Fifth Amendment applies to transfer proceedings is revealed by the conclusion of the Supreme Court in *In re Gault*, 386 U.S. 1, 87 S. Ct. 1428, 18 L. Ed. 2d. 527 (1967). In *Gault*, the court ruled that juveniles are entitled to the Fifth Amendment's protection against self-incrimination in juvenile proceedings themselves, despite the non-criminal nature of those proceedings.

"Finally, in order to safeguard the defendants' Fifth Amendment rights, the government must take stringent steps to ensure that no impermissible use of statements made by those these defendants during psychiatric interviews is made. . . . In order to ensure that the use of these statements is confined to the constitutional purposes for which they will be compelled, the government should keep all records pertaining to the psychiatric interviews separate from its other investigatory files, and prevent the use of any of the information obtained during those interviews in the investigation or prosecution of any matters, including the present and all subsequent proceedings, concerning these defendants. Most immediately, these statements must not be used by the agency to which these juveniles are now committed for study in connection with that agency's investigation of the non-psychological factors to be explored. Agency employees charged with those areas of investigations are to have no access to the psychiatric files. The government will have the burden of proving that it had fulfilled this obligation . . ."

CASE SIGNIFICANCE: This case is significant because the court upheld the statute that provided for the commitment of juveniles for study as constitutional, but found that the statute as applied to these juvenile defendants violated their Fifth Amendment rights. The court recognized the constitutionality of collecting information about juveniles when they are being considered for transfer to the adult court, but also recognized that the need for information to determine the amenability of transfer cannot be so broad and overriding as to violate the rights of the juveniles with regard to self-incrimination.

Matter of Seven Minors
664 P.2d 947 (Nev. 1983)

Transfer decisions should be made based on clear and convincing evidence, using such factors as seriousness, criminal history, and social history of the juvenile.

FACTS: This case consolidates the fact situations of seven cases that focus on the issue of transfer decisions:

1. Thomas R., 17 years old, was charged with residential burglary. He had a number of prior adjudications for felony offenses, beginning at age 10. His offenses tended to fall into the burglary range, some with a weapon, and an arson adjudication at an early age. He had been placed in a restrictive juvenile facility, but showed no improvement.

2. Michael S., 17 years old, and three other juveniles were charged with two residential burglaries that took place on the same day. His only prior of-

fense was the theft of a bicycle several years previously. He had never been placed in a juvenile disposition placement and had strong support from his family. His criminal career was influenced by peer pressure and the use of marijuana.

3.   Terry M., 17 years old, was charged with residential burglary after being found hiding under the victim's house. His record shows that he was a persistent offender, with adjudications for possession of stolen property, burglary, and possession of a controlled substance. He had previously been committed to a restrictive juvenile placement that was willing to continue working with him.

4.   Brett G., 17 years old, was accused of two residential burglaries. He had an extensive delinquency history, consisting primarily of burglary incidents. He was a heavy drug user and had been treated in restrictive juvenile facilities previously.

5.   Parris W., 17 years old, was charged with residential burglary. He had previously been adjudicated delinquent for possession of stolen property and was on probation at the time of the most recent burglaries. His probation officer sought to keep him on the probation caseload, saying that the youth had had very little time on probation and had not yet exhausted the full range of services available. He had strong family support and was nearing graduation from high school with an admission acceptance to the University of Nevada-Las Vegas.

6.   Sandra C., 17 years old, was charged with grand larceny in the theft of $118.00 worth of clothing from a retail store. Her record indicates that she had previously been adjudicated delinquent for petty larceny and attempted larceny from a person. No juvenile placement had been attempted and no issues of community safety were involved.

7.   Amanda C., 17 years old, was charged with picking the pockets of a man while engaging in prostitution. She had no juvenile record of any kind and therefore had received no services from the juvenile justice system.

In these cases state transfer procedures allowed the juvenile court to transfer a 16- or 17-year-old to adult court for any act that would be a felony if committed by an adult. Such transfers were entirely up to the discretion of the juvenile court judge, with little or no guidelines or procedural standards in place to ensure appropriate transfer decisions.

ISSUE: What are the appropriate criteria and standard of proof necessary for a transfer decision?

DECISION: The appropriate criteria for transfer of juveniles from juvenile to adult court are threefold: (1) the nature and seriousness of the charges; (2) the persistency and seriousness of past adjudications of criminal behavior; and (3) subjective factors such as age, level of maturity, and family relationships. All of these elements should be weighed using the "clear and convincing" standard of proof.

REASON: "Transfer has played an important role in juvenile court jurisprudence since its earliest days and has acted as a safety valve through which offenders who were within the statutory age of juvenile court jurisdiction could in appropriate circumstances be held accountable for their criminal acts by referral to the adult criminal justice system. The transfer process is based upon the sound idea that there is no arbitrary age at which all youths should be held fully responsible as adults for their criminal acts and that there should be a transition period during which an offender may or may not be held criminally liable, depending on the nature of the offender and the offense. Other than the requirement of a 'full investigation,' the statute places no limitations on the discretion of the juvenile courts in such matters. The latitude of this discretion has been limited in some degree by our opinion in *Lewis v. State*, 478 P.2d 168 (1970), wherein we adopted the so-called *Kent* criteria (*Kent v. United States*, 383 U.S. 541 [1966]) to be followed by juvenile courts in transfer matters.

"In transfer matters, then, we hold that the juvenile court should consider a decisional matrix comprised of the following three categories: first, nature and seriousness of the charged offense or offenses; second, persistence and seriousness of past adjudicated or admitted criminal offenses; and third, what we will refer to as the subjective factors, namely such personal factors as age, maturity, character, personality and family relationships and controls. As in the sentencing process, primary and most weighty consideration will be given to the first two of these categories. By focusing on the youth's criminal activity, past and present, the court is in a better position to make objective judgments in differentiating between the hard-core offender and the majority of 16- and 17-year-old youths who do not, in the public interest, necessarily have to suffer the consequences of adult prosecution. By stressing objective records rather than subjective clinical factors, the court will be adopting much safer and fairer criteria for transfer decisions."

CASE SIGNIFICANCE: Although the criteria established in *Kent* provide procedural guidelines for making transfer decisions from juvenile court to adult criminal court, it did little in the way of defining the factors upon which to base such transfers. This case builds on the one concern that should drive a transfer decision—public safety. It set up a decision matrix composed of three considerations:

1.   nature and seriousness of the current offense;
2.   persistency and seriousness of past offenses;
3.   demographics factors such as age, maturity, character, personality, and family relationships.

The court in this case also adopted the *clear and convincing* standard of proof as necessary at transfer hearings in the juvenile justice system. The "clear and convincing" standard, however, is not required by the Constitution in transfer cases.

State v. Muhammad
703 P.2d 835 (Kan. 1985)

If a juvenile is notified of a transfer hearing, is given the right to be present, and is represented by counsel, due process is not violated if that juvenile does not appear at the hearing and is transferred to criminal court.

FACTS: Seventeen-year-old Shima Muhammad was arrested as a juvenile for allowing friends and members of her family to take merchandise through her cashier line at a Venture store without payment or for reduced payment. The state filed a motion for transfer of jurisdiction. The court appointed an attorney and set the hearing for January 26, 1984. After continuances, the hearing was held on February 7, 1984. While her attorney was present, neither Shima nor her parents were present. The attorney offered the court the explanation that he had heard that Shima was mistakenly arrested on a warrant issued for her sister and was being detained elsewhere. The court allowed the hearing to take place and her attorney made no requests for another continuance or objections. He cross-examined the witnesses that the state presented, but offered no defense testimony. The court waived the case to the adult court, juvenile proceedings were dismissed, and the district attorney filed criminal charges against Shima that led to her criminal conviction. The defendant appealed.

ISSUE: Was the defendant denied due process rights when the court waived jurisdiction to the adult court without the juvenile being present? NO.

DECISION: When the juvenile is notified of the hearing, given the right to be present, and is represented by counsel, due process and fair treatment requirements are met, even if the juvenile does not appear.

REASON: "At the outset it should be noted that appellant makes no attack upon the factual determination that she was not amenable to juvenile proceedings and should be tried as an adult. The thrust of the appellant's argument is that her constitutional right to due process was violated when the hearing was held without her presence, not that there was insufficient evidence to support a waiver of juvenile jurisdiction. . . .

"Only a few courts have considered the question of whether a juvenile has the absolute right to be present at a waiver hearing. As might be expected there is a split in the results reached in this decision. . . .

"Some courts have seized upon the language in *Kent* that a waiver may not be granted without a hearing and 'without the participation or any representation of the child' to determine that the presence of the child is not necessary if counsel is present . . .

"From what has been said, it appears obvious that a juvenile waiver proceeding is a critically important proceeding which requires a hearing, notice and an opportunity to be present in person or by counsel or by both. We note that K.S.A. 1984f Supp. 38-1606(a) requires an attorney 'at every stage of the proceedings' under the juvenile offenders code. It is equally clear that a juvenile may waive his or her appearance if such waiver is knowingly and voluntarily made. The critical question here is whether the court may conduct a hearing without a voluntary waiver of appearance by the juvenile if counsel is present and allowed to participate on the juvenile's behalf. We hold that it may."

CASE SIGNIFICANCE: In this transfer case, the juvenile was not present at the transfer hearing. Her attorney was present, and commented that he thought his client might be detained elsewhere. Although the juvenile was not there, the hearing was held and the defense offered no objection. The juvenile was waived to the adult court. The question raised in the appeal was whether the juvenile was denied due process rights when the transfer hearing was held in her absence.

The court stated that the waiver hearing "involves a substantial right subject to the requirements of due process, it is not adjudicatory in nature in that it does not result in any determination of guilt or innocence or in confinement or punishment." The court added that the waiver hearing was a preliminary process that determines what will follow at a later date. Under Kansas statutes regarding juvenile transfer, the requirement is that the juvenile be represented and that the attorney must be present for the hearing, but not the juvenile. The court held that the spirit of *Kent* was satisfied even though the juvenile failed to appear. The significance of the case is in the holding by the court that the due process rights of the juvenile were upheld in the transfer hearing as long as the counsel for the juvenile was present, even if the juvenile was absent from the proceeding. The court stated: "Only a few courts have considered the question of whether a juvenile had the absolute right to be present at a waiver hearing. As might be expected, there is a split in the results reached in those decisions." Nonetheless, this court decided that the due process right of the juvenile was not violated because her lawyer was present during the transfer hearing.

R.H. v. State
777 P.2d 204 (Alaska App. 1989)

The privilege against self-incrimination is violated when a juvenile is forced to participate in a psychological evaluation as part of transfer proceedings.

FACTS: R.H., 16 years and 10 months old, and another minor burglarized a business, stealing a pistol, ammunition, and an extra clip. They decided to rob a taxi for drug money and kill the driver, which they did, shooting him five times at point-blank range and stealing his taxi. R.H. was questioned two days after the murder and gave a videotaped confession to both the burglary and the murder. The state then moved to transfer R.H. from children's court, based on the severity of the charges—murder in the first degree, robbery in the first degree, and other offenses stemming from the burglary and shooting.

As part of its transfer request, the state asked for a psychiatric evaluation of R.H., arguing that expert testimony concerning R.H.'s psychological condition would be relevant in determining his amenability to treatment. Counsel for R.H. opposed the evaluation, citing the Fifth Amendment protection against self-incrimination. The judge, in ordering the examination, took precautions to protect R.H.'s right to counsel and privilege against self-incrimination, including allowing counsel to be present and sealing the reports for viewing by the court only after screening by R.H.'s counsel. R.H.'s waiver hearing was held in two stages—stage one focused on whether there was probable cause to believe that R.H. committed the delinquent acts alleged. The second stage focused on the minor's amenability to treatment in the juvenile system. Upon conclusion of the transfer hearings, the court found that there was probable cause to believe that R.H. had committed the alleged acts and that R.H. was not amenable to juvenile system treatment. The court's ruling relied heavily on the psychiatric evaluation for support of the transfer. R.H. appealed, preserving his original objections to being subjected to the evaluation.

ISSUES:

1. Do the involuntary psychiatric evaluations of a juvenile for use in certification proceedings violate the Fifth Amendment to the U.S. Constitution? YES.

2. Do the involuntary psychiatric evaluations of a juvenile for use in certification proceedings violate the Sixth Amendment to the U.S. Constitution? NO.

DECISIONS:

1. The juvenile's privilege against self-incrimination was violated by the court.

2. The juvenile's Sixth Amendment right to counsel was not violated because his counsel was permitted to accompany him and consult with him throughout the evaluation process.

REASON: . . . "[J]uvenile waiver hearings are hardly 'neutral proceedings.' Rather, they are fully adversarial proceedings in which the burden of establishing a child's probable unamenability to treatment is formally allocated to the state. . . . Nor can juvenile waiver proceedings realistically be said to affect 'only the forum where the issue of guilt will be adjudicated.' A juvenile waiver proceeding is the only available avenue by which the state may seek to prosecute a child as an adult.

 . . . "[I]f R.H. were prosecuted as a child he would face approximately three years of confinement in the relatively benign and treatment-oriented setting of a juvenile detention facility. If prosecuted as an adult and convicted of first-degree murder, he would face a maximum term of ninety-nine years in a penitentiary, and a mandatory minimum sentence of twenty years' imprisonment. . . . Admission of the psychiatric evidence against R.H., as an adult, thereby exposed him to potential punishment far more severe than could otherwise have been visited upon him. The state's reliance at the waiver hearing on the court-compelled evidence was 'plainly adverse' to R.H.

 . . . "Although the Alaska Supreme Court has noted the possible desirability of psychiatric examination in waiver proceedings, . . . it has never suggested that an examination may be conducted against the wishes of a child, nor has it held that expert testimony is a necessary precondition to waiver. To the contrary, the Alaska Supreme Court has expressly recognized that the state need not present any psychiatric evidence to meet its burden of proving that a child is unamenable to treatment.

"The evidence relating to the circumstances surrounding the offense and to R.H.'s history of delinquent behavior would certainly be sufficient, standing alone, to support the superior court's decision to waive children's court jurisdiction. In fact, this evidence may be far more compelling than the predictions expressed by the expert witness. As we have noted in prior cases, an offender's past conduct can be a more reliable indicator of future behavior than psychological prognostication."

CASE SIGNIFICANCE: This case dealt with a juvenile's right to be free from self-incrimination and his right to counsel during judicially required examinations related to transfer decisions. In this case, the examination was a psychiatric examination required by the juvenile court, despite the juvenile's and his legal counsel's objections.

Even with the elaborate protections mandated by the juvenile judge, the issue of self-incrimination remained and the appellate court did not approve of the juvenile court forcing the juvenile to involuntarily participate in a potentially incriminating process.

This case established a certification hearing as a "critical phase" in the juvenile justice process. Therefore, the process must be accompanied by appropriate constitutional protections in order to ensure protection for the juvenile.

People v. P.H.
582 N.E.2d 700 (Ill. 1991)

The gang-transfer provision of a transfer statute is constitutional.

FACTS: P.H. was arrested and charged in Illinois with two counts of attempted murder in the first degree, "two counts of aggravated battery, two counts of aggravated battery with a firearm and one count of armed violence." The state filed a motion to transfer jurisdiction to the criminal court under the "gang-transfer" provision of the juvenile code. The "gang-transfer" statute requires transfer to criminal court if the juvenile has a prior adjudication of delinquency for a felony and is subsequently charged with a felony "in furtherance of gang activity." The Cook County circuit court denied the transfer, stating that the "gang-transfer" provision is in contradiction of the statute that allows for "discretionary transfer." The court held that the provision was unconstitutional in that it violated separation of powers.

ISSUE: Is the gang-transfer provision of the statute constitutional? YES.

DECISION: The "gang-transfer" provision of the statute is constitutional. It does not violate constitutional provisions on separation of powers, double jeopardy, equal protection, or due process.

REASON:
Separation of Powers. "We do not believe that the 'gang-transfer' provision is an infringement upon the inherent powers of the judiciary. In so concluding, we are mindful that juveniles have neither a common law nor a constitutional right to adjudication under the Juvenile Court Act. (*People v. M.A.* (1988), 124 Ill. 2d 135, 124 Ill. Dec 511, 529 N.E.2d 492.) The Act is a purely statutory creature whose parameters and application are defined solely by the legislature.
    Double Jeopardy. "The linchpin of defendant's argument is that the 'gang-transfer' hearing is tantamount to an adjudicatory hearing. Defendant first points out that the juvenile court in *Breed* found that the allegations in the delinquency petition were true and that the standard of proof to sustain the allegations was beyond a reasonable doubt. Therefore, defendant reasons that since the 'gang-transfer' provision requires that the juvenile court judge determine that the allegations in the motion are 'true,' the standard of proof for transfer is also beyond a reasonable doubt.
    "We find no authority to support such a conclusion and reject the assertion as being supported by *Breed*. The reasonable standard in *Breed* applied to proof of the allegations of delinquency in the petition, not to the decision for transfer.
    Equal Protection. "Defendant advances a singular argument to support his claim that the 'gang-transfer' provision violates the equal protection guarantee. He asserts that the provision arbitrarily and capriciously punishes some more harshly than others who are guilty of the same or more serious offenses. Specifically, defendant argues that when a minor is excluded from the juvenile court under the 'automatic exclusion' provisions (Ill. Rev. Stat. 1989, ch. 37, pars. 805-4(6)(a), (7)(a)), but is later convicted only of an offense not covered by the exclusion provision, the court must proceed with disposition under the Juvenile Court Act (Ill. Rev. Stat.1989, ch. 37, par. 805-4(6)(c), (7)(c)). However, the 'gang-transfer' provision contains no similar 'transfer back' provision.
    "However, even broadly concluding that the two groups of offenders, because of their tender age, are alike, we find no equal protection violation. As we have stated, equal protection does not preclude different treatment for like persons where there is a rational basis for so doing. We believe that that standard is met here.
    "The Juvenile Court Act seeks to protect the minor offender from the negative spiraling down effects of criminal conduct, thereby benefiting the child

and society. It was not designed to protect the minor who, secure, in the knowledge of possible avoidance of criminal prosecution, contends himself to engage in a lifestyle of deviant behavior. Rather, the Act was intended to protect the child, who without thought of consequence for his conduct, violates the law. Those goals are not compromised by enactment of the 'gang-transfer' provision.

"For the reasons stated, we conclude that defendant has failed to satisfy his burden of establishing the invalidity of the 'gang-transfer' provision. Accordingly, the judgment of the circuit court of Cook County is reversed, and the cause remanded for proceedings consistent with this opinion."

CASE SIGNIFICANCE: In this case, the Illinois transfer statute was challenged because of a section that called for transfer of juveniles to adult court if the child is adjudicated delinquent for a felony offense and is then subsequently charged with another felony "in furtherance of gang activity." The issues were whether the "gang-transfer" statute violated constitutional rights on many grounds: separation of powers, double jeopardy, equal protection, substantive due process, vagueness, and procedural due process. The court found that it did not.

This case is significant because of court statements that "gang transfer" provisions of state law are valid. Some states are revising their transfer statutes, adding statutes regarding gang-related crimes and gang affiliation as criteria for transfer to adult court. Many states legislatures feel that these statutes are necessary to reduce gang activity and gang criminal activity. From this case, it appears that as long as the statute is well drafted, courts will likely uphold it.

<hr>

People v. R.L.
634 N.E.2d 733 (Ill. 1994)

The required prosecution in adult court of juveniles charged with possession or possession with intent to sell of drugs within 1,000 feet or on the property of public housing does not discriminate against a class, despite its disparate impact, and is constitutional.

FACTS: In 1992, D.W. a 16-year-old black male, was arrested and charged with delivering less than one gram of cocaine, a Class 2 felony. He was also charged with performing the crime on a public way within 1,000 feet of a public housing project. This enhanced the penalty for the crime to a Class 1 felony and made it a non-probationable offense.

At the end of 1991, R.L., a 16-year-old black male, was arrested and charged with possessing 15.6 grams of cocaine with intent to deliver, a Class X felony, which is a non-probationable offense, and with performing the crime within 1,000 feet of public housing property.

Because both were juveniles at the time of their offenses, they would normally have been adjudicated in juvenile court, but one exception to juvenile court jurisdiction involved the possession or sale of controlled substances on residential property owned, operated, or managed by a public housing agency or on a public way within 1,000 feet of such property. The Illinois Controlled Substance Act stated: "These charges and all other charges arising out of the same incident shall be prosecuted in the criminal division of circuit court." Both juveniles were found guilty as adults and both appealed, alleging denial of equal protection under the Fourteenth Amendment.

ISSUE: Does the required transfer to adult court of cases of 15- and 16-year-old minors charged with drug offenses committed within direct proximity to public housing violate the equal protection clause of the Constitution? NO.

DECISION: Even if the statute allowing 15- and 16-year-old minors to be automatically tried as adults for committing a drug offense on a public way within 1,000 feet of public housing had a racially disparate impact, there is insufficient proof that the legislature purposely intended to racially discriminate in enacting the law. Therefore, the law is constitutional and does not violate the equal protection clause.

REASON: "Under both the Federal and Illinois Constitutions, the guarantee of equal protection requires that the government treat similarly situated individuals in a similar manner. Equal protection prohibits the State from according unequal treatment to persons placed by a statute into different classes for reasons wholly unrelated to the purpose of the legislation. . . . However, equal protection does not preclude different treatment for like persons where there is a rational basis for so doing . . .

. . . "It is true that a discriminatory purpose can be inferred from the totality of the relevant facts, including a racially disproportionate impact. . . . Sometimes a clear pattern, unexplainable on nonracial grounds, emerges from the effect of a statute, even when the law is facially neutral. However, 'such cases are rare.' . . . A facially neutral and otherwise valid law does not violate the equal protection clause simply because the law may affect a greater proportion of one race than another. Disproportionate impact is relevant, but it is not the sole determinative factor of unconstitutional racial discrimination. Disproportionate impact alone does not trigger strict scrutiny.

"Under the rational basis test, a statutory classification need only be rationally related to a legitimate State goal. A statute must have only a rational basis for distinguishing the class to which the law applies from the class to which the law does not apply. Under this test, the court's review of legislative classification is limited and generally deferential. The legislature, under the State's police power, has wide discretion to classify offenses and prescribe penalties for those offenses. Thus, if any set of facts can reasonably be conceived to justify the statute, it must be upheld. . . . Further, the State may direct a law against what it considers to be a problem as it actually exists. The statute need not cover the whole field of possible abuse. The Legislature may enact a law that addresses the area of concern that seems most acute. . . . We conclude that a rational basis exists for the classification created by section 5-4(7)(a) of the Juvenile Court Act of 1987. The classification at issue here is based on the location of the charged offense. This is a permissible distinction . . . Prosecuting 15- and 16-year-old minors as adults is also a reasonable means of accomplishing such deterrence."

CASE SIGNIFICANCE: This case dealt with the required transfer of juvenile cases to adult court based on the location of the offense. The transfer in this case dealt with the possession, or possession with intent to sell, of drugs within 1,000 feet of public housing. The juveniles allege that the law under which they were automatically tried in adult circuit court and therefore subject to harsher penalties was unconstitutional on the grounds of racial discrimination.

The court ruled that even though the equal protection clause requires similar treatment for similar offenders in the criminal justice system, it allows for exceptions as long as there is a rational reason for the exception. In this case, the court saw a rational basis for such exception based on the proliferation of drugs in public housing and the vulnerability of juveniles to influences in such environments.

The court further found that even acknowledging that in some circumstances a law might be discriminatory on its face, this law was not discriminatory in its intent even though its application may have resulted in some discrimination. Disproportionate impact is a relevant factor in determining an equal protection violation but is not the sole determinant of unconstitutionally discriminatory practices.

The significance of this case lays in the law being upheld as constitutional despite the fact that its application will inevitably discriminate against minorities and low-income individuals. The court declared the law "facially neutral" and therefore valid. Disparate impact, says this case, does not, in and of itself, make an ordinance unconstitutional.

C.M. v. State
884 S.W.2d 562 (Tex. App. 1994)

The trial judge has discretion in determining the weight to be given to the various factors considered by the court in a transfer hearing.

FACTS: C.M. and a friend were walking through a public housing project in San Antonio when they came across Rogelio Garcia, Jr. and others who were spray-painting graffiti on a wall. C.M. and Garcia belonged to rival gangs, and Garcia had assaulted C.M. one week prior. C.M. asked Garcia why he was painting the walls. Garcia approached C.M., pushed him to the ground, and they began to fight. C.M. pulled out a .25 semi-automatic handgun, shot approximately five times, and struck Garcia twice. Garcia died at the hospital. C.M. was charged with "intentionally and knowingly" causing the death of the victim by shooting him. C.M. was certified to stand trial as an adult. In the course of the certification trial, a juvenile probation officer and a clinical psychologist both testified that the juvenile would have a better chance of rehabilitation if he stayed in the juvenile system. C.M. argued that the trial court abused its discretion in ordering the transfer because both aforementioned witnesses testified that he was a good candidate for rehabilitation in the juvenile system.

ISSUE: Did the judge err in ordering C.M.'s transfer? NO.

DECISION: There was sufficient evidence in the case for the trial court to make the decision to transfer the youth to the adult system.

REASON: "The requirements for transferring a case from juvenile court to the district court are:

1. the child is alleged to have violated a penal law of the grade of felony;
2. the child was 15 years of age or older at the time he [or she] is alleged to have committed the offense and no adjudication hearing has been conducted concerning that offense; and
3. after full investigation and hearing the juvenile court determines that there is probable cause to believe that the child before the court committed the offense alleged and that because of the seriousness of the offense *or* the background of the child the welfare of the community requires criminal proceedings.

Texas Fam. Code Ann. Sec. 54.02(a) (Vernon Supp. 1994).

"In making the transfer determination, the trial court appropriately considered the factors set forth in section 54.02(f) of the Family Code, and made the following findings of fact:

1.   the offense was against a person;
2.   the offense was committed in an aggressive and premeditated matter;
3.   there was sufficient evidence upon which a grand jury could be expected to return an indictment;
4.   appellant was sufficiently mature and sophisticated to confer with his attorney and assist with his own defense;
5.   there were no prior offenses;
6.   it was unclear whether the public would be adequately protected if appellant were not transferred to criminal district court.

See Tex. Fam. Code Ann. Sec. 54.02(f) (Vernon 1986).

"Most importantly, the trial court found that 'because of the seriousness of the offense, the welfare of the community' required transfer."

CASE SIGNIFICANCE: In this case, the child was ordered to stand trial as an adult for knowingly and intentionally causing the death of another person. During the course of the transfer hearing, two witnesses testified that the juvenile had a better chance of rehabilitation if he were to be kept in the juvenile system. The issue raised was whether the court abused its discretion in making the decision to transfer despite the testimony of the two witnesses. The court held that the trial judge had the discretion to transfer a youth based on consideration of the factors stated in the Family Code. Furthermore, the court held that consideration could include differential weighting of the importance of the factors. In other words, it was within the judge's discretion to transfer the child on the belief that the seriousness of the offense outweighed the child's level of amenability to treatment within the juvenile system.

This case is significant because it addresses the issue of the factors that judges are to consider in transfers to the adult system. There are various factors that judges must consider in the transfer hearing. One issue in this case was whether all the factors must be weighed equally. In this case, the appellate court held that the judge had the discretion to transfer based on the factor of seriousness of the charges, even if the background of the child suggested amenability to treatment in the juvenile system. This case suggests that judges are to consider all the factors that must be considered in transfer decisions, but they do not all have to be equally weighed. Note, however, that conditions for waiver to adult court are usually governed by state law. They may therefore vary from state to state.

Laswell v. Frey
45 F.3d 1101 (6th Cir. 1995)

Admitting to charges pending in the course of a detention hearing does not turn that detention hearing into an adjudication hearing; thus, jeopardy does not attach.

FACTS: Marie Anne Laswell and two co-defendants were arrested in conjunction with a robbery and double murder that occurred one month earlier. On July 26, Laswell was arraigned in the Union County District Court during the juvenile session and charged with two counts of complicity to commit first degree robbery. During this hearing, Laswell was represented by counsel. During the hearing, the court advised Laswell of her constitutional rights to an attorney, to remain silent, to confront witnesses, to appeal the determination of the court, and to examine any reports filed with the court and to question the report writers. The Court next asked the defendant if she would "admit to or deny" the charges. Laswell admitted to the charges. The disposition hearing was apparently set for August 15, 1991.

After the initial hearing, the state added two counts of murder and moved to transfer the jurisdiction of the case to adult court. Her defense attorney objected, stating that the initial July 26th hearing had been an adjudication hearing, and therefore transfer would invoke the double jeopardy clause. The court disagreed and scheduled the youthful offender hearing for August 29, 1991. On August 29, 1991, the case was waived to adult court. "The grand jury indicted Laswell on two counts of complicity to commit capital murder, and complicity to commit first degree robbery as well as complicity to receive stolen property, over $100 and tampering with physical evidence."

Laswell later filed a writ of habeas corpus arguing that the first hearing had been an adjudication hearing and the subsequent adult hearing would violate the double jeopardy clause.

ISSUE: Was the preliminary hearing an adjudication hearing and, if it was, would the subsequent adult hearings held after the transfer hearing constitute double jeopardy? NO.

DECISION: Admitting to the charges in the preliminary hearing did not automatically transform a detention hearing into an adjudication, therefore there was no double jeopardy in the above proceeding.

REASON: "Upon review, this court notes that an adjudication demands a determination of the truth or falsity of the allegations, and that a determination of the truth requires more than the simple verbal admission at the detention hearing at issue in the instant case. The Court is persuaded that, because no inquiry was made of the veracity of the charges or admission, because no inquiry was made to determine if the 'plea' was voluntarily made, and because no inquiry was made as to the nature of the charges, that the proceedings cannot later be transformed from a determination of probable cause for detention into an acceptance of a valid guilty plea.

"The District Court found that appellant was simply trying to fashion a guilty plea after the fact based on events subsequent to her admission. This Court agrees. The juvenile court inquired into the matter of probable cause by asking appellant whether she admitted or denied the offenses at that time. The admission established probable cause for detention only. At that time and under the circumstances, it was insufficient to establish guilt, and thus jeopardy did not attach at the July 26, 1991, hearing."

CASE SIGNIFICANCE: In this case, the child admitted at the detention hearing that she committed the acts with which she was charged. After that hearing, the juvenile was charged with some serious additional charges, and the state moved to transfer the case. The attorney for the juvenile objected, saying that the detention hearing had been an adjudication hearing and that the juvenile had been adjudicated delinquent for the initial charges. The court disagreed and the juvenile was waived to the adult court. The juvenile was indicted for several offenses and her attorney challenged that the first hearing had been an adjudication hearing and thus the juvenile was placed in jeopardy because the subsequent adult hearing would constitute double jeopardy. The court held that just because the juvenile admitted to the charges in the preliminary hearing that hearing did not automatically become an adjudication hearing.

The court noted that the function of the adjudication hearing is to determine the truth of the allegations. The determination of the truth "requires more than the simple verbal admission at the detention hearing" as was the heart of the issue in this case. The court held that "no inquiry was made of the veracity of the charges or admission, because no inquiry was made to determine if the 'plea' was voluntarily made, and because no inquiry was made as to the nature of the charges, that the proceeding cannot later be transformed from a determination of probable cause for detention into an acceptance of a valid guilty plea."

This case demonstrates that the various juvenile court hearings can be confusing to the defendants and the other participants. The court recognized that "[W]e may have a questionable and atypical point of law as far as exactly when everything takes place." When faced with the question of whether the detention hearing could have been construed as an adjudication hearing, the United States Court of Appeals found that the elements of an adjudication hearing were not present, hence no double jeopardy attached.

Adjudication 7

Introduction

In juvenile court, the adjudicatory hearing is defined as "a fact-finding hearing at which the court determines the existence or nonexistence of the allegations contained in the petition."[1] Adjudication is the juvenile justice equivalent of an adult trial. According to recent statistics, 495,000 youths were adjudicated through juvenile courts in 1994. This represents 58 percent of all cases in which a petition was filed.[2]

The juvenile adjudication hearing did not begin as a clone of the adult trial. As you will discover in this chapter, the procedure of the adjudication hearing was changed through court intervention. According to Bartollas and Miller, "[t]he adjudicatory hearing today is a blend of the old and the new."[3]

When the first juvenile court was created in 1899, the Illinois Juvenile Court Act called for juvenile court hearings to be handled informally. The entire process was designed to be different from that in the adult court. For example, there were no lawyers present, no formal rules of procedure, and juveniles enjoyed no legal rights.[4] The child and what he or she needed, in terms of future rehabilitation, was the focus of the court process.[5] Thus, much less important in the eyes of the court was what the child had done to first come to the attention of the court. Therefore, the act that brought the child into the system, and the "proving" of that act, was not of paramount importance in the juvenile court.

Once the juvenile court was created in 1899, the informal process and the judicial philosophy that dictated that process remained unchallenged until the 1960s.[6] Many of the cases concerning the due process rights of juveniles were decided by the Supreme Court in the late 1960s and early 1970s. The 1967 landmark Supreme Court case, *In re Gault*, offers basic constitutional rights to juveniles facing an adjudication hearing that might result in incarceration in a juvenile facility. In 1970, in *In re Winship*, the Supreme Court held that juvenile adjudication hearings should hold the same burden of proof as adult hearings—beyond a reasonable doubt. In 1972, *Ivan v. City of New York* held that the Court's holding in *Winship* should be applied retroactively to all cases in the appellate process.

In 1971, the Supreme Court decided to keep some fundamental differences between the juvenile and adult court when it held in *McKeiver v. Pennsylvania* that juveniles did not have a constitutional right to trial by jury. *United States v. Torres,* in 1974, is an example of a lower court's decision to extend the *McKeiver* holding (no constitutional right to a jury trial) to juveniles being processed through the federal juvenile courts. Today, one of the basic fundamental differences between juvenile and adult court is that juveniles do not enjoy a constitutional right to trial by jury. Ten states, however, allow juveniles a jury hearing by virtue of state law.[7]

The 1992 case of *In re Montrail M.* is included to demonstrate some of the other questions regarding the adjudicatory processes that confront courts. *Goss v. Lopez* (1975) held that due process must be given to juveniles even in short-term suspension cases. The last two cases presented here, *Boyd v. State* (1993) and *In re Marven C.* (1995) deal with the applicability of other adult trial issues to juvenile proceedings. While the courts changed the face of the juvenile court with the cases heard in the late 1960s and early 1970s, there are still many issues regarding juvenile adjudication hearings that are being addressed or will be addressed in both the courts and the legislatures. These issues include the opening of juvenile court hearings to the public, the erosion of confidentiality of juvenile hearings, and disclosure of juvenile records (Chapter 11, Privacy and Confidentiality of Juvenile Records and Proceedings).

Notes

[1]   Samuel M. Davis, *Rights of Juveniles: The Juvenile Justice System* (1980) at 5-1.

[2]   Jeffrey A. Butts, Howard N. Snyder, Terrence A. Finnegan, Anne L. Aughenbaugh, and Rowen S. Poole, *Juvenile Court Statistics 1994*. Washington, DC: National Center for Juvenile Justice. Office of Juvenile Justice and Delinquency Prevention. U.S. Department of Justice, Office of Justice Programs. (1994).

[3]   Clemens Bartollas and Stuart J. Miller, *Juvenile Justice in America* (1994) at 103.

[4]   Cliff Roberson, *Exploring Juvenile Justice: Theory and Practice* (1996).

[5]   Cliff Roberson, *Exploring Juvenile Justice: Theory and Practice* (1996).

[6]   George L. Kelling, "The Historical Legacy." In *From Children to Citizens: Volume I: The Mandate for Juvenile Justice*. (Mark Harrison Moore, ed. 1987).

[7]   Clemens Bartollas, *Juvenile Delinquency*, Fourth Edition (1997).

I.   UNITED STATES SUPREME COURT CASES

In re Gault
387 U.S. 1 (1967)

Juveniles must be given four basic due process rights in adjudication proceedings that can result in confinement in an institution in which their freedom would be curtailed.

FACTS: On June 8, 1964, a 15-year-old named Gault and a friend were taken into custody as a result of a complaint that they had made lewd phone calls. Gault's parents were not informed that he was in custody. The parents were never shown the complaint that was filed against their son. The complainant did not appear at any hearing and no written record was made at the hearings. Gault was committed to the State Industrial School as a delinquent until he reached majority, a total of six years from the date of the hearing. The maximum punishment for an adult found guilty of the same offense was a fine from $5 to $50, or imprisonment for a maximum of two months.

ISSUE: Is a juvenile entitled to procedural due process rights during the adjudication stage of a juvenile delinquency proceeding? YES.

DECISION: Juveniles are entitled to procedural rights in proceedings (such as adjudication of delinquency) that might result in commitment to an institution in which their freedom would be curtailed. These rights are:

1.   Right to reasonable notice of the charges;
2.   Right to counsel, his or her own, appointed by the state if indigent;
3.   Right to confront and cross-examine witnesses;
4.   Privilege against self-incrimination, including the right to remain silent.

REASON: "The right of the state, as *parens patriae* to deny to the child procedural rights available to his elders was elaborated by the assertion that a child, unlike an adult, has a right 'not to liberty but to custody.' If his parents default in effectively performing their custodial functions—that is, if the child is 'delinquent'—the state may intervene. In doing so, it does not deprive the child of any rights, because he has none. It merely provides the 'custody' to which the child is entitled. On this basis, proceedings involving juveniles were described as 'civil,' not 'criminal,' and therefore not subject to the requirements which restrict the state when it seeks to deprive a person of his liberty.

"Accordingly, the highest motives and enlightened impulses led to a peculiar system for juveniles, unknown to our law in any comparable context. The constitutional and theoretical basis for this peculiar system is—to say the least—debatable. And in practice, as we remarked in the *Kent* case, *supra*, the results have not been entirely satisfactory. Juvenile Court history has again demonstrated that unbridled discretion, however benevolently motivated, is frequently a poor substitute for principle and procedure. . . . The absence of substantive standards has not necessarily meant that children receive careful, compassionate, individualized treatment. The absence of procedural rules based upon constitutional principles has not always produced fair, efficient, and effective procedures. Departures from established principles of due process have frequently resulted not in enlightened procedures, but in arbitrariness.

"Failure to observe the fundamental requirements of due process has resulted in instances, which might have been avoided, of unfairness to individuals and inadequate or inaccurate findings of fact and unfortunate prescriptions of remedy. Due process of law is the primary and indispensable foundation of individual freedom. It is the basic and essential term in the social compact which defines the rights of the individual and delimits the powers which the state may exercise . . .

". . . We do not mean by this to denigrate the juvenile court process or to suggest that there are not aspects of the juvenile system relating to offenders which are valuable. But the features of the juvenile system which its proponents have asserted are of unique benefit will not be impaired by constitutional domestication. For example, the commendable principles relating to the processing and treatment of juveniles separately from adults are in no way involved or affected by the procedural issues under discussion . . .

"Further, it is urged that the juvenile benefits from informal proceedings in the court. The early conception of the Juvenile Court proceeding was one in which a fatherly judge touched the heart and conscience of the erring youth by talking over his problems, by parental advice and admonition, and in which, in extreme situations, benevolent and wise institutions of the State provided guidance and help 'to save him from a downward career.' Then as now, goodwill and compassion were admirably prevalent. But recent students have, with surprising unanimity, entered sharp dissent as to the validity of this gentle conception. They suggest that the appearance as well as the actuality of fairness, impartiality and orderliness—in short, the essentials of due process—may be a more impressive and more therapeutic attitude as far as the juvenile is concerned. . . . Of course, it is not suggested that juvenile court judges should fail appropriately to take account, in their demeanor and conduct, of the emotional and psychological attitude of the juveniles with whom they are confronted. While due process requirements will, in some instances, introduce a degree of order and regularity to Juvenile Court proceedings to determine delinquency, and in contested cases will introduce some elements of the adversary system, nothing will require that the conception of the kindly juvenile judge will be replaced by its opposite, nor do we rule upon the question of whether ordinary due process requirements must be observed with respect to hearings to determine the disposition of the delinquent child.

". . . [I]t would be extraordinary if our Constitution did not require the procedural regularity and exercise of care implied in the phase 'due process.' Under our Constitution, the condition of being a boy does not justify a kangaroo court."

CASE SIGNIFICANCE: *In re Gault* is the most important case ever to be decided by the Supreme Court in juvenile justice and is the most widely known case on the rights of juveniles. It basically says that juvenile proceedings, even though civil in nature, require many due process protections that are afforded adults in criminal proceedings. Since the *Gault* case, the Court has decided other cases extending most constitutional rights to juvenile proceedings, such that at present the only rights not extended to juveniles are the right to a grand jury indictment, the right to bail, the right to a jury trial, and the right to a public hearing. All other constitutional rights have been given to juveniles by the Court in various cases.

This case represents a significant erosion of the pure *parens patriae* approach that characterized juvenile proceedings since the founding of the first juvenile court in Chicago in 1899. *Gault* was decided in 1967, indicating that for a long time the Court respected the *parens patriae* approach and adopted a "hands-off" attitude in juvenile proceedings.

What led to the erosion of *parens patriae*? The answer lays in a footnote in the *Gault* case. Quoting an earlier case (*Kent v. United States*, 383 U.S. 541 [1966]), the Court said: "There is evidence . . . that there may be grounds for concern that the child receives the worst of both worlds; that he gets neither the protections accorded to adults nor the solicitous care and regenerative treatment postulated for children." In the face of this concern, the court abandoned the pure *parens patriae* approach and injected due process into juvenile proceedings. Once that approach was taken, other constitutional rights for juveniles followed.

Gault must be understood in the proper context, which is that it applies only in proceedings that might result in the commitment of a juvenile to an institution in which his or her freedom would be curtailed. The rights given in *Gault* do not apply to every juvenile proceeding. For example, most CHINS (Children in Need of Supervision), MINS (Minors in Need of Supervision), and PINS (Persons in Need of Supervision) proceedings need not give juveniles *In re Gault* rights if these proceedings, because of the provisions of state law or agency policy, do not result in the juvenile losing his or her freedom. What *In re Gault* says is that in adjudication proceedings that might result in institutionalization, a juvenile must be given basic due process rights. In a proceeding that does not result in institutionalization, the juvenile is not entitled under the Constitution to due process rights, but they may be given (and are usually given) by state law.

———

In re Winship
397 U.S. 358 (1970)

Proof beyond a reasonable doubt, not simply a preponderance of the evidence, is required in juvenile adjudication hearings in cases in which the act would have been a crime if it were committed by an adult.

FACTS: During an adjudication hearing, a New York Family Court judge found that the juvenile involved, then a 12-year-old boy, had broken into a locker and stolen $112 from a woman's purse. The petition, which charged the juvenile with delinquency, alleged that his act, "if done by an adult, would constitute the crime or crimes of larceny." The judge acknowledged that guilt might not have been established beyond a reasonable doubt but that the New York Family Court Act required that the verdict need only be based on a preponderance of the evidence. At the dispositional hearing (the equivalent of sentencing), the juvenile was ordered to be placed in training school for an initial period of 18 months, subject to annual extensions of his commitment until his eighteenth birthday.

ISSUE: Does the due process clause of the Fourteenth Amendment require proof beyond a reasonable doubt in a juvenile adjudication? YES.

DECISION: Proof beyond a reasonable doubt, not simply a preponderance of the evidence, is required during the adjudicatory stage, if a juvenile is charged with an act that would constitute a crime if committed by an adult.

REASON: "The requirement of proof beyond a reasonable doubt has this vital role in our criminal procedure for cogent reasons. The accused during a criminal prosecution has at stake interests of immense importance, both because of the possibility that he may lose his liberty upon conviction and because of the certainty that he would be stigmatized by the conviction . . .

"We turn to the question whether juveniles, like adults, are constitutionally entitled to proof beyond a reasonable doubt when they are charged with a violation of a criminal law. The same considerations that demand extreme caution in fact-finding to protect the innocent adult apply as well to the innocent child.

"Nor do we perceive any merit in the argument that to afford juveniles the protection of proof beyond a reasonable doubt would risk destruction of beneficial aspects of the juvenile process. Use of the reasonable doubt standard during the adjudicatory hearing will not disturb New York's policies that a finding that a child has violated a criminal law does not constitute a criminal conviction, that such a finding does not deprive the child of his civil rights, and that the juvenile proceedings are confidential. Nor will there be any effect on the informality, flexibility, or speed of the hearing at which the fact-finding takes place. And the opportunity during the post-adjudicatory or dispositional hearing for a wide-ranging review of the child's social history for his individualized treatment will remain unimpaired. Similarly, there is no effect on the procedures distinctive to juvenile proceedings that are employed prior to the adjudicatory hearing."

CASE SIGNIFICANCE: Juvenile proceedings are civil proceedings and as such are supposedly to be decided by a "preponderance of the evidence" standard. In this case, the Court said that in juvenile cases in which a juvenile is charged with an act that would constitute a crime if committed by an adult, the standard of proof is not a preponderance of the evidence, but proof beyond a reasonable doubt. The implication is that although juvenile proceedings generally are considered civil proceedings, they are in fact treated like criminal proceedings in some instances. This gives credence to the assertion by some writers that juvenile proceedings are civil only in name and that in reality they are criminal proceedings and are considered such by the United States Supreme Court.

This case does not hold that all juvenile proceedings require proof beyond a reasonable doubt. What it says is that all juvenile proceedings in which a juvenile "is charged with an act that would constitute a crime if committed by an adult" are subject to a higher standard of proof—proof beyond a reasonable doubt. Any other juvenile proceeding that does not fall under this category is governed by the preponderance of the evidence standard unless state law provides otherwise. The reason for this distinction is the seriousness of the offense and the possible punishment. Most cases in which a juvenile is charged with an act that would constitute a crime if committed by an adult constitute juvenile delinquency, which can result in institutionalization and therefore a deprivation of freedom. On the other hand, CHINS (Children in Need of Supervision), MINS (Minors in Need of Supervision), or PINS (Persons in Need of Supervision) cases (usually relatively minor offenses) result in probation or other forms of non-punitive rehabilitative sanctions and therefore are not subject to the proof beyond a reasonable doubt standard. The exception is if proof beyond a reasonable doubt is required by state law even for minor offenses or violations.   In these cases, state law prevails.

McKeiver v. Pennsylvania
403 U.S. 528 (1971)

Juveniles have no constitutional right to trial by jury, even in a delinquency proceeding.

FACTS: In 1968, 16-year-old Joseph McKeiver was charged with robbery, larceny, and receiving stolen goods—all acts of juvenile delinquency. Under Pennsylvania criminal law, these offenses were felonies. McKeiver was represented by counsel at his adjudication hearing. He requested but was denied trial by jury. The judge ruled that McKeiver had violated a law of the commonwealth and was adjudged a delinquent. He was placed on probation.

ISSUE: Do juveniles have a constitutional right to trial by jury in a delinquency proceeding? NO.

DECISION: Juveniles do not have a constitutional right to trial by jury, even in a juvenile adjudication hearing.

REASON: "All the litigants agree that the applicable due process standard in juvenile proceedings, as developed by *Gault* and *Winship*, is fundamental fairness. As that standard was applied in those two cases, we have an emphasis on fact-finding procedures. The requirement of notice, counsel, confrontation, cross-examination, and standard of proof naturally flowed from this emphasis. But one cannot say that in our legal system the jury is a necessary component of accurate fact-finding.

"There is the possibility, at least, that the jury trial, if required as a matter of constitutional precept, will remake the juvenile proceeding into a fully adversary process and will put an effective end to what has been the idealistic prospect of an intimate, informal protective proceeding.

"The imposition of the jury trial on the juvenile court system would not strengthen greatly, if at all, the fact-finding function, and would, contrarily, provide an attrition of the juvenile court's assumed ability to function in a unique manner. It would not remedy the defects of the system. Meager as has been the hoped-for advance in the juvenile field, the alternative would be regressive, would lose what has been gained, and would tend once again to place the juvenile squarely in the routine of the criminal process.

"If the jury trial were to be injected into the juvenile court system as a matter of right, it would bring with it into that the traditional delay, the formality, and the clamor of the adversary system, and possibly, the public trial . . .

"If the formalities of the criminal adjudicative process are to be superimposed upon the juvenile court system, there is little need for its separate existence. Perhaps that ultimate disillusionment will come one day, but for the moment we are disinclined to give impetus to it."

CASE SIGNIFICANCE: Unlike other leading juvenile cases, this case does not give juveniles any constitutional rights. What it says instead is that juveniles are not entitled to a jury trial in an adjudication hearing (the equivalent of a trial) or at any stage of a juvenile proceeding. The Court gave a number of reasons for not extending the right to trial by jury to juvenile criminal proceedings. Among these:

1. Compelling a jury trial might remake the proceeding into a fully adversary process and effectively end the idealistic prospect of an intimate, informal, protective proceeding;
2. Imposing a jury trial on the juvenile court system would not remedy the system's defects and would not greatly strengthen the fact-finding function;
3. Jury trial would entail delay, formality, and clamor of the adversary system, and possibly a public trial; and
4. Equating the adjudicative phase of the juvenile proceeding with a criminal trial ignores the aspects of fairness, concern, sympathy, and paternal attention inherent in the juvenile court system.

The right to trial by jury is one of the few constitutional rights not enjoyed by juveniles. The other constitutional rights not extended to juveniles are: the right to a public trial, the right to bail, and the right to a grand jury indictment. Note, however, that although the right to a jury trial is not constitutionally required, some states, by state law, give juveniles the right to a jury trial either during the adjudication or revocation process (if the juvenile is placed on probation), or both.

Ivan v. City of New York
407 U.S. 203 (1972)

The decision in *Winship*—that juveniles are entitled to proof beyond a reasonable doubt in adjudication hearings—should be applied retroactively to all cases in the appellate process.

FACTS: Petitioner was adjudicated delinquent in the Family Court of Bronx County, New York for the delinquent act of stealing a bicycle at knifepoint from another youth. Based on the preponderance of evidence, the court found the child delinquent on the grounds that he committed an act that would be considered robbery in the first degree if the child were an adult. This case was heard before the Supreme Court that had decided *In re Winship*. On direct appeal, the adjudication was reversed by the Appellate Division, First Department, holding that *Winship* should be applied retroactively to all cases that were still in the appeal process. The New York Court of Appeals reversed. On remand to the Appellate Division, the delinquency adjudication of the appellant was upheld. The case was appealed to the Supreme Court of New York, First Judicial Division.

ISSUE: Should the *Winship* decision (holding that a juvenile is entitled to proof beyond a reasonable doubt in an adjudication hearing when charged with an act that would be a crime if committed by an adult) be applied retroactively to all cases in the appellate process? YES.

DECISION: The *Winship* decision is retroactive to all cases in the appellate process.

REASON: "Where the major purpose of new constitutional doctrine is to overcome an aspect of the criminal trial that substantially impairs its truth-finding function and so raises serious questions about the accuracy of guilty verdicts in past trials, the new rule has been given complete retroactive effect. Neither good-faith reliance by state or federal authorities on prior constitutional law or accepted practice, nor severe impact on the administration of justice has sufficed to require prospective application in these circumstances." *Williams v. United States*, 401 U.S. 646, 653 (1971). *See Adams v. Illinois*, 405 U.S. 278, 280 (1972); *Roberts v. Russell*, 392 U.S. 293, 295 (1968).

"*Winship* expressly held that the reasonable-doubt standard is a prime instrument for reducing the risk of convictions resting on factual error. The standard provides concrete substance for the presumption of innocence—that bedrock 'axiomatic and elementary' principle whose 'enforcement lies at the foundation of the administration of our criminal law.' . . . 'Due process commands that no man shall lose his liberty unless the Government has borne the burden of . . . convincing the fact finder of his guilt.' To this end, the reasonable-doubt standard is indispensable, for it 'impresses on the trier of fact the necessity of reaching a subjective state of certitude of the facts in issue.' 397 U.S. at 363-364.

"Plainly, then, the major purpose of the constitutional standard of proof beyond a reasonable doubt announced in *Winship* was to overcome an aspect of a criminal trial that substantially impairs the truth-finding function, and *Winship* is thus to be given complete retroactive effect. The motion for leave to proceed in *forma pauperis* and the petition for writ of certiorari are granted. The judgment of the Appellate Division of the Supreme Court of New York, First Judicial Department, is reversed and the case is remanded for further proceedings not inconsistent with this opinion."

CASE SIGNIFICANCE: The juvenile in this case had been adjudicated delinquent in Family Court in New York. The judge had applied the standard of a preponderance of the evidence in adjudicating the child delinquent. At the time of the hearing, the Supreme Court had not yet handed down the decision in *In re Winship*.

The question in this case was whether *In re Winship* was to be applied retroactively to cases that were in the appeal process. *Winship* held that juveniles must be adjudicated delinquent beyond a reasonable doubt when the delinquent act is something that would constitute a crime if committed by an adult. In this case, the court held that *Winship* was to be applied retroactively to all cases in the appellate process. Preponderance of the evidence (used in this case) is lower in certainty than guilt beyond a reasonable doubt (required by *Winship*).

Goss v. Lopez
419 U.S. 565 (1975)

Due process must be given to juveniles even in short-term suspension cases.

FACTS: This class action suit was filed on behalf of all students of the Columbus, Ohio Public School System (CPSS) who had been suspended for 10 days or less, with little or no due process. The only statutory requirement afforded to students suspended for 10 days or less was parental notification within 24 hours. There was no policy for administrative review or appeal.

The students' appeal asserted that they had been unconstitutionally deprived of their right to an education without a hearing of any kind, a violation of the due process clause of the Fourteenth Amendment.

ISSUES:

1. Do students facing temporary suspension from a public school possess property and liberty interests that require protection under the due process clause of the Fourteenth Amendment? YES.

2. If yes, what type of due process should be given?

DECISION: Students facing temporary suspension from a public school have property and liberty interests and are entitled to due process rights. Due process in these cases requires, at a minimum, oral or written notice of charges supporting the suspension, an explanation of evidence if the student denies involvement, and an opportunity to present the student's version. Such notice and hearing should precede the suspension but, under extenuating circumstances, may follow as soon as possible *after* the suspension.

REASON: "In holding as we do, we do not believe that we have imposed procedures on school disciplinarians which are inappropriate in a classroom setting. Instead we have imposed requirements which are, if anything, less than a fairminded school principal would impose upon himself in order to avoid unfair suspensions. . . . We stop short of construing the due process clause to require, countrywide, that hearings in connection with short suspensions must afford the student the opportunity to secure counsel, to confront and cross-examine witnesses supporting the charge, or to call his own witnesses to verify his version of the incident. Brief disciplinary suspensions are almost countless. To impose in each such case even truncated trial-type procedures might well overwhelm administrative facilities in many places and, by diverting resources, cost more than it would save in educational effectiveness. Moreover, further formalizing the suspension process and escalating its formality and adversary nature may not only make it too costly as a regular disciplinary tool but also destroy its effectiveness as part of the teaching process.

"On the other hand, requiring effective notice and an informal hearing permitting the student to give his version of the events will provide a meaningful hedge against erroneous action. At least the disciplinarian will be alerted to the existence of disputes about facts and arguments about cause and effect. He may then determine himself to summon the accuser, permit cross-examination, and allow the student to present his own witnesses. In more difficult cases, he may permit counsel. In any event, his discretion will be more informed and we think the risk of error substantially reduced. . . . Requiring that there be at least an informal give-and-take between student and disciplinarian, preferably prior to the suspension, will add little to the fact-finding function where the disciplinarian himself has witnessed the conduct forming the basis for the charge. But things are not always as they seem to be, and the student will at least have the opportunity to characterize his conduct and put it in what he deems the proper context."

CASE SIGNIFICANCE: This case dealt with short-term school suspensions that were imposed by school administrators with no initial hearing. The problem involved many students whose alleged offenses ranged from involvement in a disturbance to being in the wrong place at the wrong time. The school had no procedures to deal with minor violations of school rules of this nature other than notification of the student's parents.

The court ruled that regardless of the nature of the disciplinary infraction, schools must provide a modicum of due process to ensure that students who received short-term suspensions were actually guilty of the charges against them and that the punishment was appropriate to the rule violation alleged. Anything less than a full review of the situation from which the suspension results would be fundamentally unfair to the juvenile regardless of the nature of the rule violation. The court further indicated that the state itself had partially created the set of circumstances that required that due process be established for school rule violations by asserting that all individuals had a right under state law to avail themselves of an education, thereby creating a right to education and therefore a liberty interest when students are deprived of such education, regardless of the extent of deprivation.

The significance of this case is in its requirement by the United States Supreme Court of a due process hearing that applies to all levels of rule violations in school, including violations of this nature. However, the rights of confrontation and cross-examination were not extended to this type of rule violation hearing.

II. LOWER COURT CASES

United States v. Torres
500 F.2d 944 (2d Cir. 1974)

The federal Juvenile Delinquency Act does not violate a juvenile's rights when it holds that a juvenile who consents to an adjudication hearing gives up the right to trial by jury.

FACTS: While a resident at the New York Training School for Boys at Otisville, New York, Torres was arrested and charged with acts of juvenile delinquency in violation of various procedures of 18 U.S.C. § 474. Torres, charged with acts in violation of federal law, first had a hearing in the U.S. District Court for the Southern District of New York. He was represented by counsel during this hearing, he agreed in writing to be treated as a juvenile, the information was filed and the case assigned.

During the hearing, Torres was advised of his rights and of the consequences of agreeing to be treated as an juvenile, including the fact that he would be giving up his right to a trial by jury. Torres' counsel argued that the juvenile did have a right to trial by jury under the Sixth Amendment, and that the federal statutes were unconstitutional. The counsel also maintained that the federal Juvenile Delinquency Act, which states that a juvenile's agreeing to be treated as a juvenile automatically waives the right to trial by jury, is unconstitutional. Torres was adjudicated delinquent on the third count in the information which charged that he "unlawfully, intentionally, knowingly, and without proper authority" made an unauthorized photographic negative of the face side of a one dollar Federal Reserve Note." The case was appealed.

ISSUES:
1. Was Torres entitled to a trial by jury? NO.

2. Is the federal Juvenile Delinquency Act section which provides for the acceptance of a juvenile to be treated as a juvenile and thus deemed a waiver of right to trial by jury constitutional? YES.

DECISIONS:
1. Juveniles are not constitutionally afforded the right to trial by jury.

2. The federal Juvenile Delinquency Act does not violate constitutional rights when it holds that a juvenile who consents to juvenile delinquency hearings is consenting to "a waiver of trial by jury."

REASON: "Appellant maintains that *McKeiver v. Pennsylvania, supra*, did not determine that a juvenile had no constitutional right to a trial by jury in a federal juvenile delinquency proceeding and that the four cases in three circuits which, relying on *McKeiver*, held that a juvenile had no such right were wrongly decided. Appellant seeks to have this court hold that the provisions of the Federal Act requiring that juvenile proceedings be without a jury is unconstitutional as violative of the Sixth Amendment. This we decline to do.

"*McKeiver* held that the juvenile appellants, who had been found to be delinquent in Juvenile Court proceedings in Pennsylvania and North Carolina, had no constitutional right to a trial by jury in the adjudicative stage of such proceedings.

"The argument of the appellant in the case at bar, that proceedings under the Federal Delinquency Act are so materially different from those under state acts considered in *McKeiver* as to be criminal prosecutions subject to the Sixth Amendment guarantee, is not persuasive.

"We hold, as did the Sixth, Eighth and Ninth Circuits, that the principles applied in *McKeiver* are applicable to the Federal Juvenile Delinquency Act. Thus, the requirement that proceedings under the Act shall be tried without a jury does not violate the Sixth Amendment or due process standards of fundamental fairness, and there is no constitutional right to a jury trial in such proceedings.

CASE SIGNIFICANCE: In this case the child was charged with delinquent acts, and agreed to be treated as a juvenile under the federal Juvenile Delinquency Act. The agreement to be treated as a juvenile automatically includes agreement to forfeit a trial by jury. The questions in this case were whether the juvenile was entitled to a jury trial, and whether the federal Juvenile Delinquency Act, which precludes the trial by jury for juveniles, was constitutional?

In *McKeiver v. Pennsylvania*, the Supreme Court held that juveniles facing adjudication do not have a constitutional right to a jury trial. In this case, the court held, that juveniles adjudicated delinquent under federal law enjoy no constitutional right to trial by jury. The court held that juvenile proceedings in federal courts were not significantly different from juvenile proceedings held in state courts, and therefore did not require a different standard than the Supreme Court held in *McKeiver*.

In re Montrail M.
601 A.2d 1102 (Md. 1992)

The merger doctrine (in which the lesser offense is merged into the greater offense) applies to all juvenile cases and does not constitute double jeopardy.

FACTS: Montrail M., Harold S., and Matio C. were apprehended by police, who found crack cocaine in their possession. The juvenile court adjudicated the three delinquent because they had committed acts that constituted juvenile delinquency and were in need of "guidance, treatment and rehabilitation." The court found the three delinquent because of the possession of the crack cocaine and also found them delinquent because they possessed the drug with the intent to distribute it. Montrail was also found in violation of motor vehicle laws by operating a vehicle without a license.

In the disposition hearing, each juvenile was ordered to be placed under the jurisdiction of the Department of Juvenile Services with specific directions of facility placement. The juveniles appealed. The Court of Special Appeals affirmed the cases of Harold S. and Matio C., but vacated the disposition of Montrail M. citing that "the disposition was based, in part on the improper adjudication" of the traffic violations. Montrail M.'s case was remanded to the circuit court for further dispositional proceedings. The defendants issued a writ of certiorari to the Court of Appeals.

ISSUES:
1.   Does the merger doctrine (in which the lesser offense is merged into the greater offense) apply to juvenile cases? YES.

2.   Did the adjudications of delinquency violate the juvenile's right to merger or double jeopardy protection? NO.

DECISION: The merger doctrine applies to juvenile cases and does not violate the prohibition against double jeopardy.

REASON: "The Doctrine of Merger was long known at the common law, and applied in criminal causes. Although a proceeding under the Juvenile Causes Act is deemed to be a civil action rather than a criminal cause, we declared in *Parojinog v. State*, 282 Md. 256, 260, 384 A.2d 86 (1978), citing *Breed v. Jones*, 421 U.S. 519, 95 S. Ct. 1779, 44 L. Ed. 2d 346 (1975), that the provisions against being twice placed in jeopardy, contained in the Fifth Amendment to the Constitution of the United States and as a part of the common law of Maryland, are 'fully applicable to juvenile adjudicatory proceedings.'

"The Fifth Amendment to the Constitution of the United States includes the clause 'nor shall any person be subject for the same offense to be twice put in jeopardy of life or limb . . .' The clause is enforceable in state criminal prosecutions through the Fourteenth Amendment. *Benton v. Maryland*, 395 U.S. 784, 794, 89 S. Ct. 2056, 23 L. Ed. 2d 707 (1969). Although the Maryland Constitution does not contain a provision prohibiting double jeopardy, the right was recognized in the common law long before the adoption of the Fifth Amendment, and was applied by our courts for many years before the decision in *Benton*. *See Thomas v. State*, 277 Md. 257, 353 A.2d 240 (1976). *See also Middleton v. State*, 318 Md. 749, 756, 569 A.2d 1276 (1990).

> Under settled Maryland common law, the usual role for deciding whether one criminal offense merges into another or whether one is a lesser included offense of the other, as well as the usual rule for determining whether two offenses are deemed the same for double jeopardy purposes, when both offenses are based on the same act or acts, is the so-called 'required evidence test.'

"In the case at hand, the required evidence test calls for the application of the doctrine of merger. The two victimless offenses, being based on the same act, are deemed to be under the same required evidence test, and merger follows as a matter of course. As it is commonly phrased, the lesser offense is merged into the greater offense. The merger, however, does not affect the *adjudications* of the circuit court based on the findings that the Petitioners had committed the two delinquent acts. The two adjudications are not inconsistent nor are they the result of successive prosecutions. We see no besmirching of the integrity of the determination that the Petitioners had committed the delinquent act of simple possession of cocaine as well as the delinquent act of possession of that substance with intent to distribute. The two adjudications stand inviolate, unaffected by the merger."

CASE SIGNIFICANCE: This case is significant because it places juveniles on the same level as adult defendants on the issues of merger of offenses and double jeopardy. The double jeopardy part of the decision reiterates the U.S. Supreme Court decision in *Breed v. Jones* that the double jeopardy protection in the Constitution applies to juvenile cases. The merger part of the decision, however, has yet to be addressed by the U.S. Supreme Court in juvenile cases.

Boyd v. State
853 S.W.2d 263 (Ark. 1993)

When a juvenile is to be tried as an adult, the rules in adult criminal trials apply.

FACTS: Boyd, a 17-year-old juvenile, was questioned by police about his involvement in the burglary of a pawn shop. He was advised of his *Miranda* rights prior to questioning, waived his rights, and gave two incriminating statements. He was charged with burglary and theft. At his trial in adult circuit court, Boyd attempted to suppress the statements made to the police because his mother failed to consent to his waiver of rights, as she would have had to do had his case remained in juvenile court. The court denied the motion and Boyd was convicted of both felonies.

ISSUE: When a minor is to be tried in adult court, do rules established for his peer age group, who are under the jurisdiction of the juvenile court, apply? NO.

DECISION: When the prosecutor uses his or her discretion to file charges against a juvenile in adult court, the juvenile becomes subject to the procedures and penalties that apply to adult criminal trials.

REASON: "[The appellant contends that the Juvenile] Code provides that a juvenile cannot waive the right to counsel unless the court finds that the custodial parent consented in writing to the decision to waive the right to counsel. His custodial parent, his mother, did not agree in writing with the decision to abandon his rights. Thus, he concludes that he could not have waived his right to counsel and that the circuit court erred in refusing to suppress his custodial statements. Appellant's argument assumes that the statutory provision requiring the custodial parent to consent to the waiver applied to proceedings in circuit court. That assumption is fallacious. The juvenile code provides that when a case involves a juvenile sixteen years old or older 'and the alleged act would constitute a felony if committed by an adult, the prosecuting attorney has the discretion to file a petition in juvenile court alleging delinquency, or to file charges in circuit court *and to prosecute as an adult.*' . . . The language is clear. A juvenile over sixteen years of age may be prosecuted 'as an adult.' When the words used in a statute have a well-defined meaning, and the wording of the statute is clear, we give those words their plain meaning . . . The plain meaning of the words 'the prosecuting attorney has the discretion to file . . . in circuit court and to prosecute as an adult' is that when the prosecutor chooses to prose- cute a juvenile in circuit court as an adult, the juvenile becomes subject to the procedures and penalties prescribed for adults. The language can have no other meaning."

CASE SIGNIFICANCE: This case dealt with how a juvenile is to be tried in adult court if certified for adult trial. The case centers around the voluntary waiver of constitutional rights guaranteed under *Miranda*. Juvenile law would require consent of the juvenile's parent or custodian in order to establish a vol- untary waiver of such rights. Once certified for adult trial, however, the same *Miranda* rules that apply to adults would then also apply to the juvenile. There- fore the court concluded that as long as it is determined that the waiver of *Mi- randa* by the juvenile was knowing, intelligent, and voluntary, any information acquired during questioning was admissible in court. This is the same rule that applies in adult criminal cases.

Two factors influenced the court's decision: (1) the advanced age of the juvenile (17 years) convinced the court that he should be treated with greater latitude than would be the case had the juvenile been of a much younger age, and (2) the use of prosecutorial discretion. These two factors lessen the signifi- cance of this case in that it applies only to similar situations in which the juve- nile is older and jurisdiction has already been determined.

In re Marven C.
39 Cal. Rptr. 2d 354 (Cal. App. 1995)

The state carries a clear burden to prove that, based on such factors as age, experience, conduct, and knowledge, a juvenile under the age of 14 clearly has the capacity to appreciate the wrongfulness of his or her conduct.

FACTS: Marven C., believed to be between 13 and 14 years old, was charged with murder and discharging a firearm at an occupied vehicle. The incident involved a dispute between gang members. It started with pushing and shoving. A gun was produced and in the resultant car chase, Marven C. fired three times into the rival gang's car, killing one of the occupants. Marven C. was found delinquent on both counts, declared a ward of the court, and committed to the California Youth Authority for a period not to exceed 29 years to life. He appealed, saying that the court had failed to show clear proof that he knew the wrongfulness of his act.

ISSUE: Who has the burden of establishing proof of knowledge and understanding of the wrongfulness of a juvenile's act in cases in which the statute clearly sets a presumption that a minor under the age of 14 is incapable of committing a crime?

DECISION: The state carries a clear burden to prove that, based on such factors as age, experience, conduct, and knowledge, a juvenile under the age of 14 clearly has the capacity to appreciate the wrongfulness of his or her conduct.

REASON: "The trial court found: '[T]he facts do impute a knowledge of the wrongfulness of this act.' . . . The manner in which this was conducted, the speed with which it was conducted, firing and departing the scene, all do impute a knowledge of the wrongfulness of the act. Shooting at someone several times in a public place to kill them would not be something that even a two-year-old would think would be all right. A minor as street-smart as this individual has shown himself to be does leave him to the imputation of knowledge of the wrongfulness of his acts.

"We conclude there is substantial evidence to support the trial court's finding. The Guatemalan birth certificate was credited. It established that appellate was at least 13 years and 8 months old at the time of the shooting. '[I]t is only reasonable to expect that generally the older a child gets and the closer [he] approaches the age of 14, the more likely it is that [he] appreciates the wrongfulness of his acts.' . . . The evidence established that appellant carried a concealed weapon to the school and displayed it to Ivan, pulling it from 'his stomach.' When a school security guard appeared, the blue Mustang departed.

Thereafter, appellant fired three shots at the occupants in the Subaru on three separate occasions as the cars drove in the area of school. Each time, appellant leaned far out of the car window to fire the gun."

CASE SIGNIFICANCE: This case dealt with the level of certainty needed to prove that a juvenile under the age of 14 was capable of understanding the wrongfulness of his act. The court ruled that in order to defeat the assumption that a juvenile under the age of 14 is incapable of committing crime, the state must show by clear proof that when the juvenile committed the act for which he was charged and that he knew of its wrongfulness.

The court further found that, in this case, substantial evidence existed to support the juvenile court's finding that the juvenile, who was under age 14 at the time of the act, knew the wrongfulness of his act and was therefore within the juvenile court's jurisdiction despite the juvenile's contention that the manner in which he committed the crime did not demonstrate knowledge of wrongfulness.

As in criminal cases, the state bears the burden of establishing knowledge of the wrongfulness of an offender's act. This is particularly true in cases involving juveniles because the concept of intent or knowledge becomes more difficult to prove the lower the age of the offender.

Disposition of Juveniles   8

I.   United States Supreme Court Cases

Eddings v. Oklahoma (1982)
Thompson v. Oklahoma (1988)
Stanford v. Kentucky (1989)

II. Lower Court Cases

Board of Managers of Arkansas Training School
   for Boys v. George (1967)
United States ex rel. Murray v. Owens (1972)
Baker v. Hamilton (1972)
State in the Interest of D.G.W. (1976)
Thompson v. Carlson (1980)
In re Marcellus L. (1991)
In re Binh L. (1992)
Matter of Shawn V. (1993)
P.W. v. State (1993)
In re Jamont C. (1993)
G.A.D. v. State (1993)
A.S. v. State (1993)
United States v. Juvenile No. 1 (LWQ) (1994)
State in Interest of T.L.V. (1994)
In re Tyrell J. (1994)

Introduction

Most states require that *disposition* (the equivalent of sentencing in an adult case) be made in a bifurcated hearing process separated from the adjudication hearing. The reasons for this separation center around the need to emphasize nonlegal issues in disposition decisionmaking, such as educational level, age, maturity, and prevailing problems such as drug or alcohol addiction, etc.

The disposition process has not received much attention from the courts. None of the landmark Supreme Court decisions dealing with juvenile justice issues has dealt with the disposition process or the variety of dispositional options available in a given state juvenile justice system. Therefore, if there is variation to be found in juvenile justice processing, in all likelihood the greatest variation will be found in the process of determining appropriate disposition and in the dispositional options available for juveniles in a particular jurisdiction. Those options range from probation to community service, to specific need treatment, to institutionalization in a secure juvenile facility.[1]

The authority to order dispositional alternatives stems from juvenile law in each state. Within the broad options offered, courts generally have unfettered discretion in determining the appropriate placement for each case brought before the court. Unlike adult sentencing, which usually focuses on the seriousness of the offense committed, juvenile sentencing is fundamentally indeterminate with a focus on the juvenile and his or her involvement in crime.[2]

Disposition is one of the most visible aspects of criminal justice processing of juveniles. The juvenile justice system is generally shielded from public scrutiny. Little or no information is given to the general public regarding the juveniles who come under the jurisdiction of the court, the types of cases dealt with by the court, or the processes involved in a particular case. The punishment (euphemistically called "disposition") meted out to a juvenile, however, is often made public once that decision is made.

Cases in this chapter deal with every aspect of disposition and punishment, from the constitutionality of the death penalty to the appropriate credentials for caregivers in a juvenile institution. Three United States Supreme Court cases start this chapter. *Eddings, Thompson,* and *Stanford* direct attention on the ultimate of all punishments—the death penalty—and its application to juveniles. *Eddings,* which was the first case to deal with juveniles and the death penalty, required that courts consider age and relevant social history as mitigating factors in the sentencing phase of capital cases. *Thompson* and *Stanford* established the age for juveniles who are subject to the penalty of death, the Court in *Thompson* ruling it unconstitutional to sentence a juvenile who is 15 years or younger at the time of the offense to death. A year later, the Court in *Stanford* held that it is constitutional to sentence a 16-year-old or older juvenile to death.

Other cases in this chapter deal with the legality of placing juveniles in adult jails and prisons, the relationship between juvenile sentencing and adult sentencing, and the balance between risk to the public and needs of the juvenile in making disposition placement decisions. Subsequent cases deal with issues of restitution and indigency and the overlap with the adult system.

The cases included in this chapter represent the diversity of disposition and punishment options—from restitution to the death penalty. These cases identify emerging trends in juvenile dispositional options, focusing on punishment and control of juvenile offenders on the one hand and the protection of society on the other.

Notes

[1]   Peter C. Kratcoski and Lucille D. Kratcoski, *Juvenile Delinquency* (1996).

[2]   Mary Clement, *The Juvenile Justice System: Law and Process* (1997).

I.   UNITED STATES SUPREME COURT CASES

Eddings v. Oklahoma
455 U.S. 104 (1982)

Mitigating circumstances, including age and relevant social history, must be considered in juvenile capital cases.

FACTS: Eddings, age 16, and several younger minors stole a car and ran away from home in Missouri. Eddings had a shotgun and several rifles in the car, which he had stolen from his father. Due to bad driving, an Oklahoma Highway Patrol officer pulled Eddings over, whereupon Eddings pointed a shotgun out the driver's window and shot and killed the approaching highway patrol officer. Eddings was certified as an adult and charged with murder in the first degree. He pleaded *nolo contendere*. During the sentencing phase, Eddings' social history was introduced as a mitigating factor. His parents had divorced when he was five, he stayed with his alcoholic and promiscuous mother until he was 14 when he was sent to his father who, unable to control him, resorted to physical abuse. Likewise, Eddings' age was introduced as indicative of his capacity to be rehabilitated. The state offered the following aggravating circumstances:

1.   that the murder was especially heinous, atrocious, or cruel,
2.   that the crime was committed for the purpose of avoiding or preventing a lawful arrest,
3.   that there was a probability that the defendant would commit criminal acts of violence that would constitute a continuing threat to society.

The judge accepted the factor of age as a mitigating factor; rejected social history as irrelevant; weighed age against the aggravating factors and sentenced Eddings to death.

ISSUE: Must mitigating circumstances, such as age and social history, be considered in the sentencing phase of a capital case? YES.

DECISION: The court must consider any and all mitigating factors in determining the sentence in a juvenile capital case. The weight and relevance of such factors are discretionary, but total exclusion of a mitigating factor is improper.

REASON: "In *Lockett v. Ohio*, 438 U.S. 586 (1978), Chief Justice Burger writing for the plurality, stated the rule that we apply today:

We conclude that the Eighth and Fourteenth Amendments require that the sentencer . . . not be precluded from considering, as a mitigating factor, any aspect of a defendant's character or record and any of the circumstances of the offense that the defendant proffers as a basis for the sentence less than death. Id., at 604. Recognizing 'that the imposition of death by public authority is . . . profoundly different from all other penalties,' the plurality held that the sentencer must be free to give 'independent mitigating weight to aspects of the defendant's character and record and to circumstances of the offense proffered in mitigation . . . Id., at 605.

"The trial judge recognized that youth must be considered a relevant mitigating factor. But youth is more than a chronological fact. It is a time and condition of life when a person may be most susceptible to influence and to psychological damage. Our history is replete with laws and judicial recognition that minors, especially in their earlier years, generally are less mature and responsible than adults.

"Even the normal 16-year-old customarily lacks the maturity of an adult. In this case, Eddings was not a normal 16-year-old; he had been deprived of care, concern, and paternal attention that children deserve. On the contrary, it is not disputed that he was a juvenile with serious emotional problems, and had been raised in a neglectful, sometimes even violent background. In addition, there was testimony that Eddings' mental and emotional development were at a level several years below his chronological age. All of this does not suggest an absence of responsibility for the crime of murder, deliberately committed in this case. Rather, it is to say that just as the chronological age of a minor is itself a relevant mitigating factor of great weight, so must the background and mental and emotional development of a youthful defendant be duly considered in sentencing."

CASE SIGNIFICANCE: In this case, the Court held that all reasonably relevant mitigating factors must be considered in a sentencing determination of this magnitude. This includes social history factors that may or may not have an impact on the behavior that resulted in the current charge of murder in the first degree.

The Court did not say what weight should be given to specific evidence, choosing instead to leave such decisions up to the judge in whose court the case is tried. It did, however, require that there be proof in the record of the case that all relevant mitigating evidence was considered by the court prior to sentencing.

The Court ruled that "age" is a relevant mitigating factor to consider. It also held that, in cases involving juveniles, all social history mitigating factors must be seriously considered by the court prior to sentencing. While a judge usually enjoys discretion in determining which mitigating factors are to be considered during sentencing, that discretion is narrowed in capital cases involving juveniles.

Thompson v. Oklahoma
487 U.S. 815 (1988)

It is unconstitutional to sentence a juvenile to death if he or she was 15 years of age or younger at the time of the commission of the offense.

FACTS: In concert with three other persons, Thompson, age 15, participated in the brutal murder of his former brother-in-law, whose body was found in a river weighted by a concrete block, with multiple gunshot wounds, a slashed throat, chest, and abdomen, multiple bruises, and a broken leg. Thompson, due to his age, was considered a child under Oklahoma law, but the state moved for transfer to try him as an adult, which was granted. Thompson was convicted of first degree murder and sentenced to death, as were the other three participants in the crime.

ISSUE: Is a sentence of death a cruel and unusual penalty for a crime committed by a 15-year-old? YES.

DECISION: The Eighth and Fourteenth Amendments to the United States Constitution prohibit the execution of a person who was 15 years of age at the time of his or her offense.

REASON: "Most relevant, . . . is the fact that all States have enacted legislation designating the maximum age for juvenile court jurisdiction at no less than 16. All of this legislation is consistent with the experience of mankind, as well as the long history of our law, that the normal 15-year-old is not prepared to assume the full responsibilities of an adult.

". . . [W]e accept the premise that some offenders are simply too young to be put to death, . . . When we confine our attention to the 18 States that have expressly established a minimum age in their death penalty statutes, we find that all of them require that the defendant have attained at least the age of 16 at the time of the capital offense.

"Although the judgments of legislatures, juries, and prosecutors weigh heavily in the balance, it is for us ultimately to judge whether the Eighth Amendment permits imposition of the death penalty on one such as petitioner who committed a heinous murder when he was only 15 years old. . . . In making that judgment, we first ask whether the juvenile's culpability should be measured by the same standard as that of an adult, and then consider whether the application of the death penalty to this class of offenders 'measurably contributes' to the social purposes that are served by the death penalty. . . . It is generally agreed that punishment should be directly related to the personal culpability of the criminal defendant. . . . There is also broad agreement on the proposition that adolescents as a class are less mature and responsible than adults. . . . Thus, the Court has already endorsed the proposition that less culpability should attach to a crime committed by a juvenile than to a comparable crime committed by an adult. The basis for this conclusion is too obvious to require extended explanation. Inexperience, less education, and less intelligence make the teenager less able to evaluate the consequences of his or her conduct while at the same time he or she is much more apt to be motivated by mere emotion or peer pressure than is an adult. The reasons why juveniles are not trusted with the privileges and responsibilities of an adult also explain why their irresponsible conduct is not as morally reprehensible as that of an adult."

CASE SIGNIFICANCE: Any offender who is 15 years old or younger at the time the offense was committed cannot be sentenced to death, regardless of the nature or heinousness of the offense. The Court took into account the fact that the statutes of approximately 18 states require that the defendant be at least 16 years old at the time of the commission of the offense for the death penalty to be imposed, saying that "it would offend civilized standards of decency to execute a person who was less than 16 years old at the time of his or her offense." In a concurring opinion, however, Justice O'Connor noted that "the Federal Government and 19 states have authorized capital punishment without setting any minimum age, and have also provided for some 15-year-olds to be prosecuted as adults." This indicates, she said, that there was no consensus about whether 15-year-olds should be subject to the death penalty.

This decision did not indicate the age when a juvenile could be executed or whether juveniles could be executed at all. Opponents of the law in this case wanted the Court to ban the use of the death penalty as a sentence for juveniles. The Court did not go that far. The earliest age at which a juvenile could be sentenced to death remained unanswered until the Court decided *Stanford v. Kentucky*, 492 U.S. 361 (1989), one year later.

Stanford v. Kentucky
492 U.S. 361 (1989)

It is constitutional for a state to impose the death penalty on a juvenile who was 16 years old or older at the time the crime was committed.

FACTS: This case consolidates two fact situations:

1. Stanford, age 17 years and 4 months, was accused of murder, sodomy, robbery, and receiving stolen property in the robbery of a gas station. Due to his age, he was within the jurisdiction of the juvenile court. The state sought and received a transfer to allow Stanford to be tried as an adult. Stanford's social history indicated that he came from an unstable family background, had used drugs since the age of 13, had been placed in juvenile treatment programs on numerous occasions, lacked age-appropriate social interaction skills, and lacked family support and supervision. Stanford was convicted and sentenced to death plus 45 years in prison.

2. Wilkins *(Wilkins v. Missouri)* was 16 years and 6 months old at the time he was accused of first degree murder, armed criminal action, and carrying a concealed weapon in the robbery of a convenience store. Due to his age, under Missouri law the juvenile court had to terminate jurisdiction and certify Wilkins for trial as an adult. The state sought and acquired such action, after which Wilkins pled guilty to all charges. At his sentencing hearing, he himself urged the court to impose the death penalty. Upon review of Wilkins' competence to enter such a plea, the court upheld the guilty plea and sentenced Wilkins to death.

ISSUE: Is the imposition of the death penalty for a crime committed at the age of 16 or 17 cruel and unusual punishment? NO.

DECISION: It is not cruel and unusual punishment for a state to impose a sentence of death on an offender who was 16 or 17 years old at the time the crime was committed.

REASON: "To begin with, it is absurd to think that one must be mature enough to drive carefully, to drink responsibly, or to vote intelligently, in order to be mature enough to understand that murdering another human being is profoundly wrong, and to conform one's conduct to that most minimal of all civilized standards. But even if the requisite degrees of maturity were comparable, the age statutes in question would still not be relevant. They do not represent a social judgment that all persons under the designated ages are not responsible enough to drive, to drink, or to vote, but at most a judgment that the vast majority are not. These laws set the appropriate ages for the operation of a system that makes its determinations in gross, and that does not conduct individualized maturity tests for each driver, drinker, or voter. The criminal justice system, however, does provide individualized testing. In the realm of capital punishment in particular 'individualized consideration [is] a constitutional requirement' . . . and one of the individualized mitigating factors that sentencers must be permitted to consider is the defendant's age. . . . Twenty-nine States, including both Kentucky and Missouri, have codified this constitutional requirement in laws specifically designating the defendant's age as a mitigating factor in capital cases. Moreover, the determination required by juvenile transfer statutes to certify a juvenile for trial as an adult ensure individualized consideration of the maturity and moral responsibility of 16- and 17-year-old offenders before they are even held to stand trial as adults. The application of this particularized system to the petitioners can be declared constitutionally inadequate only if there is consensus, not that 17 or 18 is the age at which most persons, or even almost all persons achieve sufficient maturity to be held fully responsible for murder; but that 17 or 18 is the age before which no one can reasonably be held fully responsible. What displays society's views on this latter point are not the ages set forth in the generalized system of driving, drinking, and voting laws cited by petitioners . . . but the ages at which the States permit their particularized capital punishment systems to be applied.

"We discern neither a historical nor a modern societal consensus forbidding the imposition of capital punishment on any person who murders at 16 or 17 years of age. Accordingly, we conclude that such punishment does not offend the Eighth Amendment's prohibition against cruel and unusual punishment."

CASE SIGNIFICANCE: This case resolves the issue that the Court refused to address in *Thompson v. Oklahoma*, 487 U.S. 815 (1988)—whether a defendant who was of juvenile age (in these cases 16 and 17) at the time the offense was committed could be sentenced to death. The Court's ruling is unequivocal, stating that "the imposition of capital punishment on an individual for a crime committed at 16 or 17 years of age does not constitute cruel and unusual punishment under the Eighth Amendment." In so deciding, the Court set the minimum age at 16 if the state is to impose the death penalty. Juveniles who are age 15 or younger at the time of the offense cannot be sentenced to death.

In reaching this conclusion, the Court relied on "evolving standards of decency that mark the progress of a maturing society." It concluded that there was no consensus against the execution of 16- and 17-year-olds, stating that "of the 37 states that permit capital punishment, 15 states decline to impose it on 16-year-olds and 12 on 17-year-olds." The Court stated that "this does not establish the degree of national agreement this Court has previously thought sufficient to label a punishment cruel and unusual."

Thompson v. Oklahoma and *Stanford v. Kentucky* settle the issue of whether a juvenile can be given the death penalty by state law. These cases say this: executing a juvenile who committed a crime at 15 years of age or younger is cruel and unusual punishment and therefore unconstitutional. Executing a juvenile who committed a crime at 16 years of age or older is constitutional.

II. LOWER COURT CASES

Board of Managers of Arkansas Training School for Boys v. George
377 F.2d 228 (8th Cir. 1967)

Disposition placements based solely on race are unconstitutional.

FACTS: This was a class action suit on behalf of all black males alleging that they had been racially discriminated against in dispositional placement. The state of Arkansas established two disposition placements: one for white male youths and one for black male youths. By law, placement was based solely on race. The facilities were designed by law to be equal, but there was no possibility of transfer between the two. Plaintiffs alleged they were denied access to equal treatment, privileges, and opportunities, by the state of Arkansas, based on race.

ISSUE: Is it constitutional to make disposition placements to equal juvenile disposition facilities based solely on race? NO.

DECISION: The establishment and use by judges of separate juvenile disposition facilities is unconstitutional if assignment of juveniles is based solely on race.

REASON: ". . . [I]t is initially urged that appellees have not stated a claim for relief since the Arkansas training schools are not 'educational' but 'penal' institutions, and therefore the 'policy' of federal court non-interference with 'penal' institutions should be applied. . . . Although we do not base our decision upon a determination that these training schools are educational institutions, we only comment that it is the legislative declaration of the Arkansas people that these schools are not to be considered as 'penal' in nature. . . . By legislative fiat these schools are an integral part of the educational system in the State of Arkansas.

Their responsibilities are equal to any other public institutions of learning in educating young people to assume useful roles in society.

"To the extent that . . . the Arkansas statutes require segregation of juveniles to white schools or colored schools, based solely upon the race of the individual involved, the statutes are clearly unconstitutional; to the extent that the statutes require commitment to segregated facilities, they are clearly unconstitutional; to the extent that the statutes require maintenance of segregated facilities, they are clearly unconstitutional. No injunction need issue to an individual judge, board manager, or any person in light of our holding at the present time. The statutes are not void in their entirety and commitment of juveniles for dependency and delinquency may still be enforced . . . However, under no circumstances should race become a determinative factor in assignment."

CASE SIGNIFICANCE: This case exemplifies discriminatory practices in the dispositional placement of juveniles. The sole determinant here for placement was race—with white males being sent to one location and black males being sent to another location.

The court clearly stated that segregated dispositional placements and all laws, rules and regulations, policies, and criteria based on race are unconstitutional.

The court found no problem in the operation of two facilities or with criteria that would allow placement of juveniles with "like peers," as long as the foundation for the establishment of "like peers" contained no factors related to race or any references to race as a factor of consideration for placement.

In this case, the federal Court of Appeals stated that no racial discrimination would be tolerated by the system in dispositional placements or in any other facet of formal processing. The decision is consistent with the United States Supreme Court ruling that "separate but equal" educational facilities for blacks and whites violate the equal protection clause and is unconstitutional. (*Brown v. Board of Education*, 347 U.S. 483 [1954]).

United States ex rel. Murray v. Owens
465 F.2d 289 (2d Cir. 1972)

The New York statute that permitted a 15-year-old juvenile who had committed an act equivalent to a serious crime to be tried without a jury and sent to a correctional facility used for adult offenders did not constitute a denial of due process and was therefore constitutional.

FACTS: A 15-year-old male was adjudicated delinquent in juvenile court for acts equal to a serious crime as defined in the New York Criminal Code, specifically, robbery, burglary, and menacing possession of a dangerous weapon. His request for a jury trial in juvenile court was denied and he was sentenced to a three-year term in the Elmira Reception Center, an adult male prison facility.

ISSUE: Can a juvenile adjudicated in juvenile court without the benefit of all constitutional rights available in adult court be sentenced to an adult correctional facility? YES.

DECISION: The New York statute that permits a 15-year-old juvenile who committed an act equivalent to a serious crime to be tried without a jury and sent to an institution of confinement used for adult offenders did not constitute a denial of due process and is therefore constitutional.

REASON: "We think the conclusion is inescapable that the Supreme Court in no way implied that jury trials were constitutionally required if the ultimate disposition following an adjudication of delinquency was the same as for older offenders. The Court's determination that trial by jury would not effectively improve the fact-finding process during the adjudicatory stage is not altered by whether the juvenile, once adjudged a delinquent, is committed to a juvenile or an adult facility. The advantages sought by the juvenile system do not begin and end with the treatment considered appropriate once an adjudication of delinquency has been reached: they include 'the idealistic prospect of an intimate, informal protective proceeding,' . . . and, we should add, one which disposes of the issues promptly and without all the time-consuming procedures which accompany trial by jury. Furthermore, where rehabilitation is doubtful, jury trials will not speed its attainment.

". . . the Supreme Court in *McKeiver* emphasized the disruptive, formalizing influence the introduction of jury trials would work on the juvenile system, and . . . were [unwilling] to give up entirely on the system and in effect return the juvenile to the criminal courts. The Supreme Court noted that 'perhaps that ultimate disillusionment will come one day, but for the moment we are disinclined to give impetus to it.' . . . We see no need to break ground so recently declared off limits by the Supreme Court. Other factors which weigh against jury trials in cases such as this are the greater delay which would take place before the case was reached for trial and the much longer time consumed in trying the issues before a jury."

CASE SIGNIFICANCE: This case addressed the state's practice of processing 15-year-old juveniles in juvenile court where the constitutional right to a jury trial does not extend, and upon adjudication subjecting them to possible incarceration in a young adult correctional facility where 16-year-old and older youths, who were tried in adult court with the opportunity for a jury trial, are housed.

The court, relying on *McKeiver*, which denied juveniles the constitutional right to jury trials in juvenile court found that disparate treatment of juveniles based on age is permissible as long as it bears a reasonable relationship to a legitimate state objective. In this case, that objective was the appropriate dispositional placement of "criminally mature" youth so as not to further adversely affect younger juvenile offenders housed in state juvenile institutions. This case does not deal as much with the right of a juvenile to a jury trial as it does with the right of a juvenile to a jury trial compared with other juveniles who were considered adults. The court said that this variance among juveniles in the right to trial by jury was constitutional.

Baker v. Hamilton
345 F. Supp. 345 (W.D. Ky. 1972)

Placement in an adult jail, without total separation from adults, is unconstitutional.

FACTS: A class action suit was filed on behalf of several juvenile males who were subject to dispositional confinement in the Jefferson County Jail with adults. The juveniles were generally confined for short periods (several days) but were not segregated from adult inmates. The general condition of the jail constructed in 1907 was poor, with insufficient ventilation, lighting, inoperable locks, cramped quarters, no outside exercise or recreation areas, and no internal opportunities for recreation. The plaintiffs wanted all such placements to cease immediately.

ISSUE: Was the dispositional placement of a juvenile in an adult jail constitutional? NO.

DECISION: Even for limited periods, dispositional placements in adult jails are a clear violation of the Fourteenth Amendment because they treat the juvenile as an adult without affording him or her the due process rights afforded adults. Furthermore, a sentence in this particular jail, which was in deteriorating condition and lacked programs, violated the Eighth Amendment ban on cruel and unusual punishment.

REASON: ". . . [T]he Court takes note of the fact that the Jefferson County Jail does not provide separate rooms or wards for juveniles. It takes note of the fact that it is a penal institution designed primarily for punishment rather than re-habilitation, [and that] . . . selective placement of forty-five juveniles in the Jefferson County Jail in pre-dispositional matters and of fifteen juveniles as a dispositional matter, even though these commitments be for limited periods of time, constitutes a violation of the Fourteenth Amendment in that it is treating for punitive purposes the juveniles as adults and yet not according them the due process the rights accorded to adults.

"This Court . . . is of the opinion that there are sufficient elements present in the Jefferson County Jail to hold that confinement therein as to juveniles constitutes cruel and unusual punishment. Specifically, these elements are as follows—cramped quarters, poor illumination, bad circulation of air, broken locks, no outdoor exercise or recreation, and no attempt at rehabilitation, in addition to the condition of the 'hole' . . ."

CASE SIGNIFICANCE: This case addressed both the pre-dispositional and post-dispositional placement of juveniles in an adult jail environment in which no attempt at separation of the juvenile and adult residents was made. The court determined that the Fourteenth Amendment prohibited the use of adult jails as dispositional options for juveniles.

The Fourteenth Amendment violation in this case was worsened by the deteriorating conditions of the jail facility and the lack of services and programs appropriate to and designed for juveniles. This case involved both the Eighth Amendment's prohibition against cruel and unusual punishment and the Fourteenth Amendment's guarantees of due process and equal protection. The practice of placing juveniles and adults together in detention facilities is now also prohibited by federal law for agencies receiving federal funds.

State in the Interest of D.G.W.
361 A.2d 513 (N.J. 1976)

The juvenile court is authorized to impose restitution as long as due process is observed.

FACTS: D.G.W., a minor, along with three other juveniles, was charged with four counts of breaking and entering a residence and school buildings and with theft and destruction of property therein worth thousands of dollars. One charge was dismissed and guilty pleas were entered on the remaining three charges. The court placed D.G.W. on probation for one year and ordered restitution to the victim of one of the offenses. The court ordered that the specific amount of restitution, based on damages incurred, be "worked out" with the probation department. The probation department developed a list of damages from the school buildings totaling $626.00. Because there were four juveniles involved, the probation department divided the total by four, requiring each juvenile to pay $156.50. D.G.W. appealed.

ISSUES:
1.   Is restitution as a condition of juvenile probation constitutional? YES.

2.   If yes, what due process rights, if any, should be given?

DECISION: Restitution as a condition of a juvenile's probation is within the jurisdiction of the juvenile court when accompanied by appropriate due process procedures. When imposing restitution, the court should direct the probation department to conduct an investigation of the incident(s) contained in the complaint in order to determine the nature and extent of personal or property damages or other losses (e.g., financial) that were caused by the offender. The results of this investigation would then be summarized in a report similar to a presentence report for use by the court in setting the terms of probation.

REASON: "In the case before us we need not pause to distinguish between the application of due process protections to property interests and to liberty interests since both are implicated where restitution is imposed as a condition of probation. The juvenile has an obvious 'property' interest in his earnings or other income to be paid over in satisfaction of the restitutionary amount. Additionally he has an obvious 'liberty' interest in his continued probationary 'freedom' which is subject to termination upon his unjustified failure or refusal to meet the restitutionary condition. We are satisfied that deprivation of these interests triggers the juvenile's entitlement to due process and it remains only to decide what process is due.

"To protect his interest in his earnings and income and his interest in continued liberty the juvenile, minimally, is concerned about (1) the amount of damage he will be held responsible for, (2) the method of determining value, (3) his pro rata share where several defendants are involved and (4) a reasonable method of repayment which realistically assesses his ability to pay. Balanced against these concerns is the State's interest in maintaining a disposition procedure which, while always preserving the offender's right to be heard, is not unduly encumbered. We are satisfied that a balance can be struck short of a full-blown adversarial procedure. . . ."

CASE SIGNIFICANCE: This case dealt with the imposition of restitution and what, if any, due process rights attach to the setting of restitution amounts and payment plans. In this case, the juvenile court ordered the payment of restitution and left the process of determining how much restitution to pay and how the distribution of payment should be divided solely up to the probation officer.

The court disapproved of the total delegation of responsibility to the probation officer in setting the restitution amount and the distribution plan. It found the delegation inherently flawed and required that the juvenile court retain responsibility for the actual decisionmaking, with the probation officer supplying information to the court as appropriate on both the damages associated with the offense and the ability to pay restitution on the part of the juvenile offenders. The result is that the juvenile court must retain all decision-making responsibilities and cannot delegate any such responsibilities to any member of the court staff without ultimate review and approval by the court itself. The setting of probation conditions, including restitution, is a judicial function and cannot be delegated to probation officers. The only possible exception is if such delegation is clearly allowed by law.

Thompson v. Carlson
624 F.2d 415 (3d Cir. 1980)

The subsequent adult conviction of a juvenile supersedes any youthful offender provisions attached to an earlier sentence.

FACTS: Richard Thompson, then 17 years old, was convicted on an Indian reservation of assault with intent to rape. He received an eight-year sentence under the Youth Corrections Act, which allowed him to be housed in an adult correctional facility, but which required his segregation from adult offenders. In 1977, Thompson was convicted of first degree murder for his participation in the stabbing death of a fellow inmate and was sentenced as an adult to a term of life in prison. The court specifically ruled that he could no longer benefit from the provisions of the Youth Corrections Act. Thereafter, Thompson was held without segregation from adult inmates. Thompson filed a habeas corpus petition alleging that the confinement was illegal until he completed his term under the Youth Corrections Act because of the lack of segregation from adult offenders.

ISSUE: Does a second conviction and sentence as an adult supersede the provisions of a previous sentence that affords special considerations for youthful offenders? YES.

DECISION: An individual who is sentenced to a consecutive sentence of life in prison as an adult offender while serving a federal Youth Corrections Act sentence can be returned to the general population and thereafter be treated as an adult if the judge who sentenced the prisoner for the original crime makes a specific finding that the individual would no longer benefit from treatment under the Act.

REASON: "Under the statute, a judge sentencing a youthful offender, defined as 'a person under the age of twenty-two at the time of conviction' (18 U.S.C. sec. 5006[d]), must determine whether the youthful offender will benefit from treatment under the YCA. . . . In *Dorzynski v. United States* (418 U.S. 424, 1974), the Court held that the statute requires an explicit finding of 'no benefit' as a condition precedent to sentencing an eligible offender as an adult, but also held that the sentencing judge need not accompany such a finding by supporting reasons. When the sentencing court does find that the youthful offender could derive benefit from the YCA, the Act provides the sentencing court with options additional to those ordinarily available (418 U.S. at 441-42). In the *Dorzynski* case, the Supreme Court reviewed in detail the history of the Act and described the options of treatment and probation made available to the federal sentencing court under the Act.

". . . [T]he purpose of the Act was 'to provide a better method for treating young offenders convicted in federal courts in [the] vulnerable age bracket [between 16 and 22 years of age], to rehabilitate them and restore normal behavior patterns' (418 U.S. at 433).

"We conclude that the judicial determination that Thompson could not benefit from the YCA, and must therefore serve the second sentence as an adult prisoner, was a finding that *continued* service of the original sentence under YCA conditions is no longer beneficial. Because that represented a judicial reevaluation in light of currently available information, we hold that Thompson can be returned to an adult prisoner population for the remainder of the YCA sentence."

CASE SIGNIFICANCE: This case deals with a unique yet increasingly common situation—sentenced offenders committing additional crimes while in state custody, receiving additional sentences while serving their first term, and the conflicts that occur when the provisions of the first sentence are in any way restrictive or protective of the juvenile involved. The juvenile justice system is known for giving opportunities to juveniles, while the adult system is less tolerant of offenders who may waste opportunities.

The court found that adult punishment can be meted out to a juvenile who has successive offenses and is now of age to be considered an adult. In case of conflict, the adult sentence takes precedence over the punishment imposed by the juvenile court.

In re Marcellus L.
278 Cal. Rptr. 901 (Cal. App. 1991)

Evidence obtained from an otherwise illegal search may be introduced in juvenile court because the minor was subject to search at any time as a condition of probation and therefore had no reasonable expectation of privacy.

FACTS: A police officer observed Marcellus L., a minor, and two other individuals sitting on the stoop of a known crack house during the middle of a school day. Approaching the group, the officer asked Marcellus L. why he was not in school. The minor replied that he was between transfers. The officer, suspecting truancy, asked Marcellus L. his name and pertinent school information, but first conducted a pat-down search for safety reasons. Marcellus L. did nothing that could be construed as a threat and the officer had no reason to believe that the minor was armed or dangerous. During the pat-down search, the officer detected a lump in the minor's pants pocket, felt it, and found that it was consistent with crack cocaine. The officer then retrieved the suspicious substance, bagged it, and subsequently determined it to be 1.68 grams of cocaine base. Throughout this process, the officer was unaware that Marcellus L. was on probation for eight months and was subject, as a condition of that probation, to "submit his person, any vehicle under the minor's control, and residence to search and seizure by a peace officer at any time of the day or night with or without a warrant." The juvenile moved to suppress the evidence seized, saying that the search was unconstitutional.

ISSUE: When there is no probable cause to justify a pat-down search, does a probation condition allowing unlimited searches by any peace officer justify the search of a juvenile? YES.

DECISION: The search, standing alone, was unconstitutional. However, because the juvenile in question had given up his Fourth Amendment right to privacy as a condition of probation, the juvenile had no expectation of privacy. Therefore, he had no right to object to the search.

REASONS: "Contrary to the minor's assertion, we do not think the validity of his search condition is dependent upon the searching officer's knowledge of that condition. . . . we are unaware of any relevant authority which invalidates the search of a probationer who is duty bound to subject himself or herself to search upon request by a peace officer, because that peace officer did not know the subject was on probation and subject to a search condition.

"We cannot say that Officer Dobie's lack of knowledge concerning the minor's probationary status rendered his pat-search without any rehabilitative or reformative effect; without question the frisk advanced a legitimate law enforcement purpose. Officer Dobie explained he wanted to pursue the school attendance matter with the minor but first decided to pat-search him, that being his standard practice when he contacted anyone in that particular location. There was no harassment or other improper motive on officer Dobie's part. Finally, although the search was not occasioned by any suspicious or threatening conduct by the minor, we conclude a preventive frisk in the course of questioning a minor about school attendance when encountered near a suspected crack house falls within the 'other legitimate law enforcement purposes' language of *People v. Bravo*, 43 Cal. 3d 600 (1987)."

CASE SIGNIFICANCE: This case upholds the legality of the search of a juvenile who was on probation, based on the court's view that probationers, even juveniles, have no reasonable expectation of privacy and therefore should be prepared to be searched regardless of the legality of the search. The admissibility of evidence from a search such as this rests entirely on the status of the juvenile as a probationer and who is subject to the conditions and supervision of the juvenile court.

Furthermore, the "knowledge-first" rule, which would require that the authority conducting the search be aware of the probationary status of the juvenile, is burdensome on the system and renders the condition itself meaningless. If police officers had to be personally aware of every juvenile in the community who is serving a sentence of probation before they could search them subsequent to a condition of probation, law enforcement would be hamstrung and the condition itself would be useless.

The court also found that even if the search had been otherwise illegal, the fact that the juvenile was on probation and was aware of the search condition attached to his probation made any evidence seized in the search admissible in any judicial proceeding against the juvenile.

In re Binh L.
6 Cal. Rptr. 2d 678 (Cal. App. 1992)

Unjustified searches can be valid if the juvenile is subject to search as a condition of probation.

FACTS: In November 1990, Binh L. was declared a ward of the juvenile court on the basis of his admission that he had stolen one car and had been in possession of another stolen car. He was placed on probation with the condition that he "submit to search and seizure anytime, day or night, with or without a warrant by any peace officer or school official." In January 1991, Binh L. was continued as a ward of the court based on his admission of having stolen a third car. In March 1991, a police officer, with no knowledge of the minor's probationary status or of the search condition attached, found the juvenile in an automobile under what the officer considered suspicious circumstances. Upon investigation, he concluded that Binh L. was truant and in the course of a pat-down search found a loaded pistol on Binh L.'s person. Based on the discovery of the weapon, the juvenile was committed to a juvenile rehabilitation facility. He appealed.

ISSUE: When a juvenile is required, as a condition of probation, to submit to a search "anytime, anywhere," is a search by a police officer who has no knowledge of the probation condition, nor probable cause for the search, unconstitutional? NO.

DECISION: When a juvenile is subject to search as a condition of probation and an officer conducts a pat-down search with little or no probable cause, any incriminating evidence seized is admissible in a court of law even if the officer was not aware of the search condition, the juvenile being searched was aware of the condition and therefore knew the risks.

REASON: ". . . [W]e conclude, the probation search condition was both statutorily and constitutionally valid. Because the search condition was tailored for and expressly made known to and individually imposed upon the minor, the search condition must be deemed to have had an impact on the minor's reasonable expectation of privacy far more direct than that of a parole condition automatically imposed on every parolee. The minor knew, by a direct and valid order of the juvenile court, that he was subject to warrantless search at any time or place by any probation or police officer. And if he associated the likelihood of warrantless search with any particular circumstances, surely it would be with his presence in or use of a motor vehicle, inasmuch as all of his difficulties with the law appear to have involved unlawful taking of motor vehicles. In short, if there were any circumstances in which the minor could reasonably have expected his decision to carry a loaded pistol to remain private from the police, this was certainly not such a circumstance: Riding in a car only four months after he had acknowledged a probation search condition in an order arising out of admitted vehicle thefts."

CASE SIGNIFICANCE: This case dealt with the search of juvenile who had been placed on probation for delinquent acts. One of the conditions was the waiver of the right to privacy through the juvenile's consent to be searched at any time, anywhere, with or without a warrant, by authorized government officials (police officers, school officials, etc.).

The court ruled that juveniles can waive their Fourth Amendment right to privacy because, unlike parole, probation is a privilege and therefore greater intrusion can be expected in order to maintain the privilege of community supervision. The court further ruled that under situations such as this, any evidence acquired could be admitted in court because the juvenile was aware of the risk of possible search prior to the search and agreed to the condition as part of his or her probation.

Matter of Shawn V.
600 N.Y.S.2d 393 (A.D. 1993)

When determining appropriate disposition under a least restrictive standard, a balance must be struck between the needs of the juvenile and the need for public safety.

FACTS: The juvenile was adjudicated delinquent after admitting guilt to a charge of petit larceny. He was placed in a secure state juvenile facility for a period of 12 months, based primarily on his past record of school suspensions, aggressive, assaultive, and antisocial behavior, and his varied displays of aggressive sexual behavior. The court ruled that Shawn V. was a risk to himself and to the general public. He appealed, claiming that the court violated "the least restrictive mandate" for dispositional placement.

ISSUE: Should public safety be considered when determining dispositional placement under the least restrictive placement alternative plan? YES.

DECISION: In determining the least restrictive alternative for placing juveniles adjudicated delinquent, the court is not to be guided solely by the best interests of the juvenile, but also by the need to protect the community, thereby creating a balance between the two.

REASON: "All of the professionals who evaluated respondent strongly recommended secure placement and indicated that direct placement in the community was unwise because it may easily result in continued antisocial conduct.

". . . [W]hen viewed as a whole there can be little doubt that ample evidence exists to support Family Court's conclusion that the least restrictive available alternative which would best meet respondent's needs and those of the community was to place him in a Division of Youth facility."

CASE SIGNIFICANCE: This case presents an example of the debate between the juvenile justice system's mandate to consider the best interests of the juveniles and the public's right to safety. Traditionally, dispositional placement for juveniles has been tied to the needs of the juvenile rather than to public safety.

However, as a result of an increasing emphasis on balancing the needs of the juvenile with the public's need for safety, the primary motivation for dispositions has been reversed, with the seriousness of the crime and public safety being the primary factors for disposition and the characteristics of the juvenile offender being merely secondary. This approach started in the 1980s and is expected to continue for some time to come.

P.W. v. State
625 So. 2d 1207 (Ala. Cr. App. 1993)

Reasonable court costs and fines can be assessed in juvenile court as long as issues of indigency, when relevant, are addressed.

FACTS: P.W., 17 years old, was adjudicated a serious juvenile offender on charges of theft of property, burglary of a motor vehicle, and possession of burglar's tools. He was ordered to pay court costs and fines and was sent to the Department of Youth Services for evaluation and placement. He appealed the order to pay court costs and fines, alleging that he was a juvenile and therefore indigent and thus should not be expected to pay such costs. He contends on appeal that he was being incarcerated because of his indigency. His record showed that he owed $1,494 in court costs and fines from 28 appearances before the juvenile court.

ISSUES:
1. Can court costs and fines be levied against a juvenile in juvenile court?
   YES.

2. If yes, can a juvenile be incarcerated for failure to pay court costs and
   fines? NO.

DECISIONS:
1. The imposition of reasonable court costs and fines is discretionary with the
   court. However, if imposed, indigency must be considered.

2. Incarceration for failure to pay if the juvenile is unable to pay is unconstitutional.

REASON: ". . . [W]e find that the juvenile was not incarcerated because of his
indigency. . . . Under the particular facts of this case, it appears to this court that
the juvenile court was offering the nonrepentant juvenile one last opportunity to
demonstrate some sign of remorse or to indicate that he acknowledged and accepted responsibility for his actions. The juvenile court was merely allowing
the juvenile to provide a mitigating or redeeming factor that was not present
when the juvenile was adjudicated a delinquent and sentenced. If anything, it
appears to this court that the juvenile court was merely trying to impress this
juvenile with the 'hardness' of the 'brick wall' he had just hit, for, from the record, it appears that no one harbored even the slightest hope that the accumulated
court costs would be paid.

"We do note that had the juvenile court's action actually been an attempt to
collect previously imposed court costs, it would have been improper. '[T]he
imprisonment of an indigent offender for failure to pay his fine is generally recognized as constitutionally impermissible.' *Williams v. Illinois*, 399 U.S. 235
(1970).

CASE SIGNIFICANCE: This case dealt with the constitutionality of using
fines as a dispositional option in juvenile court and the application of court costs
to juvenile court processing. Both have been used sparingly in juvenile court
because juveniles generally have few personal assets and the imposition of fines
and court costs would become the responsibility of the parents of the juvenile,
thus diminishing the impact of this rehabilitative effort.

While upholding the use of fines and court costs in juvenile court, the court
considered unconstitutional any attempt by the juvenile court to incarcerate an
indigent juvenile for failure to pay such fines and court costs. This is consistent
with the United States Supreme Court decision stating that indigent probationers
cannot have their probation revoked for failure to pay fines or court costs be-

cause to do so would violate the equal protection clause of the Fourteenth Amendment (*Bearden v. Georgia*, 461 U.S. 660 [1983]).

In re Jamont C.
17 Cal. Rptr. 2d 336 (Cal. App. 1993)

The probation condition that permitted searches without individualized suspicion did not violate the juvenile's Fourth Amendment right to privacy.

FACTS: Jamont C., a minor, challenged the probation search condition imposed upon him by the juvenile court. The probation condition requires that the probationer "submit his person, property, residence, or any vehicle owned by said minor or under said minor's control to search and seizure at any time of the day or night by any peace officer or school official, with or without a warrant." Jamont C. claimed that the probation was unconstitutionally intrusive on his Fourth Amendment right to privacy, to the extent that it permits searches without individualized suspicion.

ISSUE: Did the probation search condition violate a juvenile probationer's Fourth Amendment right to privacy when permitted without individualized suspicion? NO.

DECISION: The condition imposed on the juvenile, which permitted searches without individualized suspicion, did not violate the juvenile's Fourth Amendment right to privacy even though a juvenile cannot refuse probation and thus such a search is not consensual. Such searches are justified by the state's interest in promoting the health and welfare of minors.

REASON: "A probation condition which encroaches upon constitutionally protected rights is subject to special scrutiny. . . . Since an adult probationer has the right to refuse probation, his or her acceptance of an order of probation which carries with it a search and seizure condition constitutes a waiver of Fourth Amendment rights in exchange for the benefit of avoiding a state prison term. . . . However, a juvenile's 'acceptance' of probation does not constitute a waiver of Fourth Amendment rights because a juvenile has no right to refuse probation. . . . Consequently, intrusions on a juvenile's Fourth Amendment rights by the imposition of a probation search condition are constitutionally valid only to the extent that such intrusions are justified by legitimate governmental interests. . . .

"The state's operation of a probation system implicates 'special needs' which justify warrantless searches on less than probable cause. . . . The protection against invasions of privacy offered by the warrant and probable cause requirements of the Fourth Amendment which probationers would otherwise enjoy is outweighed by the government's legitimate interests in rehabilitating probationers and protecting the public from further victimization.

"The state's involvement in guiding juvenile delinquents along the path to productive citizenship justifies relaxing barriers to effective supervision of these juveniles. An individualized suspicion requirement for searches pursuant to juvenile probation search conditions would thwart the state's efforts. Consequently, the balance of interests favors obviation of any individualized suspicion requirement for searches pursuant to juvenile probation search conditions."

CASE SIGNIFICANCE: This case upheld the use of an unlimited search condition in juvenile probation, justifying it as consistent with the state's interest in promoting the health and welfare of minors. This case reinforced the limitations on Fourth Amendment rights to privacy for juveniles who are on probation.

The statute allowing such searches in this case was very broad. It included the juvenile, his property, his residence, and any vehicle under his control at the time of contact. Although the language was broad, the court upheld such a search, saying that probation is not a right, but a privilege.

G.A.D. v. State
865 P.2d 100 (Alaska App. 1993)

Public protection prevails over a juvenile's right to a least restrictive placement.

FACTS: G.A.D., 13 years old, was adjudicated delinquent for sexually abusing his three-year-old brother. He was initially placed in a non-secure residential sex offender treatment program, where he failed to show improvement and eventually escaped. In juvenile court on the escape charge, G.A.D. was recommended by numerous experts for state placement in a secure facility that had a sex offender treatment program. G.A.D.'s attorney recommended placement in foster care with a day sex offender treatment component. The juvenile court placed G.A.D. in the secure facility, with participation in the sex offender treatment program as part of the order, based on the fact that G.A.D. had failed to respond to previous treatment, needed constant supervision, had victimized other youth in treatment programs, was extremely self-centered and showed little regard for others, had no concept of the seriousness of his conduct, and refused to accept responsibility for his behavior. G.A.D. appealed.

ISSUE: Does public protection prevail over the right of a juvenile to the least restrictive placement? YES.

DECISION: The public's right to protection prevails. The court can institutionalize a juvenile if the state presents substantial evidence that lesser placements will likely fail to meet the dual goals of rehabilitating the juvenile and protecting public safety.

REASON: "When the State seeks institutionalization of a delinquent minor, the State bears the burden of proving, by preponderance of the evidence, that less restrictive alternatives will not satisfy the twin goals of rehabilitating the minor and protecting the public. . . . Judge Reese's remarks at the conclusion of the hearing show that he was well aware of his duty to view institutionalization as the disposition of last resort.

". . . G.A.D. contends that Judge Reese lacked a substantial basis for ordering him placed at McLaughlin. However, . . . G.A.D's mother, his therapist, . . . his probation officer, . . . and his guardian ad litem all testified in favor of institutionalization.

"The record contains substantial evidence supporting Judge Reese's decision to commit G.A.D. to the McLaughlin Youth Center as the least restrictive alternative consistent with G.A.D.'s rehabilitation and protection of the public."

CASE SIGNIFICANCE: This case is an example of an attempt on the part of the court to balance the goal of the juvenile justice system to place delinquent juveniles in the least restrictive dispositional placement with the need to protect society. It presents no issue of difference in programming or inadequacy to treat the juvenile. The court notes that the less restrictive program and the more restrictive program are virtually identical, with only the environment for treatment being different. In this case, the juvenile court had attempted less restrictive placements with this juvenile with little or no success. The juvenile himself was primarily to blame for the past failure of programming efforts. Institutionalization was the more prudent course to take.

A.S. v. State
627 So. 2d 1265 (Fla. App. 1993)

Parents of a convicted juvenile are not responsible for restitution to the victim unless the court finds evidence of a lack of good faith effort on the part of the parents to raise the juvenile.

FACTS: A.S. was convicted of aggravated battery in circuit court for his role in a schoolyard fight in which the victim suffered a broken nose. As part of his sentence, A.S. was required to pay restitution in the amount of $4,986.60 for medical expenses incurred by the victim's family. As part of the order, A.S.'s mother was required to pay $2,500.00 of the $4986.60. The statute that allowed the assessment of restitution on parents for acts of their children read in part:

> The liability of a parent under this paragraph shall not exceed $2,500 for any one criminal episode. A finding by the court, after a hearing, that the parent has made diligent good faith efforts to prevent the child from engaging in de-linquent acts shall absolve the parent of liability for restitution under this paragraph.

ISSUE: Can parents of minors who commit acts that result in restitution judg-ments be required to pay restitution even though they [the parents] have a good parental record? NO.

DECISION: The parents of a convicted juvenile cannot be held partially re-sponsible for restitution to a victim under a statute allowing the court to impose such liability, unless the court can justify such assessment based on a lack of good faith effort on the part of the parents to raise the juvenile.

REASON: "On the subject of the mother's liability, the court simply said at the end of the hearing that he was going to hold the mother responsible for $2,500.00 of the restitution.

". . . the evidence is one-sided. Hence, the issue might properly be viewed as whether the court could make the mother liable simply by not believing her testimony. Strangely, that is not what the state argues. Instead, it contends that the mother could have anticipated the boy's delinquent acts and that she 'had the burden to establish a degree of effort above and beyond the normal parenting tasks to establish her diligence by the greater weight of the evidence.' . . . If all the evidence shows that the child is otherwise well-behaved, then surely it should be enough for the parent to show merely that she had accomplished the 'normal parenting tasks' to escape liability for restitution under this statute. To do otherwise would be to impose strict liability on parents for all delinquent acts of their minor children. If the legislature had intended that result, it would have chosen a different text than the one it had adopted at the time."

CASE SIGNIFICANCE: The court decided that the parents could be assessed a reasonable amount of restitution as part of a delinquency finding. However, the statute itself provided that the juvenile court, in assessing such restitution, must make a finding of "lack of good faith effort" on the part of the parents to raise the juvenile before assessing restitution on them for the actions of their children.

The significance of this case is twofold. First, the juvenile court clearly has the power, as recognized in this case, to assess restitution on parents of juveniles who are found delinquent. Second, prior to assessing restitution, the juvenile court must make a finding of parental defect amounting to a lack of good faith on the part of the parent to raise the juvenile, thus excusing parents who have attempted to guide their children, but holding accountable parents whose efforts do not amount to good faith.

The provision allowing parents to be held liable only if there was a lack of good faith on their part in raising the juvenile is a requirement under state law. The United States Supreme Court has not decided whether "good faith" is a constitutionally valid defense in these cases.

United States v. Juvenile No. 1 (LWQ)
38 F.3d 470 (9th Cir. 1994)

A probation condition prohibiting a juvenile from carrying a gun is valid under the First Amendment.

FACTS: Juveniles #1 and #2, members of the Confederated Tribes of the Umatilla Indian Reservation, were adjudicated delinquent for a simple assault in which, while drunk, they broke into a house in search of money, knocked the elderly female owner to the floor, and set the house on fire. They left her unable to move until she was rescued by neighbors. The two juveniles were sentenced to probation with one of the conditions being that they could not possess a fire-arm until they reached the age of 21. The juveniles objected on the grounds that tribal religious customs required participation in a "hunt," and thus such a con-dition violated their First Amendment right to freedom of religion.

ISSUE: Is the prohibition against possessing a gun as a condition of probation in violation of the First Amendment? NO.

DECISION: The condition of probation prohibiting the juveniles from possessing firearms until they are 21 years old reasonably serves the statutory goals of punishment, deterrence, and public protection. It does not severely limit the juveniles' religious freedom under the First Amendment, and is therefore constitutional.

REASON: "Without deciding whether a tribal hunt is a religious exercise protected by the First Amendment, we reject the juveniles' argument. Deciding how to shape conditions of probation is essentially a task for the district court. . . . Here, the district court considered the juveniles' request to except tribal hunts from its firearm prohibition order. It chose not to create such an exception. We cannot say the district court abused its discretion in making this choice. The juveniles may still participate in tribal hunts. They may even take part in killing game, by using a bow and arrow or any other weapon which is not a firearm."

CASE SIGNIFICANCE: This decision shows that in juvenile cases the First Amendment freedom of religion is not an absolute right. In this case, a tribal religious custom that required young males to engage in a religious "hunt," in which guns were commonly used clashed with a probation condition. The probation condition prohibited possession or use of a firearm under any circumstances, with no exceptions.

The court saw the wisdom of enforcing the condition even when it was in direct conflict with one of the most basic of constitutional rights. It offered the juveniles several alternatives to participate in the hunt, including the use of bows and arrows, but rejected their contention that the conditions were set by the juvenile court to interfere with their constitutionally protected religious freedoms.

The significance of this case is that when faced with a choice of maintaining public safety as a condition of a juvenile disposition and upholding a basic constitutional right of a juvenile that could be accommodated in other ways, the court will likely choose to protect the public.

State in Interest of T.L.V.
643 So. 2d 290 (La. App. 1994)

Juvenile courts are not bound by the state's mandatory adult sentencing guidelines.

FACTS: T.L.V. and a companion planned to snatch a purse to obtain money. They chose as their victim a 75-year-old female in a mall parking lot. In an attempt to steal her purse, T.L.V. hit the victim on the head, causing a substantial wound, and knocked her to the ground, breaking her arm. The juveniles then fled to a nearby apartment. When contacted, the resident of the apartment identified the juveniles and offered to give them a message telling them to turn themselves in. T.L.V. came to the police station with his mother and confessed to his part in the purse snatching. He pled guilty in juvenile court and was sentenced to the Louisiana Department of Public Safety and Corrections for three years on the purse snatching and one year on the battery charge, to be served consecutively. He appealed, stating that his sentence was excessive.

ISSUE: Was the sentence excessive in light of the state's sentencing guidelines used in adult criminal court? NO.

DECISION: Juvenile courts are not required to follow felony sentencing guidelines that are mandatory for adult criminal courts in similar offenses.

REASON: ". . . [T]he record here shows that the defendant was a 10th grade student at Booker T. Washington high school. He was passing his courses and even had a 'B' in world geography. He apparently had complied with the house arrest order pending the hearing date. Defendant told the court he was sorry for the victim and he wrote an apology letter to the victim. The court found defendant came from a good family. However, the court also found that defendant and his companion planned the event for some time and lay in wait for their victim who was an elderly person. The court considered that the act endangered human life and caused grave harm to the victim.

"It seems obvious from the juvenile court's discussion of the offense that the court found the delinquent conduct could be contemplated to cause or threaten harm, that there was no strong provocation, that there were no grounds tending to justify the conduct, and that the victim neither induced nor facilitated the offense.

"Here, the trial court apparently was swayed by the facts that defendant planned the purse-snatching offense in advance, but then resorted to violence and inflicted severe injuries when his elderly victim proved less complacent than he had hoped. Defendant, had he been an adult, would have faced up to ten years on the attempted purse snatching and up to five years for the simple battery. The disposition imposed is in the far lower range of what an adult would have faced."

CASE SIGNIFICANCE: The issue in this case is whether juvenile courts are bound by sentencing guidelines that are mandatory in adult criminal courts. The court found that juvenile courts are not bound by such guidelines, based on the need of the juvenile justice system to balance the needs of the juvenile with protection of society. Balancing those two factors is unique to the juvenile justice system and requires a different rationale than that used in drafting the mandatory adult criminal court sentencing guidelines.

The court found nothing wrong with juvenile judges informally using such sentencing guidelines as guideposts in a particular case; neither did the court discourage the development of a similar set of dispositional guidelines for use exclusively in juvenile court. But the court also said that adult sentencing guidelines do not apply to juvenile cases, unless specified otherwise by law. Some states have sentencing guidelines for adult offenders, other states do not.

In re Tyrell J.
876 P.2d 519 (Cal. 1994)

Evidence obtained by the police in a questionable search may be admissible in court if the juvenile was subject to a probation condition to submit to a search with or without a warrant.

FACTS: Tyrell J. was declared a ward of the court on the basis of a misdemeanor battery on school grounds. He was placed on probation subject to a variety of conditions, including that he "submit to a search of his person and property, with or without a warrant, by any law enforcement officer, probation officer or school official." During a football game between two rival schools, two officers noticed Tyrell J. and two male friends acting suspiciously, mainly because one of the juveniles was wearing a heavy quilted jacket and the temperature was 80 degrees. One of the officers identified them as members of a gang that had caused trouble at a football game the previous week. The officers asked the trio to "hold up," pulled up the jacket and found a large hunting knife on the person of one of the juveniles. The officers then escorted all three to a fence nearby. During the pat-down search of Tyrell J., the officer noticed that his fly was partially unzipped and noticed a soft package object protruding from his pants. The officer retrieved the object and found that it was a rolled up bag of marijuana approximately three inches in diameter and 12 inches long. Tyrell J. was adjudicated delinquent and again declared a ward of the court.

ISSUE: Can the fruits of an otherwise questionable search be admitted into evidence against a juvenile if the juvenile was subject to a probation search condition, even though the officer had no knowledge of such condition? YES.

DECISION: Because the juvenile was subject to a valid condition of probation that required him to submit to a warrantless search by any law enforcement officer, he had no reasonable expectation of privacy over the cache of marijuana in his pants, therefore, the evidence was admissible in court.

REASON: "We conclude a juvenile probationer subject to a valid search condition does not have a reasonable expectation of privacy over his person or property. In this case, Tyrell J. was subject to a valid search condition, directly imposed on him by the juvenile court in a prior matter. We presume he was aware of that limitation on his freedom, and that any police officer, probation officer, or school official could at any time stop him on the street, at school, or even enter his home, and ask that he submit to a warrantless search. There is no indication the minor was led to believe that only police officers who were aware of the condition would validly execute it. The minor certainly could not reasonable have believed Officer Villemin would not search him, for he did not know whether Villemin was aware of the search condition. Thus, any expectation the minor may have had concerning the privacy of his bag of marijuana was manifestly unreasonable."

CASE SIGNIFICANCE: In this case, the juvenile was subject to search at any time, by authorized governmental officials. Unlike previous cases, there was no obvious connection between the crime of delinquency and the search condition, but nonetheless the juvenile was subject to search and knew he was subject to search at any time, with or without a warrant, by authorized officials.

The juvenile contended that such searches were legal only when made in connection with his probation and therefore any officer or officials who searched him should be aware of his probationary status in order for the search to be valid.

The court disagreed, saying that due to the conditions of probation imposed and agreed to by the juvenile, he had little expectation of privacy regardless of who was conducting the search, and that to require that searches as a condition of probation be conducted only by those who are aware of the probation and the conditions attached was ludicrous. The court added that, contrary to the juvenile's assertion, rejecting the "knowledge first" rule would not result in more illegal warrantless searches and that requiring knowledge first on the part of all law enforcement officers, probation officers, and school officials would greatly impair the ability of the system to utilize a very effective tool of the juvenile justice system in stopping repetitive delinquent behavior.

Conditions of Confinement and Liability for Failure to Protect 9

I. No United States Supreme Court Cases

II. Lower Court Cases

Introduction

The first facility to house juveniles in the United States was the House of Refuge, which opened in New York City in 1825.[1] These institutions were founded by private organizations concerned with the welfare of children who were handled in the adult court system. The institutions operated on the philosophy that juveniles needed to be institutionalized separately from adults and placed in a facility that provided discipline and education.[2] Ensuing decades found state and local governments assimilating Houses of Refuge that had been previously established, and the concept of the state training, industrial, or reform school was born.[3]

By the 1890s, every northern state had followed this concept and reform or industrial schools were the norm of juvenile correctional institutes.[4] In 1899, when the first juvenile court was created in Chicago to deal with the problems of troubled children, the juvenile justice system was born with the institution at its core.

Juvenile correctional institutions continue to play a big role in America's juvenile justice system. One result of the "conservative reform agenda" that the juvenile justice system experienced in the late 1970s and early 1980s was "a significant increase in the number of youth in juvenile correctional facilities."[5]

Although the juvenile institutions were designed to care for juveniles in their best interests, they have historically been the target of persistent and sometimes inconsistent criticisms. Criticisms of the training schools center on many issues, among them: that they do not rehabilitate, they do not punish, they are costly, they are abusive, they do not protect the public, and they contribute to future delinquency.[6]

The criticism of the institutions as abusive usually refers to conditions of confinement. The 1970s saw many states experiencing lawsuits dealing with the conditions of confinement in juvenile facilities. The cases chosen for inclusion in this chapter are representative of many similar suits. In 1972, *Inmates of the Boys' Training School v. Affleck* questioned the isolation of boys in dark, cold isolation cells that contained only a mattress and a toilet, as well as whether confinement in a former women's reformatory was anti-rehabilitative. *Morales v. Turman*, decided in 1974, questioned many rules and practices found in the juvenile correctional facilities of the Texas Youth Council. Included among those were the use of physical brutality (including the use of corporal punishment, mace, and tear gas), disciplinary procedures used, lack of assessment and placement, overuse of psychotropic drugs, and concerns about staff quality and training. Also decided in 1974, *Nelson v. Heyne* focused on the use of corporal punishment, specifically a fraternity paddle, and the use of psychotropic drugs. Included in this suit was the question of a constitutional right to treatment for confined juveniles. The case of *Cruz v. Collazo* (1978) is included to demonstrate that there are other issues and practices that have been called to the attention of the courts. Recent research by the Office of Juvenile Justice and Delinquency Prevention suggests that juvenile correctional facilities, including juvenile detention centers, reception centers, training schools, camps, ranches, and farms, still face significant conditions of confinement concerns.[7] This research also suggests that "there are several areas in which problems in juvenile facilities are substantial and widespread—most notably living space, health care, security, and control of suicidal behavior."[8]

On liability issues, *State ex rel. Southers v. Stuckey* (1993) held that public administrators are immune from civil liability in the performance of discretionary duties. *C.J.W. by and through L.W. v. State* (1993) held that the state has a duty to protect the juveniles who come under its custody. Failure to provide information that results in a child's injury places potential liability on the state.

Notes

[1]   Barry Krisberg, *The Juvenile Court: Reclaiming the Vision.* The National Council on Crime and Delinquency (1988).

[2]   Cliff Roberson, *Exploring Juvenile Justice: Theory and Practice* (1996).

[3]   Barry Krisberg, *The Juvenile Court: Reclaiming the Vision.* The National Council on Crime and Delinquency (1988).

[4]   Barry Krisberg, *The Juvenile Court: Reclaiming the Vision.* The National Council on Crime and Delinquency (1988).

[5]   Barry Krisberg and James F. Austin, *Reinventing Juvenile Justice* (1993) at 50.

[6]   Clemens Bartollas, *Juvenile Delinquency*, Fourth Edition. (1997). Robert M. Regoli and John D. Hewitt, *Delinquency in Society*, Third Edition. (1997). Allen F. Breed and Barry Krisberg, "Juvenile Corrections: Is There a Future?" *Corrections Today.* December 48:8:14-20 (1986).

[7]   Dale G. Parent, Valerie Leiter, Stephen Kennedy, Lisa Livens, Daniel Wentworth, and Sarah Wilcox, *Conditions of Confinement: Juvenile Detention and Corrections Facilities*. Washington, DC: Office of Juvenile Justice and Delinquency Prevention. U.S. Department of Justice, Office of Justice Programs. (1994).

[8]   Dale G. Parent, Valerie Leiter, Stephen Kennedy, Lisa Livens, Daniel Wentworth, and Sarah Wilcox, *Conditions of Confinement: Juvenile Detention and Corrections Facilities*. Washington, DC: Office of Juvenile Justice and Delinquency Prevention. U.S. Department of Justice, Office of Justice Programs. (1994).

I. NO UNITED STATES SUPREME COURT CASES

II. LOWER COURT CASES

Inmates of Boys' Training School v. Affleck
346 F. Supp. 1354 (D.R.I. 1972)

Cruel and unusual conditions of confinement are anti-rehabilitative and unconstitutional.

FACTS: The boys being held in the training school were committed to the school for various reasons: voluntarily committed by their parents, pending trial, adjudicated delinquent, declared wayward by the court, or found to be dependent and neglected. The school became concerned with discipline and escape problems, so some of the youth were sent to institutions known as "Annex B, Annex C, Annex C cellblock, and the Maximum Security building of the Adult Correctional Institution (ACI)." The transfer of youth to the various institutions was carried out without administrative or judicial hearing or prior notice. Five juveniles sought a preliminary injunction to stop confinement of the juveniles in the Adult Correctional Institution. Conditions of confinement in the training school were also challenged.

ISSUES:
1. Did conditions of confinement at the training school violate the prohibition of cruel and unusual punishment offered by the Eighth Amendment? YES.

2. Did the confinement of the juveniles in the former women's reformatory violate the equal protection and the due process clauses of the Constitution? YES.

DECISIONS:
1. At the boys training school, isolation of juveniles in cold, dark isolation cells containing only a mattress and a toilet constituted cruel and unusual punishment.

2. Confinement of juveniles in a former women's reformatory were anti-rehabilitative and in violation of due process and equal protection.

REASON: "Conditions in Annex B were deplorable, as defendants themselves must have recognized in stopping its use. Lest defendants find themselves pressing Annex B into use again because of lack of adequate facilities elsewhere, this court enjoins the use of Annex B and orders that it be closed. . . .

"Further, this court holds that because the conditions of confinement in Annex B are anti-rehabilitative, use of Annex B is enjoined as a violation of equal protection and due process of law. . . .

"This court is greatly disturbed by the testimony of two plaintiffs who have been confined to the ACI that they have learned little there other than how to better commit crimes, that they were threatened with homosexual attacks, and that they had not participated in any rehabilitative programs. Such a situation surely cannot be in society's best interest. I note that a report by a committee appointed by the Governor of Rhode Island strongly recommended that the practice of incarcerating juveniles at the ACI be stopped.

"Whatever the reasons, confinement in Annex C and its cellblock is punishment. The conditions of confinement are themselves detrimental to rehabilitation. . . .

"In closing, the Court emphasizes that this judgment does not reflect on defendants' choice of theory of rehabilitative techniques being employed in cottages at the Training School proper. The court realizes that defendants have been handicapped by lack of adequate facilities and trained personnel to deal with the plaintiff class, and that the remedy for this situation will involve the expenditure of state funds. The issue is not the good faith of defendants, but rather the issue is of the protection of the constitutional rights of these boys."

CASE SIGNIFICANCE: This case represents an early conditions-of-confinement case heard during the beginning of the period of courts' "hands-on" and judicial intervention into conditions of juvenile confinement. The case reflects the growing concern about juvenile correctional institutions and the violation of the Eighth Amendment as early as 1972, when the rights of prisoners in general and of juveniles in particular had not as yet been clarified or established. Even then the court concluded that the conditions of confinement in this facility constituted cruel and unusual punishment. This conditions-of-confinement case reaffirms *parens patriae* and the original rehabilitative ideal of the juvenile justice system. It also reaffirms basic constitutional rights of juveniles even under the *parens patriae* concept.

Morales v. Turman
383 F. Supp. 53 (E.D. Tex. 1974)

Conditions of confinement in Texas constituted cruel and unusual punishment and were unconstitutional. Moreover, juveniles have a constitutional right to treatment.

FACTS: On February 12, 1971, attorneys tried to confer in private with some children who were committed to the Texas Youth Council (TYC) facilities. When access to their clients was denied, the attorneys filed a civil action. The attorneys filed a motion for a "preliminary injunction—seeking to enjoin the TYC and their agents from interfering with the children's right to confer privately with counsel and from impeding in any manner their correspondence with counsel through the mail." The concern was that these children had not received the due process rights during their adjudication hearings as guaranteed in *Gault*. Questionnaire results showed that many juveniles had not received full rights, and the suit expanded to include the question of procedural due process during an adjudication hearing.

Some of the questionnaires returned contained allegations of abuse within the institutions. The judge then approved a number of unique investigative requests by the plaintiffs to get into the institutions and determine whether practices within the institutions violated the Eighth Amendment prohibition against cruel and unusual punishment. The judge allowed juveniles within TYC institutions to be interviewed about how they were treated within the institutions, and also granted permission for Participant Observation Teams of professionals to observe conditions of confinement in some selected institutions.

The trial took place in the summer of 1973; TYC lost. The judge addressed many practices of TYC. The issues were numerous and included corporal punishment, the use of mace and tear gas, segregation, solitary confinement, visitation, and screening of prospective staff. The court found that the practices at TYC constituted cruel and unusual punishment, and that juveniles were denied their right to treatment. The judge, among other actions, ordered two juvenile institutions closed.

ISSUE: Did the Texas Youth Council engage in policy and practices that violated the Eighth Amendment's prohibition against cruel and unusual punishment? YES.

DECISION: Juveniles confined in the facilities of the Texas Youth Council have a right to proper treatment. Some of the practices and procedures of TYC constituted cruel and unusual punishment.

REASON: "The Court of Appeals for the Fifth Circuit has recently held that a person involuntarily committed to a state mental hospital in a civil proceeding had the constitutional right to receive such individual treatment as will give him a reasonable opportunity to be cured or to improve his mental condition. . . . In the instant case, the state is charged with a statutory duty to provide a 'program of constructive training aimed at rehabilitation and re-establishment in society of children adjudged to be delinquent.' Tex. Rev. Civ. Stat. Ann. art. 5143d (1971). This basis for commitment—to rehabilitate and reestablish the juvenile in society—is clearly grounded in a *parens patriae* rationale. Thus, under the *parens patriae* theory, the juvenile must be given treatment lest the involuntary commitment amount to an arbitrary exercise of governmental power proscribed by the due process clause.

"Schools under the jurisdiction of the TYC, particularly Mountain View and Gatesville, have been the scenes of widespread physical and psychological brutality. In the emergency interim relief order, several practices found to be in violation of the Eighth Amendment's proscription of cruel and unusual punishment were enjoined on the grounds that such practices were so severe as to degrade human dignity; were inflicted in a wholly arbitrary fashion; were so severe as to be unacceptable to contemporary society; and finally, were not justified in serving any necessary purpose. *See Furman v. Georgia*, 408 U.S. 238, 257–306, 92 S. Ct. 2726, 33 L. Ed. 2d 346 (1972) (Brennan, J.); *see also Jackson v. Bishop*, 404 F.2d 571 (8th Cir. 1968).

"Practices found by this court to violate the Eighth Amendment were: the widespread practice of beating, slapping, kicking, and otherwise physically abusing juveniles in the absence of any exigent circumstances, *see Ingraham v. Wright*, 498 F.2d 248 (5th Cir. July 29, 1974); the use of tear gas and other chemical crowd-control devices in situations not posing an imminent threat to human life or an imminent and substantial threat to property; the placing of juveniles in solitary confinement or other secured facilities, in the absence of any legislative or administrative limitation on the duration and intensity of the confinement and subject only to the unfettered discretion of correctional officers; the requirement that inmates maintain silence during periods of the day merely for the purpose of punishment; and the performance of repetitive, nonfunctional, degrading and unnecessary tasks. Included as such tasks (the so-called "make work") were: requiring a juvenile to pull grass without bending his knees on a large tract of ground not intended for cultivation or any other purpose; forcing him to move dirt with a shovel from one place on the ground to another and then back again many times; and making him buff a small area of the floor for a period of time exceeding that in which any reasonable person would conclude that the floor was sufficiently buffed."

CASE SIGNIFICANCE: The judge who decided the case (Judge William W. Justice) was concerned about the totality of the conditions of confinement as a treatment issue. He took an active interest in the case and employed a number of unique legal tools. For example, he authorized the distribution of questionnaires regarding due process rights in adjudication hearings for every incarcerated juvenile, interviews of incarcerated juveniles and, finally, a participant-observation team living in some of the training schools for a short period. Finally, when the settlement agreement was reached, the judge appointed a Consultant Committee to oversee the Settlement Agreement for four years.

This was one of the earliest juvenile cases questioning the conditions in juvenile facilities. Many consider *Morales* to be the most extensive conditions-of-confinement case in juvenile justice. The judge concluded that Texas was running two unconstitutional juvenile justice facilities and ordered them to be closed. Against a backdrop of *parens patriae*, this decision was startling at that time. Since then, courts have been less reluctant in probing into allegations involving juvenile facilities. This case took almost 15 years to settle through a consent decree and is an example of how conditions of confinement cases develop and how long it takes for cases to be finally resolved.

Nelson v. Heyne
491 F.2d 352 (7th Cir. 1974)

Conditions of confinement that constituted cruel and unusual were declared unconstitutional.

FACTS: The suit was filed against the Indiana Boys' School, which was a medium-security juvenile correctional facility designed to hold boys 12 to 18 years old. About one-third of the boys in the facility were non-criminal offenders.

The school consisted of about 16 cottages and an academic building, vocational building, gymnasium, and administrative building. Children confined to the Indiana Boys' School stayed an average of six and one-half months. The population at the school generally numbered around 400 boys, although the capacity of the Boys' School was less than 300.

The complaint alleged that the juveniles' rights were violated under the Eighth and Fourteenth Amendments. "Plaintiffs moved for a temporary restraining order to protect them from defendants' corporal punishment and use of control-tranquilizing drugs."

ISSUES:

1. Does corporal punishment that is inflicted with a "fraternity paddle" constitute cruel and unusual punishment? YES.

2. Is the use of a "tranquilizing drug administered intramuscularly by staff, without trying medication short of drugs and without adequate medical guidance and prescription" cruel and unusual punishment? YES.

3. Do juveniles have a right to treatment under the due process clause of the Fourteenth Amendment and the Indiana Juvenile Court Act? YES.

DECISION: Practices in the Indiana Boys' School constituted conditions that violated the Eighth and Fourteenth Amendments.

REASON: "It is not disputed that the juveniles who were returned from escapes or who were accused of assaults on other students or staff members were beaten routinely by guards under defendants' supervision. There is no proof of formal procedures that governed the beatings which were administered after decision by two or more staff members. Two staff members were required to observe the beatings.

"In beating the juveniles, a 'fraternity paddle' between ½" and 2" thick, 12" long, with a narrow handle, was used. There is testimony that juveniles weighing about 160 pounds were struck five blows on the clothed buttocks, often by a staff member weighing 285 pounds. The beatings caused painful injuries. The district court found that this disciplinary practice violated the plaintiffs' Eighth and Fourteenth Amendment rights, and ordered it stopped immediately.

". . . The record before us discloses that the beatings employed by defendants are disproportionate to the offenses for which they are used, and do not measure up to contemporary standards of decency in our contemporary society.

"Witnesses for both the School and the juveniles testified at trial that tranquilizing drugs, specifically Sparine and Thorazine, were occasionally administered to the juveniles, not as part of an ongoing psychotherapeutic program, but for the purpose of controlling excited behavior. The registered nurse and licensed practical nurse prescribed intramuscular dosages of the drugs upon recommendation of the custodial staff under standing orders from the physician. Neither before nor after injections were the juveniles examined by medically competent staff members to determine their competence.

"We hold today that only the use of disciplinary beatings and tranquilizing drugs in the circumstances shown by this record violates plaintiffs' Fourteenth Amendment right protecting them from cruel and unusual punishment. We do not intend that penal and reform institutional physicians cannot prescribe necessary tranquilizing drugs in appropriate cases. Our concern is with actual and potential abuses under policies where juveniles are beaten with an instrument causing serious injuries, and drugs are administered to juveniles intramuscularly by staff, without trying medication short of drugs and without adequate medical guidance and prescription."

CASE SIGNIFICANCE: This case represents another conditions-of-confinement case. The court here showed concern about the use of psychotropic drugs and their distribution, and the use of corporal punishment. These are the same issues raised in other juvenile conditions-of-confinement cases. The court held that hitting juveniles with a fraternity paddle, which caused pain, was cruel and unusual punishment. Administering intramuscular drugs without the guidance of a doctor and without trying other medical remedies also constituted cruel and unusual punishment.

The court also addressed the right to treatment for incarcerated juveniles. The court reaffirmed a juvenile right to treatment under the U.S. Constitution and the Indiana Juvenile Court Act. This represents a continuing concern about the treatment of juveniles confined in the nation's juvenile correctional facilities. Many courts have held that juveniles have a constitutional right to treatment, a right adult offenders do not have. In juvenile cases, the right to treatment usually means the right to rehabilitation.

Cruz v. Collazo
450 F. Supp. 235 (D.P.R. 1978)

Transferring a juvenile from a non-secure facility into a secure facility is constitutional.

FACTS: Pedro A. Vegas Cruz, a juvenile, was placed at the Guaynabo State Home for Boys. He filed a suit alleging that he and the class he sought to represent were not receiving adequate rehabilitative treatment. He also claimed infringements upon his rights pursuant to the Fourth, Eighth, Ninth, and Thirteenth Amendments. While this case was pending, Cruz escaped from the Guaynabo State Home for Boys. A motion was filed alleging that his escape prevented him from representing the other residents of the institution. Cruz returned to the Guaynabo State Home for Boys, and escaped again about two months later. When Cruz returned this time, he was transferred to the Industrial School for Boys in Mayaguez. Plaintiff filed a motion for a Temporary Restraining Order "alleging therein that the Mayaguez Industrial School was a maximum-security juvenile institution which housed hardened delinquents." He also alleged that he had been sent there in violation of his due process and equal protection rights.

ISSUE: Does the transfer of a juvenile (who has been committed) from a non-secure facility to a secure facility without a judicial hearing violate the due process and equal protection provisions of the Constitution? NO.

DECISION: The juvenile did not have a liberty expectancy under the law of Puerto Rico to remain in one juvenile institution, so the transfer without a judicial hearing did not violate due process or equal protection rights.

REASON: "We find the precise issue here in question, the transfer from one juvenile institution to another, albeit a maximum security one, is of first impression. The cases cited by the parties in support of their respective contentions involve either the transfer of juveniles to adult penal institutions or of mentally ill patients from minimum to maximum security confinements or for indeterminate periods. Both lines of cases present the risk of losing perspective of the proper analysis to be made in view of the constitutional right involved. Thus, in the present case a proper definition of the right involved is essential to trigger the correct analysis.

"Much as we would like to rule otherwise, under *Meachum v. Fano*, the statute's omission in creating a liberty expectancy to remain in one given juvenile institution compels us to decide that there is no such liberty interest at stake. There is no creation by omission.

CASE SIGNIFICANCE: The juvenile in this case was in the custody of a state home when he escaped from that home twice. After the second escape, he was transferred to a more secure facility. A motion was filed, stating that the child had been transferred in violation of his rights. The court held that the child had not had his rights violated by being transferred to a more secure facility without a judicial hearing.

The court in this case said that no due process rights were needed prior to the transfer of a juvenile from a nonsecure facility to a secure facility, because the juvenile was not entitled to this right either under the U.S. Constitution or under the laws of Puerto Rico. This holding is similar to what the U.S. Supreme Court said in *Meachum v. Fano*, 427 U.S. 215 (1976)—that a transfer from one facility to another within the state does not require giving the prisoner due process rights such as a hearing.

C.J.W. by and through L.W. v. State
853 P.2d 4 (Kan. 1993)

The state has a duty to protect the juveniles who come under its care and custody. Failure to provide information that results in the injury of a minor places potential liability on the state.

FACTS: On two separate occasions, a 12-year-old juvenile male was allegedly brutally assaulted, raped, and sexually molested by a 17-year-old male, while in the custody of the Johnson County Juvenile Hall. The 17-year-old assailant had an extensive history of aggression that dated back at least seven years, with known escalation of violence and a propensity for sexual aggression. Upon his detention at the Johnson County Juvenile Hall, no information regarding his behavior patterns was provided to detention staff by either the state or his assigned caseworker. The first attack on the 12-year-old occurred on the first day of the 17-year-old's admission to the juvenile hall. Even after contact with the detention staff by the assigned caseworker, no mention of such a behavior pattern was brought to the attention of the juvenile hall authorities. The plaintiff contended that C.J.W. suffered personal injury, mental anguish, emotional distress, psychiatric disorders, embarrassment, humiliation, and social withdrawal as a result of the attacks, which would likely affect him for the rest of his life. They further contended that the state, which had knowledge of the violent and sexually aggressive nature of the 17-year-old, failed to fulfill its obligation by not affirmatively informing the juvenile hall authorities of such tendencies and providing factual documentation of such past behavior. The state contended that it was immune from liability in this case because it had no obligation to release such information unless directly asked by the juvenile detention staff.

ISSUES:
1. Did the state have an obligation to ensure the safety of a minor placed in its care by taking reasonable steps to convey known information regarding the history of an aggressive and sexually deviant juvenile with whom the minor was likely to come into contact? YES.

2. Is the state liable under state law for the injuries suffered by the minor due to its failure to convey known relevant information to the appropriate authorities? YES.

DECISIONS:
1. The state owed a duty to the 12-year-old minor who was sexually assaulted while in a juvenile detention facility by a 17-year-old fellow inmate, to warn the juvenile detention authorities of the 17-year-old inmate's pro-

pensity for violence and sexually deviant conduct and to take reasonable steps to protect the juvenile from such an inmate when such information was known by both the juvenile caseworker and the Social and Rehabilitation Services Department.

2. Such negligence by the state can lead to liability under the State Tort Claims Act.

REASON: "The Kansas Tort Claims Act makes liability the rule and immunity the exception, and the burden is on the State to establish its entitlement to any of the exceptions. . . . The State argues that the decision to inform Juvenile Hall of Randy's history was within Sharon Minor's discretion. To support this proposition, the State relies upon excerpts of testimony from Minor's deposition where she states that the Kansas Manual for Youth Services requires SRS to provide a case history on a child under SRS supervision to a facility which undertakes physical custody of the child only upon the facility's request for information. Minor also testified in her deposition that SRS caseworkers were permitted to share information on a child's history with a facility housing the child at the discretion of the caseworker's supervisor. The State asserts that, according to Minor's testimony, the manual allowed her discretion in providing information concerning Randy to Juvenile Hall, and, in exercising her discretion, she chose not to provide any information. The State maintains that as Minor's actions were a discretionary function, the State shall not be liable for damages . . . Because the State's duty to control Randy, to warn others about his dangerous propensities, and to protect persons in the position of the plaintiff is imposed by law and is ministerial, not discretionary, the State is not entitled to the protection afforded by the discretionary function exception. SRS cannot rely upon its manual to avoid liability for its acts regarding a duty imposed by law."

CASE SIGNIFICANCE: This case dealt with a state's responsibility to guarantee the care and safety of juveniles in its custody. Liability attached for failure to do so. The state argued that it was immune from liability and that the policy manual of the state agency involved covered the proper procedure for such exchanges of information, placing discretion on the caseworker assigned to the case. The court disagreed, saying that the state was liable unless it could justify why an exception should be made, which in this case the state could not.

This court held that the state can be held liable for injuries inflicted on a juvenile due to the negligence of its officers. States generally are protected from liability based on the doctrine of sovereign immunity. Many states, however, waive immunity through a State Tort Claims Act such as the one involved in this case. The provisions of State Tort Claims Acts vary and therefore liability must be determined on a case-by-case basis. In this case, liability was imposed under the Kansas State Tort Claims Act. If this case had taken place in another state, the State Tort Claims Act of that state would determine whether liability would be imposed.

State ex rel. Southers v. Stuckey
867 S.W.2d 579 (Mo. App. 1993)

Public administrators are immune from civil liability in the performance of discretionary duties.

FACTS: A juvenile runaway from a residential youth facility operated by the State Division of Youth Services assaulted a woman in her home and then set her house on fire. The victim and her husband sued the administrator of the residential youth facility for negligence in the performance of her duties, saying that she:

> Consistently, negligently, and deliberately failed to maintain adequate security at the facility and supervision of the residents in numerous respects, including, but not limited to, the following: she did not provide for an adequate number of staff to supervise the residents of the facility; she did not provide adequate security measures to prevent the residents from leaving the building without authorization, she did not provide for adequate physical barriers to prevent escapes of residents such as locks on the doors, bars on the windows and a perimeter fence of the area encompassed by the facility, and she did not make adequate provisions to ensure that staff were trained in security procedures . . .

The plaintiffs characterized such duties as "mandatory, ministerial and non-discretionary" and asked the court to grant relief due to the administrator's "negligent and reckless acts." The administrator claimed protection under the official immunity doctrine, which provides that a public official is not civilly liable to members of the public for negligence arising out of the performance of discretionary duties.

ISSUE: Was the administrator liable to private citizens for the actions of an escaped juvenile who was under state custody and care at the time of the escape? NO.

DECISION: A residential youth facility administrator's regulatory duty to report a runaway to police and others is a duty owed to the state, not to the victims. Therefore the public duty doctrine barred the victims from suing the facility administrator for actions of a juvenile while on escape status.

REASON: "The general rule of official immunity is that: 'public officers acting within the scope of their authority are not liable for injuries arising from their discretionary acts or omissions, but they may be held liable for torts committed when acting in a ministerial capacity.' . . . Missouri courts have applied official immunity to circumstances similar to those faced by the relator. . . . it is clear that the allegations against relator should be dismissed based upon official immunity."

CASE SIGNIFICANCE: This case dealt with the question of official immunity in the case of the administrator of a youth residential facility from which a juvenile escaped and committed additional crimes before his recovery. The state maintained that the administrator fulfilled her duty to the public by notifying the appropriate law enforcement entities and asking the residential staff to search for the escapee. The couple, whose house was burned, alleged that the administrator had a duty to inform the citizens of such an escape, especially citizens who lived close to the residential facility.

The court ruled that the administrator was immune from individual liability as long as she carried out her duties, as she had in this case. The court further ruled that any obligation of notice was strictly aimed at notifying the appropriate agencies who were in a position to assist in the search for the escaped youth and that no duty existed to inform individual citizens no matter how closely they lived to the facility.

This case explored the legal relationship between juvenile residential facilities and residents of the neighborhoods surrounding them. It held that failure to inform the immediate neighborhood in case of an escape does not lead to liability as long as administrators follow procedure, appropriately notify the authorities, and have an emergency plan in place to deal with incidents such as escapes.

Release and Revocation of Juveniles   10

I. No United States Supreme Court Cases

II. Lower Court Cases

Introduction

Aftercare in the juvenile justice system is the equivalent of parole in the adult criminal justice system. Juveniles who are released from an institution either in the form of early release or after completion of their sentence are placed on aftercare status, which usually involves supervision for a specific period and continuation of certain conditions unique to the individual juvenile, such as drug or alcohol abuse treatment.[1] Probation is a disposition that allows the juvenile to remain in the community under supervision and subject to certain terms and conditions designed to deal with the difficulties encountered by the juvenile and his or her involvement in criminal activity.

There is no standard for determining when a juvenile should be released from a juvenile facility. Because juvenile sentencing is fundamentally indeterminate in nature, the length of time held and the conditions attached to release vary from case to case with little regard for issues of equity between similarly situated juveniles.[2]

Should a juvenile violate the terms of his or her probation or release from an institution on aftercare, revocation proceedings may be initiated, resulting in either a continuation of community supervision or a return of the juvenile to a secure facility for a indefinite period. Although revocation procedures vary, the formality of the hearing and the rights extended to juveniles during such hearings are diminished from previous juvenile justice procedures. Generally, adult revocation processes in place in each state govern the structure of juvenile revocation hearings.[3]

This chapter deals with issues that affect the release of juveniles and potential revocation of community-based dispositions. Many of the cases included here came to the court in the form of traditional *habeas corpus* cases (in which the juvenile seeks release from detention), while others are Section 1983 cases (cases alleging violations of constitutional rights and seeking improvement of conditions and/or monetary damages) contesting policies and practices of incarcerating agencies.

There are no landmark cases from the U.S. Supreme Court to guide lower courts in making decisions in release and revocation cases. The variety of cases reviewed in this chapter is indicative of the volume of legal activity in this area. Cases include the issues of right to indigency appeal, the criteria for aftercare release decisions, and due process prior to revocation.

Several cases focus on institutional issues of *good time* as it applies to sentence reduction, the calculation of minimum release dates, facility responsibility to fulfill legislative mandates as they apply to specialized groups of offenders, and the impact of concurrent juvenile and adult sentences on time served. One reflects a trend in juvenile penalty statutes. *J.R.W. v. State*, a 1994 case from Texas, declares valid "rollover statutes," which allow juveniles adjudicated delinquent in juvenile court to be sentenced to a juvenile facility for the duration of their minority status and then to be transferred to an adult prison upon attaining adulthood. Tired of violent juvenile crime, states are experimenting with more punitive methods. Whether they will work is debatable.

Notes

[1] Larry J. Siegel and Joseph J. Senna, *Juvenile Delinquency: Theory, Practice & Law* (1991).

[2] Mary Clement, *The Juvenile Justice System: Law and Process* (1997).

[3] Peter C. Kratcoski and Lucille D. Kratcoski, *Juvenile Delinquency* (1996).

I. NO UNITED STATES SUPREME COURT CASES

II. LOWER COURT CASES

Reed v. Duter
416 F.2d 744 (7th Cir. 1969)

Juveniles seeking release from institutionalization have the same right to indigency appeal and counsel as adults.

FACTS: The appellant, now 17 years old and confined to the Wisconsin School for Girls, filed a writ of habeas corpus petition in federal court, seeking to obtain her release from custody.   The federal court denied her petition on the grounds that she had not exhausted her state remedies, but not from lack of trying.   The difficulty at hand had little to do with the merits of the petition— rather, it dealt with her right to appeal *pro bono* and the appropriate local jurisdiction for such an appeal.   On April 10, 1968, the appellant was found to be a delinquent minor and was subject to confinement until the age of 21.   At the adjudication hearing she was represented by voluntary counsel, but was not informed of any of her subsequent constitutional rights to appeal or to have representation by legal counsel.   In July 1968, the appellant filed an affidavit of indigency and a petition for appointment of counsel to assist in her appeal in the county of current confinement.   Her petition was denied, with no consideration of its merits, based on improper filing; with the court contending that such an application and filing was legally the responsibility of the appellant's prior county of residence.   Appellant then refiled both the affidavit and the petition of legal appointment in her county of prior legal residence with the same effect, denial based on jurisdiction.   In October 1968, the Supreme Court of Wisconsin issued an order for each court to show cause for denial; that process was pending at the time of this filing.

ISSUE: Do juveniles have the same right of indigency appeal and appointment of counsel as adults under the Fourteenth Amendment equal protection clause? YES.

DECISION: The equal protection clause of the Fourteenth Amendment requires that juveniles be afforded the same rights and privileges as adults in the appointment of counsel for indigency appeals.

REASON: "*Gault* must be construed as incorporating in juvenile court procedures, which may lead to deprivation of liberty, all of the constitutional safeguards of the Fifth and Sixth Amendments to the Constitution of the United States which apply, by operation of the Fourteenth Amendment, in criminal proceedings. The juvenile must be advised of the charges against him, he may not be denied the right to representation by counsel, he must be advised that counsel will be appointed to represent him, upon request, if he be indigent, the privilege against self-incrimination applies, and any finding of delinquency which may lead to deprivation of liberty cannot stand unless such finding be based upon the sworn testimony of his accusers, subject to the full opportunity for cross-examination. *In re Gault*, 387 U.S. 1, (1967) . . . We must interpret *Gault*, . . . as requiring that Wisconsin may not deny to appellant the right to an effective review of the proceedings which led to her commitment to custody. She cannot be held accountable for any consequences which might attach to the fact that the immediate avenue for review of direct appeal was lost because of her inaction, since it affirmatively appears that she was never advised that she had the right to appeal and the right to have counsel appointed for that purpose. Equal protection of the laws requires that she have an equal opportunity for a first appellate review, and that such proceeding be effective for the full protection of her constitutional rights. Wisconsin does provide preliminary judicial consideration of merit to claims of error by prisoners and does appoint counsel for indigent adult prisoners upon such claims. . . . Appellant here has not been able to obtain any consideration on the merits of her petition or of her right to counsel thereon, apparently because of concern by the courts with what public funds would be used to pay for counsel. Under *Gault*, there can be no constitutionally permissible discrimination between the adult prisoner and the juvenile defendant held in state custody."

CASE SIGNIFICANCE: The issue in this case was the extension of the basic constitutional right to counsel to juveniles who are indigent, for purpose of an appeal. The circumstances of this case were extreme and represented a system's effort to deny the juvenile the right to appeal her adjudication.

The court found that the juvenile was not properly advised of her constitutional rights at adjudication and had no way of knowing that she had constitutional protections during the adjudication process. The court said that because adults must be advised of such rights and provided appropriate assistance in cases of indigency, juveniles must likewise be advised of such rights and afforded assistance. This is logical because juveniles who are indigent deserve at least the same, if not better, protection than adults. Although the case was decided in the late 1960s, the court showed concern with basic constitutional rights and disregarded pure *parens patriae* in favor of due process.

Majchszak v. Ralston
454 F. Supp. 1137 (W.D. Wis. 1978)

Denial of parole as an adult inmate cannot be based on juvenile adjudications that were conducted without legal assistance to the juvenile.

FACTS: A writ of habeas corpus petition was filed by an inmate at the Federal Correctional Institution in Oxford, Wisconsin. The petitioner alleged that he was denied parole after having served 46 months of a 12-year sentence, based on the United States Parole Commission's reliance on his past juvenile court record. The petitioner contended that such reliance violated his Sixth Amendment right because he was not represented by legal counsel in any of his appearances before the juvenile court and was therefore adjudicated delinquent without the benefit of counsel. The petitioner further contended that the Commission's reliance on such old criminal records (1956-1964) did not adequately reflect his current status with regard to public risk and potential success on parole. His internal appeal to the Parole Commission was denied at all levels.

ISSUE: Can the denial of parole of an adult offender be based on juvenile court adjudications at which the juvenile received no legal assistance? NO.

DECISION: In making a parole decision, the United States Parole Commission should not consider juvenile delinquency adjudications made without the benefit of counsel for the juvenile. Where the parole record reflects no acknowledgment of such constitutional infirmity in unrepresented juvenile delinquency cases, but is used in support of the denial of parole, the only appropriate remedy is a new parole hearing.

REASON: "In the context of the present petition, the mandate of *In re Gault* poses three legal questions: first, whether *Gault* should be given retroactive effect; second, whether the *Gault* right to counsel attached to the particular juvenile adjudications which had been entered against this petitioner; and third, if *Gault* is to be applied retroactively, what are to be the consequences of the Commission's consideration of constitutionally defective juvenile adjudications.

"The Constitution neither prohibits nor requires retrospective application of judicial decisions. *Linkwater v. Walker*, 381 U.S. 618 (1965). The retroactive or prospective effect of a new constitutional rule of criminal procedure depends upon 'the peculiar traits of the specific rule in question.' *Johnson v. New Jersey*, 384 U.S. 719 (1966) . . . The resolution of the retroactivity of the right to counsel . . . requires no elaborate analysis. The right to counsel is designed to insure the fundamental fairness of a judicial proceeding. . . . The Court has abided by this principle in requiring retroactive application of its right to counsel decisions where it has been clear that the lack of counsel threatened the integrity of the adjudicatory process. *See Gideon v. Wainwright*, 372 U.S. 335 (1963) . . . Given the affinity between *Gideon* and *Gault*, there can be little question that *Gault*, like *Gideon*, falls within the category requiring retrospective decisions."

CASE SIGNIFICANCE: This case involved the use of juvenile adjudications of delinquency to deny parole to an adult offender years after those adjudications took place. Those juvenile adjudications were made without counsel.

The court ruled that if such adjudications were in fact used by the U.S. Parole Commission in making a determination as to whether to grant parole, they were used inappropriately. However, there was confusion on the part of the court as to whether the denial of parole was in fact based in part on the juvenile adjudications in question because the offender also had several convictions, incarcerations, and parole revocations as an adult. Nonetheless, the court said that if the U.S. Parole Commission had in any way considered any of the juvenile adjudications that were conducted without the benefit of counsel in determining amenability for parole, then the process was tainted. The only recourse the court offered was to hold a new parole hearing using none of the tainted information resulting in a clear parole decision based on usable information.

This case addressed the issue of the use of questionable juvenile adjudications and information in any adult proceeding. If the juvenile process was flawed, the information acquired is tainted and cannot be used against the offender in a subsequent parole proceeding. This is however, only a federal district court decision and is not binding even in other federal district courts. Other federal district courts may decide this same issue differently. What it shows is that in the late 1970s, some courts had interjected due process into proceedings involving former juveniles.

United States v. Riggans
746 F.2d 1379 (9th Cir. 1984)

Due process is not violated by long delays in the service of a probation violation warrant as long as the delay is within statutory guidelines.

FACTS: Riggans, as a juvenile sentenced under the Youth Corrections Act (YCA) to probation, violated that probation. A bench warrant remained unserved for four years, even though Riggans was never a fugitive and filed all change of address forms with the U.S. Post Office. When Riggans finally appeared in court in response to the warrant, he was no longer the juvenile seen by the court four years earlier and was sentenced to three years as an adult. On appeal, that sentence was vacated. Upon remand, the court sentenced Riggans to the custody of the United States Attorney General as a "youth." Riggans contended that the four-year delay in service of the warrant was entirely at the hands of the government because he never tried to hide his residence at any time during the period. The government contended that Riggans failed to perform his obligation to contact his probation officer on a regular basis and thus his failure caused the delay.

ISSUE: Was the four-year delay in the service of a warrant for probation revocation a violation of the appellant's due process rights? NO.

DECISION: The juvenile identified no prejudice other than the unwarranted interruption of his life after he thought he had been forgotten by the government. In this case, the issuance and execution of the warrant fell clearly within an established five-year period provided for by statute and therefore there was no deprivation of due process.

REASON: "In *United States v. Wickham*, 618 F.2d 1307, 1310 (9th Cir. 1979), we said:

> Ordinarily, to challenge a revocation proceeding, the delay must have been caused by government action that was not the result of the probationer's own criminal conduct. In addition, the delay must have prejudicially affected the probationer's ability to contest revocation. Prejudice might result from delays causing probationers difficulty in contesting the alleged facts constituting a violation of their release conditions; hardship in finding and presenting favorable witnesses; or inability to produce evidence of mitigating circumstances which might result in continued probation despite the violation.

"Riggans has pointed to no prejudice other than the unwanted interruption of his life after he thought he had been forgotten by the government.

"Recently, we considered delay between the issuance of a probation bench warrant and its execution in the context of the district court's jurisdiction and announced guidelines in determining whether jurisdiction was retained. *United States v. Hill*, 719 F.2d 1402 (9th Cir. 1983). In *Hill*, the bench warrant was not issued until four years after the probation violation and was not executed for another two and a half years, at a time when a five-year period provided by 18 U.S.C. § 3651, 3653 (1976 & Supp. III 1979) had expired. We held that the

issuance of the bench warrant long after the probation violation and shortly before the running of the five years would not toll the five years to give the government unlimited leisure in which to arrest a defaulting probationer. In the
case at bar, issuance and execution of the warrant fall clearly within the five-
year period provided by the statute . . . We find no deprivation of due process.
The sentence may appear to be somewhat at odds with conventional approaches
to rehabilitation, but we cannot characterize it as an abuse of discretion or a
violation of any constitutional or statutory right."

CASE SIGNIFICANCE: The question in this case related to the service of a
warrant for the violation of a juvenile probation term. The statute governing
service of warrants allowed the government five years after the violation in
which to serve a revocation warrant. The warrant was served four years after
the juvenile violated his probationary term.

The juvenile contended that the delay in service of the warrant was entirely
the fault of the government because he had never tried to conceal his whereabouts and had faithfully registered change of address forms with the United
States Post Office after each change in residence. The government maintained
that the juvenile's failure to contact his probation officer on a regular basis
constituted a breach of his obligation to the court and therefore caused the delay
in service.

The court ruled in favor of the government, saying that, procedurally,
service of the warrant any time prior to the five-year expiration date negates any
contention of lack of due process on the part of the government. The court
noted some confusion about the intent of service of the warrant four years after
the violation of probation, although it appeared that the juvenile made significant strides in turning his life around. However, even though the court questioned the rationale for such action, it could find no basis for reversing the juvenile court's decision and allowed the service of the warrant and the consequences therefrom to stand.

The reasons behind such service after four years are questionable. By all
accounts, the juvenile in this case had succeeded and was rehabilitated, yet he
was subjected to penalty after four years of success on probation after the violation. Whether the action taken was wise is open to debate, but its constitutionality was upheld.

Watts v. Hadden
627 F. Supp. 727 (D. Colo. 1986)

Offenders sentenced under special laws are to be afforded the benefits of those laws until no other such offenders remain in the system.

FACTS: This was a class action case on behalf of all persons committed for treatment under the Youth Corrections Act (YCA). The appeal focused on offenders who remained incarcerated as the result of a YCA designation, even though the Act itself was repealed in October 1984. The appellants contended that as the number of YCA commitments declined, the Federal Bureau of Prisons and the United States Parole Commission focused less emphasis on those who remained in the system and their mandate as charged in the YCA, such that youthful offenders were not receiving appropriate classification to determine treatment needs, treatment needs were not being addressed, progress reports were not being developed and reported to the Parole Commission, and the Parole Commission was not assuming joint responsibility for the appropriate treatment of offenders committed under the YCA.

ISSUE: Are controlling agencies responsible for continuing treatment of the offender population sentenced under specialized acts that have since been repealed? YES.

DECISION: The Bureau of Prisons and the United States Parole Commission are jointly responsible for determining the appropriate treatment required for inmates sentenced under the YCA. This responsibility does not decrease as the affected population dwindles and stays until no YCA offenders remain in the system.

REASON: "While the YCA was repealed on October 21, 1984 . . ., the repeal is of no effect on the present issues because persons committed under the Act must be treated according to the requirements of the statute.

"For its part, the Parole Commission continues to contend that regardless of program participation, the offense severity is a primary factor, and that emphasis on offense severity is necessary to reduce disparity which erodes confidence in the criminal justice system. The YCA expressly contemplates disparity in the length of confinement of inmates convicted of the same or similar offenses. That is precisely why the Act was adopted as an alternative to the sentence which would otherwise be required by law. Again, it is necessary to emphasize that which the Supreme Court said thirteen years ago in *Dorszynski. The execution of the sentence must fit the person, not the crime for which he was convicted.*

"A second requirement is that the Director through his delegate, the Warden, or some other staff position, shall develop a system for periodic reporting on the inmate's progress in treatment, with written reports and interim evaluations to go to the Parole Commission no less frequently than at six-month intervals. Additionally, the Director shall, through the Warden or other delegate, cause a . . . recommendation for conditional release to be made to the Parole Commission, with a report of findings and sufficient statement of reasons to give the Parole Commission an understanding of the individual inmate's status and the basis for the Director's judgment. To make these periodic reports and release recommendations meaningful, the Parole Commission will be required to conduct conditional release interviews with each inmate within ninety days of the receipt of the interim reports and within sixty days of the receipt of the release recommendation.

. . . "It may well be that with the declining population the use of contract facilities will become more appropriate for the particular treatment needs of individuals under the YCA, and that for appropriate and articulated reasons, an inmate may be placed with a contract agency even though there would then be no segregation from adults. These are matters which are not now before this court in this case. They are mentioned only to remind the respondents that there are alternatives which can be considered in performing the difficult task of treating YCA inmates under the changed circumstances resulting from repeal of the Act."

CASE SIGNIFICANCE: This case dealt with the issue of a continuing obligation to implement specialized programming attached to sentencing acts even after repeal of the legislation. The Federal Bureau of Prisons was forced to continue the provisions of a youthful offender act which required that offenders declared by the court to be youthful offenders be treated differently from the general population, providing segregated housing and specialized programming designed to meet the needs of the individual youthful offender. Furthermore, the U.S. Parole Commission was required by the court to review offenders sentenced under specialized acts by the rules and criteria for return established in those acts, not prevailing adult sentencing statutes.

Even when the population of specialized offenders in the system has dwindled to a few, the requirement of special group care and consideration does not end. It ends only when there are no more offenders sentenced under such provision. Then the prison system may discontinue such programs and practices and integrate all populations into their general population.

The repeal of a law does not retroactively negate the provisions of the original sentence nor subject the youthful offender to longer periods of incarceration due to new release criteria or ignorance of the provisions of the original sentencing act, regardless of current practice. What is owed under law to a group is owed to everyone in that group. This is a case based on federal law. State courts, when faced with a similar problem, may decide differently, particularly if state law provides otherwise.

J.K.A. v. State
855 S.W.2d 58 (Tex. App. 1993)

Full due process proceedings are not required when the court reviews a violation of a probation condition for revocation purposes.

FACTS: A juvenile court found that J.K.A. had engaged in delinquent conduct by committing a burglary. The court committed him to the Texas Youth Commission (TYC) but suspended the sentence, placing him in his mother's custody under the supervision of the Juvenile Probation Department for a period of one year. Later, J.K.A. was caught with a gun at school; a violation of his probation conditions. Modification of custody proceedings were begun, alleging a violation of a rule of probation and requesting the court to enter further custody orders. The court held a revocation hearing, revoking J.K.A.'s probation and committing him to the Texas Youth Commission. J.K.A. appealed, not contesting the revocation of probation or the commitment to TYC, but instead challenging the wording of the court order. In effect, J.K.A. was asking for clarification that he had not been adjudicated delinquent on a new felony charge but was instead revoked based on his failure to meet the conditions of probation.

ISSUES:
1. In modifying the disposition proceeding, did the court find the juvenile delinquent of a new felony charge or did the court merely revoke based on a violation of a condition of probation?

2. If the juvenile was found delinquent on a new felony charge, was full due process afforded the juvenile? NO.

DECISIONS:
1. The court's order modifying the disposition and revoking probation was based on the court's finding that the juvenile had violated a reasonable and lawful order of the court.

2. The juvenile was not found delinquent based on the felony charge of possession of a weapon, even though the weapon offense was the reason for seeking incarceration of the juvenile probationer. Therefore, the court was

not required to conduct a full due process adjudication hearing to find that the juvenile had violated a rule of probation.

REASON: "We . . . hold that the trial court was not required to conduct a full due process hearing to find that J.K.A. violated a reasonable and lawful order of the court, i.e., violated a rule of probation. The trial court's judgment/order modifying disposition adjudicated that J.K.A. violated a court order, neither a felony nor a misdemeanor. Therefore, the somewhat reduced due process safeguards . . . were adequate.

"It may very well be that J.K.A. would benefit from the longer commitment to the TYC and the greater restriction. But J.K.A. is entitled to due process safeguards appropriate to the seriousness of the alleged offense and the degree of infringement on his liberty interest. If the State wants an adjudication of felonious delinquent conduct with its serious classification implications, it must afford an opportunity for a full . . . adjudication hearing. On the other hand, if the State merely wishes to modify a disposition by obtaining a finding that the youth violated a reasonable and lawful order of the court, then a . . . hearing to modify disposition is all that is required."

CASE SIGNIFICANCE: This case dealt with the type of due process necessary to adjudicate a juvenile delinquent versus the type of due process needed to revoke a juvenile's probation for a violation of a condition of probation, which is a lower category falling under Conduct In Need of Supervision (CINS) under Texas law. The juvenile in this case engaged in a new offense—carrying a gun on school property—but was not charged with or adjudicated for the crime itself, rather the crime became the basis for an order to modify a current disposition based on violating a reasonable and lawful condition of probation. However, the court's order revoking probation was unclear as to whether the juvenile was found delinquent on a new felony charge or was merely removed from probation based on a violation of the conditions of his probation.

The significance of this case rests in the distinction made between the type of due process necessary for adjudication and revocation hearings. A lower standard is needed for revocation hearings. This case also articulates the difference between adjudication for a new felony and revocation of probation based on an alleged felony. Adjudication requires more due process guarantees than does revocation. This is the same rule in adult probation cases.

In the Matter of Lucio F.T.
888 P.2d 958 (N.M. App. 1994)

The use of an adult conviction in the revocation of a juvenile's probation does not constitute double jeopardy.

FACTS: The appellant, while still a juvenile, was charged with the commission of three criminal acts, two of which were dismissed. Lucio F.T. admitted guilt to the third and was adjudicated delinquent. He was placed on two years probation by the juvenile court. Less than two hours after being placed on probation, the appellant was arrested for possession of alcohol, concealing his identity, evading an officer, and resisting arrest. Because Lucio F.T. was 18 years old at the time of the latter offenses, he was processed through municipal court. On the day of the adult filing, the juvenile court received a petition to revoke the appellant's probation based on the filing of adult charges. Lucio F.T. pled guilty to all adult charges, was fined, and he was then transferred to a juvenile detention center where two weeks later his probation with the juvenile court was revoked and he was committed to the Children, Youth and Families Department, New Mexico Boys' School for a term not to exceed two years.

ISSUE: Did the use of adult charges as the basis for revoking a concurrent juvenile probation sentence violate the constitutional prohibition against double jeopardy? NO.

DECISION: Proceedings in juvenile court to revoke prior juvenile probation due to adult offenses for which the appellant had been convicted in municipal court did not amount to new or separate punishment and therefore did not constitute double jeopardy.

REASON: "Double jeopardy protects defendants from more than one criminal prosecution for the same criminal offense. . . . A probation revocation proceeding is not a new criminal trial to impose new punishment, but instead 'is a hearing to determine whether, during the probationary . . . period, the defendant has conformed to or breached the course of conduct outlined in the probation . . . order.'

"Since probation revocation proceedings are not directed at attempting to punish the original criminal activity but merely reassess whether the probationer may still be considered a good risk, the federal courts have routinely concluded that double jeopardy is not implicated in adult probation revocation proceedings. . . . State courts in other jurisdictions have similarly concluded, with respect to adult offenders, that any punishment resulting from revocation of a defendant's probation is punishment that relates to the person's original offense, therefore, an individual's subsequent prosecution for the same conduct in a new proceeding does not violate double jeopardy principles.

"We find that no significant legal reason exists to reach a different result regarding application of the Double Jeopardy Clause to a child from the rule applied in the case of an adult."

CASE SIGNIFICANCE: This case involved a complicated set of circumstances in which charges filed against an 18-year-old, which were processed through adult municipal court, were used to support a revocation of probation in juvenile court.

The court found that charges filed as an adult can be used as the basis for revoking a juvenile's probation with no double jeopardy violation. This case highlights the increasing overlap between adult and juvenile courts at multiple levels within the system and the difficulty in determining what information is proper for use in a probation revocation hearing.

The offender in this case pled guilty to charges in adult municipal court and paying a fine. The same charges were then used against him in juvenile court to revoke his probation and send him to a secure juvenile facility for a period of two years—thus, at least superficially, punishing him twice for the same crime. However, the court, relying on a comparison to adult revocation cases, found that the revocation hearing was not an attempt to punish the offender, but merely a reassessment of risk. The rule at present is that double jeopardy applies to juvenile adjudication (the equivalent of a trial), but the use of an adult conviction in revoking a juvenile's probation does not constitute double jeopardy.

Matter of Tapley
865 P.2d 12 (Wash. App. 1994)

Different release policies do not violate the equal protection clause as long as they do not establish an expectation that the minimum release date is the actual release date.

FACTS: In 1991 and 1992 respectfully, Todd Tapley and Daniel Brixey were sentenced as juveniles under the standard sentencing range used by the juvenile court. Both juveniles were subsequently placed at the Green Hill School, a serious-offender juvenile correctional facility operated by the Department of Social and Health Services (DSHS), Division of Juvenile Rehabilitation (DJR). Upon entry to Green Hill, Tapley and Brixey were each assigned a release date based on the Treatment Behavior Contract (TBC) method in which the juvenile and a counselor meet and sign a "contract" establishing individual treatment and behavior expectations for each juvenile. Under the TBC method, a maximum initial release date is set, but by fulfilling the conditions of the "contract" the juvenile can work off days toward a minimum release date. Of the five juvenile institutions in Washington, Green Hill is the only facility utilizing the TBC method for establishing release dates; all others use a minimum release date of 60 percent of the time set by the juvenile court. The actual release date is based on the juvenile's behavior up to that point. In both Tapley and Brixey's cases, periodic reviews of their agreed-upon conduct "contract" found both juveniles in non-compliance with the agreed-upon goals, and thus each received less than the maximum number of "good time" days allowed. Both juveniles filed suit, challenging the release procedures in place at Green Hill School.

ISSUE: Does an institutional release policy utilizing a progressive behavior contract system violate a juvenile's due process and equal protection rights? NO.

DECISION: Release policies of this nature do not deprive juveniles of their right to due process as long as administrative regulations and policies do not create an expectation that a juvenile's release date will be the minimum amount of time possible. The procedural differences used by juvenile facilities regarding the manner in which juvenile minimum release dates are calculated do not violate the equal protection clause.

REASON: ". . . [W]e find that . . . the DJR policy guidelines do not create an expectation or protected interest in being released at the minimum. . . . Clearly, [the] provision contemplates some form of procedure in the setting of release dates beyond the minimum term. When read in its entirety, however, this provision does not create an expectation that a juvenile's release date will be set at the minimum in the absence of a formal administrative review. Rather, this provision simply provides a procedure whereby a juvenile is entitled to an opportunity to review the material being considered and to be told why a release date beyond the minimum is being established. . . . [T]he TBC method is not so inconsistent with the procedural requirements of DJR [guidelines] to raise a colorable due process issue.

"Even assuming that petitioners have established membership in a class, we must reject their equal protection claim in light of the fact that no showing of disparate treatment under the law has been established. While the manner by which Green Hill juveniles receive their initial release date differs from the approach taken at other facilities, Green Hill juveniles, nevertheless, are not penalized or treated differently from the juveniles at other facilities. Rather, at all institutions, including Green Hill, a juvenile's behavior is determinative. That is, despite minor differences in procedure, all juveniles must earn their minimum release date through good behavior."

CASE SIGNIFICANCE: This case focuses on the methods of determining release in juvenile institutions. There was conflict between a minimum release date system and a progressive behavior contract system, both of which were used in juvenile facilities in a single state. The juveniles in this case contended that they were denied equal protection due to their placement in the facility that used the progressive behavior contract system. They further alleged that their incarceration under such a system resulted in a longer stay in the institution in comparison to their peers who were housed in facilities that utilized the minimum release date system.

The court ruled in favor of the state, saying that they found no indication of the existence of an expected date of release or a protected liberty interest in setting such a date. Instead it found that at all institutions the date of release, whether articulated or not, was merely a target date and that the actual date of release was based on the juvenile's behavior during the institutionalization. Even though the actual process using a progressive behavior contract system was different, it was not in conflict with the minimum release date system in use at other sites and therefore was a constitutional exercise of discretion by the state.

J.R.W. v. State
879 S.W.2d 254 (Tex. App. 1994)

A trial court does not exceed its authority in transferring a juvenile to prison on his or her eighteenth birthday, as allowed by state law.

FACTS: A juvenile court adjudicated the appellant delinquent after a jury found that he committed attempted capital murder, aggravated kidnapping, and unauthorized use of a motor vehicle. The jury recommended and the court imposed a 30-year determinate sentence to the Texas Youth Commission (TYC). After serving 22 months (near his eighteenth birthday), the court held a release hearing. At that hearing the court had essentially three options: (1) discharge the juvenile from court jurisdiction; (2) transfer the juvenile to the Texas Department of Criminal Justice (TDCJ) (to an adult correctional facility); or (3) remand to TYC without a determinate sentence, allowing TYC to release when it deems appropriate. The court heard testimony from state officials in support of continuation with TYC in a less restrictive setting, even though those who testified acknowledged that J.R.W.'s behavior during the 22 months in TYC custody had been less than exemplary—he slept through some group sessions, was lazy and uncooperative, had problems with authority, and appeared to admire only those with money and power. On the positive side, during his 22 month stay with TYC he had completed his GED and received a welding certificate. The court also heard testimony from law enforcement officials involved in the original case and from the victim's girlfriend attesting to the public risk associated with the appellant's release and the harm caused to the victim by the appellant. Based on all the evidence presented to the court, the court ordered the appellant transferred to TDCJ for incarceration in an adult facility upon his eighteenth birthday. The juvenile appealed.

ISSUE: Did the court exceed its authority in deciding to continue custody of a juvenile adjudicated delinquent in prison upon his turning 18? NO.

DECISION: Trial courts in juvenile proceedings have broad power and discretion. The decision to transfer the delinquent juvenile to an adult prison on his eighteenth birthday, as authorized by state law, was supported by the evidence presented. The court did not abuse its discretion by not following the recommendations of the staff. The responsibility for proper placement of the juvenile was with the court.

REASON: "Under an abuse of discretion review, we reverse the trial court only if the trial court has acted in an unreasonable or arbitrary manner. We may not reverse for an abuse of discretion because we disagree with the trial court's decision as long as that decision was within the trial court's discretionary authority. . . . The record shows the trial court decided to transfer appellant to TDCJ based on the considerations listed in parts (d) and (j) of section 54.11. The trial court followed the guiding statute in deciding the issue. . . . After review of the entire record, we conclude the trial court did not abuse its discretion in transferring appellant to TDCJ."

CASE SIGNIFICANCE: This case dealt with the issue of "roll-over" statutes, which afforded the juvenile court the option of adjusting a juvenile delinquent's sentence as he nears the age of majority. In this case, one of the options was to continue institutionalization of the juvenile in an adult state prison. This is the option the juvenile court chose. The court's decision caused the juvenile to be moved from his present location to a prison facility with adult offenders.

The court, using the "abuse of discretion standard," upheld the juvenile court's ruling, finding that the juvenile court acted reasonably. The court followed Texas law by reviewing evidence indicating that the juvenile had problems with authority, had previously violated court orders, was very self-centered, and was not concerned about the impact of his actions upon others.

The appellate court went on to say that even if it disagreed with the juvenile court's decision, it would still uphold the decision because its role is not to second-guess the juvenile court, but rather to ensure adherence to any procedure, guiding rules and principles, or other due process issues as relevant.

This case was decided under the Texas Determinate Sentencing Law, which allows the adjudication of a juvenile for a specified number of offenses in juvenile court with all the rights adults have in a criminal trial. If the juvenile is adjudicated delinquent, he or she could be sent to a juvenile facility and then, after a hearing, be transferred to an adult prison on his or her eighteenth birthday. That procedure was followed here. The appellate court held that there was basis for such a transfer.

This case is significant because it implicitly declared the law to be valid and therefore allowed the transfer. This procedure is peculiar in that the original juvenile hearing provided all the constitutional rights given to adult criminal defendants. Without those constitutional rights, the procedure would likely not be valid because juvenile cases are generally considered civil cases. The law involved here is another example of the "get tough" policies states are using with serious juvenile offenders.

In re Interest of Thomas W.
530 N.W.2d 291 (Neb. App. 1995)

A detailed written statement of evidence relied upon in a probation revocation proceeding is not essential as long as the record is preserved in some manner for appeal.

FACTS: The appellant was charged with theft, burglary, and criminal mischief. At the adjudication hearing, the juvenile pled guilty to the theft charge, and the burglary and criminal mischief charges were dropped. As a result of the delinquency finding, the juvenile was placed on 12 months probation with 75 hours of community service, and ordered to pay restitution and court costs. Ten months later, the appellant admitted to being a minor in possession of alcohol and possession of drug paraphernalia. A motion was entered with the juvenile court to revoke the appellant's probation based on the new admissions. The appellant was placed on 24 months of intensive supervision probation with specific conditions, including: attending school, without expulsion or truancy; not violating local, state, or federal law; and refraining from associating with current or former friends from Pleasant Dale, Nebraska. With the appellant's counsel and state attorney's support, the intensive supervision probation sentence served as both the revocation disposition and the disposition for the new charge. Nine months later, the state filed a motion to revoke the intensive probation in both cases, based on alleged violations of the three specific conditions in the intensive supervision order.

ISSUE: Did the juvenile court err in failing to issue a detailed written statement of the evidence it relied on and the reasons for revoking probation? NO.

DECISION: The written statement requirement for revocation of a juvenile's probation is satisfied if a judge's oral statement, recorded by a court reporter, taken together with the revocation order, reveals the evidence relied upon and the reasons for revocation. There is no need for a written statement.

REASON: ". . . [T]he Nebraska Legislature enacted sec. 43-286(4) in order to afford juveniles due process in the context of probation revocation hearings. The legislative history of [the law] reveals that the Legislature intended to afford juveniles the same procedures as were outlined in *Morrissey v. Brewer*, 408 U.S. 471 (1972) and *Gagnon v. Scarpelli*, 411 U.S. 778 (1973), including a written statement of evidence relied upon and reasons for revocation of parole. Cases subsequent to *Morrissey* and *Gagnon* have held that the written statement requirement is satisfied if the trial judge orally gives a statement of evidence relied upon and reasons for revocation, and if those oral statements are transcribed and included in the record on appeal.

"Consistent with the above authority, we find that the written statement requirement contained in sec. 43-286(4)(f) is satisfied if the judge's oral statements appearing in a bill of exceptions from the revocation hearing, as well as in the revocation order, when taken together, reveal the evidence relied upon and reasons for the revocation. We believe that our holding today adequately preserves the juvenile's due process rights by ensuring accurate fact-finding and establishing a record for appellate review. Further, our holding today allows a juvenile judge to refer to his or her oral statements made on the record rather than to regurgitate such statements word for word in a separate written statement or order."

CASE SIGNIFICANCE: The issue in this case was how detailed a written reason for revocation of a juvenile's probation a court must have in order for the revocation to be upheld on appeal. The juvenile contended that a full and detailed statement of evidence relied upon, assumptions made, and findings utilized must accompany a dispositional modification. The state responded that a mere reflection of factors utilized by the court is sufficient support for a judicial determination to revoke probation in juvenile court.

The court agreed with the state, saying that requiring the court to repeat factors and findings that support probation revocation is redundant when the court record reflects the consideration of such factors and findings and is in fact a waste of the court's time. The only exception would be a set of circumstances in which the factors, findings, etc. were not accurately reflected in the court transcripts and therefore were inaccessible to all parties unless clearly articulated by the juvenile court judge for inclusion within the judicial record. This case says that juveniles are entitled to due process prior to revocation, but such does not include a detailed written statement of the evidence relied upon for revocation.

In the Interest of D.S. and J.V., Minor Children
652 So. 2d 892 (Fla. App. 1995)

Probation restrictions on juvenile association are allowable as long as they can be reasonably enforced.

FACTS: D.S. and J.V. were found guilty in circuit court of simple battery and placed on community control. As one of the conditions of their community control sentence, they were not to associate with gang members. The juveniles appealed.

ISSUE: Are restrictions on the freedom of association of a juvenile constitutional? YES.

DECISION: The condition that juvenile delinquents not associate with gang members was proper. However, sanctions for violating such condition could be enforced only if it could be proved that the juvenile knew that the individuals with whom he was associating were gang members.

REASON: ". . . [J]ust as any violation of probation must include the element of intent, there would have to be a showing that D.S. *knew* the individuals were gang members before he could be found guilty of *knowingly* violating such a provision."

CASE SIGNIFICANCE: The sole issue in this case was the validity of a probation condition that restricted the association of a juvenile while under the supervision of probation. In this case, the condition prohibited association with gang members.

The court ruled that restrictions on association were allowable as long as they could be reasonably enforced. The state had to prove that the juvenile had prior knowledge that the person with whom he was associating was a gang member before he could be held in violation of the condition. The concept of "knowingly violating a condition" applies and requires that the state bring evidence to prove that the juvenile was actually aware of his violation of probation conditions. Prior knowledge by the probation officer or other state officials is not sufficient to prove the violation—the juvenile himself must be aware of who he is associating with, and this must be established by the state.

Privacy and Confidentiality of Juvenile Records and Proceedings

11

I. United States Supreme Court Cases

Davis v. Alaska (1974)
Smith v. Daily Mail Publishing Co. (1979)

II. Lower Court Cases

In re Smith (1970)
In re J.D.C. (1991)
United States v. Three Juveniles (1994)
State v. Acheson (1994)

Introduction

The juvenile court was created to protect the identity of the child and to ensure that the processes of the juvenile justice system protected the juvenile's privacy. Historically, the juvenile court process has been closed—juvenile court proceedings were not open to the public or the media, juvenile records were closed, and the names of juveniles and their offense records were confidential.[1]

The concept of juvenile courts being closed has been questioned. Some suggest that the protection of the juvenile's privacy by closing the juvenile justice system has allowed the system to exist with virtually no public access. Thus, the juvenile justice system has existed with virtually no accountability.[2] Others question whether the increase of serious juvenile crime warrants more public and media access to a system whose effectiveness is under question.[3] Torbet et al. suggest that the "dynamic tension" of the conflict about opening juvenile records is a result of the public's "right to know" directly confronting the juvenile's "right to privacy."[4] The reason for the tension is the demand by the public that the juvenile justice system protect society. This conflicts with the philosophical underpinnings of the juvenile system, which has historically been to protect the child.[5]

Recent changes have been made in the laws regarding the confidentiality of juvenile records and the openness of juvenile court proceedings. Today, 22 states have provisions that allow, or even mandate, open juvenile court in some circumstances. Often the case must involve a repeat, violent, or serious juvenile offender.[6] In addition, the juvenile codes of about 50 percent of the states allow for the public to receive information about juvenile records in some instances, and school administrators in 13 states have the right to some information regarding juvenile offenders who attend their schools.[7] Thirty-nine states also have provisions in their juvenile statutes for public or media release of a serious, violent, or repeat juvenile offender's name and picture.[8]

Juvenile record confidentiality is related to the issue of whether a juvenile's record should follow the juvenile into adulthood. Currently, juveniles in 48 states are allowed, in some cases, to have their records expunged or sealed.[9] One area in which there has been a major change in the handling of juvenile records is inclusion of prior juvenile records in criminal court action. The National Institute of Justice reports that "[v]irtually all states have enacted legislation requiring presentence reports to include prior juvenile records."[10]

The cases chosen for this chapter are a cross-section of the holdings of the courts on the issue of juvenile confidentiality. In 1974, the U.S. Supreme Court held in *Davis v. Alaska* that a juvenile witness who is on juvenile probation can have that status brought out in the cross-examination at a criminal trial. In 1979, in *Smith v. Daily Mail Publishing Co.*, the Supreme Court held that the state cannot make it criminal for a newspaper to publish a juvenile's name if that name is lawfully obtained. *In re Smith* (1970) is a lower court case that addressed the issues of the confidentiality of records when a petition is withdrawn for lack of evidence.

Some later cases in lower courts are included in this chapter to demonstrate that the issue of records, confidentiality, and privacy are issues with which the courts are still grappling. *In re J.D.C.* (1991) focuses on the issue of future harm from continued media exposure, and the case of *United States v. Three Juveniles* (1994) addresses the issue of blocking the media from the juvenile court. *State v. Acheson* (1994) held that juveniles can be required by state law to register as sexual offenders under state sexual offender registration laws.

The small number of cases resolved by the courts on the issues of privacy and confidentiality demonstrates that these issues are still evolving and that these issues are better resolved in legislative bodies rather than in the courts.

Notes

[1] Patricia Torbet, Richard Gable, Hunter Hurst IV, Imogene Montgomery, Linda Szymanski, and Douglas Thomas. *State Responses to Serious and Violent Juvenile Crime*. Washington, DC: National Center for Juvenile Justice. Office of Juvenile Justice and Delinquency Prevention. U.S. Department of Justice, Office of Justice Programs (1996).

[2] Ira Schwartz, *Justice for Juveniles: Rethinking the Best Interests of the Child* (1989).

[3] Robert Regoli and John Hewitt, *Delinquency in Society*, Third Edition. (1997).

[4] Patricia Torbet, Richard Gable, Hunter Hurst IV, Imogene Montgomery, Linda Szymanski, and Douglas Thomas. *State Responses to Serious and Violent Juvenile Crime*. Washington, DC: National Center for Juvenile Justice. Office of Juvenile Justice and Delinquency Prevention. U.S. Department of Justice, Office of Justice Programs (1996).

[5] Patricia Torbet, Richard Gable, Hunter Hurst IV, Imogene Montgomery, Linda Szymanski, and Douglas Thomas. *State Responses to Serious and Violent Juvenile Crime*. Washington, DC: National Center for Juvenile Justice. Office of Juvenile Justice and Delinquency Prevention. U.S. Department of Justice, Office of Justice Programs (1996).

[6] Patricia Torbet, Richard Gable, Hunter Hurst IV, Imogene Montgomery, Linda Szymanski, and Douglas Thomas. *State Responses to Serious and Violent Juvenile Crime*. Washington, DC: National Center for Juvenile Justice. Office of Juvenile

Justice and Delinquency Prevention. U.S. Department of Justice, Office of Justice Programs (1996).

[7] Robert Regoli and John Hewit, *Delinquency in Society*, Third Edition. (1997).

[8] Patricia Torbet, Richard Gable, Hunter Hurst IV, Imogene Montgomery, Linda Szymanski, and Douglas Thomas. *State Responses to Serious and Violent Juvenile Crime.* Washington, DC: National Center for Juvenile Justice. Office of Juvenile Justice and Delinquency Prevention. U.S. Department of Justice, Office of Justice Programs (1996).

[9] National Institute of Justice, *State Laws on Prosecutors' and Judges' Use of Juvenile Records.* Washington, DC: U.S. Department of Justice, Office of Justice Programs (1995).

[10] National Institute of Justice, *State Laws on Prosecutors' and Judges' Use of Juvenile Records.* Washington, DC: U.S. Department of Justice, Office of Justice Programs (1995) at 1.

I. UNITED STATES SUPREME COURT CASES

Davis v. Alaska
415 U.S. 308 (1974)

Despite state confidentiality laws, the probation status of a juvenile witness may be brought out by the opposing lawyer on cross-examination.

FACTS: Davis was convicted of grand larceny and burglary in an Alaska court. A key prosecution witness during the trial was Richard Green, a juvenile. The trial court, on motion of the prosecuting attorney, issued a protective order prohibiting the defendant's attorney from questioning Green about his having been adjudicated as a juvenile delinquent because of a burglary he had committed and about his probation status at the time of the events about which he was to testify. The Court's protective order was based on state law protecting the anonymity of juvenile offenders.

ISSUE: Does the confrontation clause of the Sixth Amendment allow a defendant in a criminal case to bring out the probation status of a juvenile witness on cross-examination, even if state law protects the anonymity of juvenile offenders? YES.

DECISION: The accused in a criminal trial is entitled to confront and cross-examine witnesses under the Sixth and Fourteenth Amendments. This right prevails over a state policy protecting the anonymity of juvenile offenders.

REASON: "The Sixth Amendment to the Constitution guarantees the right of an accused in a criminal proceeding 'to be confronted with the witnesses against him.' This right is secure for defendants in state as well as federal proceedings under *Pointer v. Texas*, 380 U.S. 400 (1965). Confrontation means more than being allowed to confront the witness physically. 'Our cases construing the [confrontation] clause hold that a primary interest secured by it is the right to cross-examination' *Douglas v. Alabama*, 380 U.S. 415, 418 (1965).

"Cross-examination is the principle means by which the believability of a witness and the truth of his testimony are tested. Subject always to the broad discretion of a trial judge to preclude repetitive and unduly harassing interrogation, the cross-examiner is not only permitted to delve into the witness' story to test the witness' perceptions and memory, but the cross-examiner has traditionally been allowed to impeach, i.e., discredit, the witness. One way of discrediting the witness is to introduce evidence of a prior criminal conviction of that witness. By doing so the cross-examiner intends to afford the jury a basis to infer that the witness' character is such that he would be less likely than the average trustworthy citizen to be truthful in his testimony. The introduction of evidence of prior crime is thus a general attack on the credibility of the witness. A more particular attack on the witness credibility is effected by means of cross-examination directed toward revealing possible biases, prejudices, or ulterior motives of the witness as they may relate directly to issues or personalities in the case at hand. The partiality of a witness is subject to exploration at trial, and is 'always relevant as discrediting the witness and affecting the weight of his testimony.' 3A J. Wigmore, *Evidence* [Sec] 940, p. 775 (Chadbourn rev. 1970). We have recognized that the exposure of a witness' motivation in testifying is a proper and important function of the constitutionally protected right of cross-examination."

CASE SIGNIFICANCE: The message in this case is clear: the constitutional right of a criminal defendant to confrontation and cross-examination prevails over state policy, embodied in state law, that assures the anonymity of juvenile offenders.

In this case, the lawyer for the petitioner wanted to introduce Green's juvenile record to show at the time that Green was assisting the police in identifying the accused, Green was on probation for burglary and therefore acted out of fear or concern of possible revocation of probation if he did not provide the testimony needed by the police. The lawyer for the accused wanted to show that Green might have made a quick and faulty identification of the accused to shift suspicion away from himself as one of the possible perpetrators, and also that Green's identification of the accused may have been made out of fear of possible probation revocation, were Green found to be somehow involved in the crime. This attempt to make public, in court, Green's probation status was denied by the trial judge because of state law providing anonymity to juveniles. The Court disagreed with the trial judge's ruling and held that because Green was a key witness, his probation status could be disclosed.

What the Court did here was balance an accused's rights to a fair trial and a juvenile's right, under state law, to anonymity. The Court concluded that "the right of confrontation is paramount to the State's policy of protecting a juvenile offender," adding that "whatever temporary embarrassment might result to Green or his family by disclosure of his juvenile record . . . is outweighed by petitioner's right to probe into the influence of possible bias in the testimony of a crucial identification witness." In sum, between an accused's constitutional right and a state policy to protect juveniles from disclosure of records, the accused's constitutional right prevails.

Smith v. Daily Mail Publishing Co.
443 U.S. 97 (1979)

A state law making it a crime to publish the name of a juvenile charged with a crime is unconstitutional.

FACTS: A 15-year-old student was shot and killed at a junior high school. A 14-year-old classmate was identified by seven eyewitnesses as the assailant and was arrested soon after the incident. The *Charleston Daily Mail* and the *Charleston Gazette* routinely monitored the police band radio frequency and, upon learning of the shooting, dispatched reporters and photographers to the scene of the shooting. Both newspapers obtained the name of the alleged assailant from various witnesses, the police, and an assistant prosecuting attorney, who were at the school.

Both newspapers published articles about the incident. The *Daily Mail*'s first article did not mention the juvenile suspect's name because of a Virginia statute prohibiting such publication without prior court approval. The *Gazette* published both the juvenile's name and picture in its article. The name of the alleged attacker was also broadcast over at least three radio stations on the days the newspaper articles appeared. Because the juvenile's name had become public knowledge, the *Daily Mail* included the information in a subsequent article it printed. An indictment was brought against both papers alleging that each had knowingly published the name of the juvenile, in violation of state statute.

ISSUE: Does a state statute that makes it a crime for a newspaper to publish, without written approval of the juvenile court, the name of any youth charged as a juvenile offender violate the First and Fourteenth Amendments to the Constitution? YES.

DECISION: The state cannot punish the truthful publication of an alleged juvenile delinquent's name lawfully obtained by a newspaper, because to do so would be a violation of the First and Fourteenth Amendments. The state's interest in protecting the anonymity of the juvenile offender cannot justify the statute's imposition of criminal sanctions on the press for the publication of a juvenile's name when lawfully obtained by the press.

REASON: "The sole interest advanced by the State to justify its criminal statute is to protect the anonymity of the juvenile offender. It is asserted that confidentiality will further his rehabilitation because publication of the name may encourage further antisocial conduct and also may cause the juvenile to lose future employment or suffer other consequences for this single offense. In

Davis v. Alaska, 415 U.S. 308 (1974), similar arguments were advanced by the State to justify not permitting a criminal defendant to impeach a prosecution witness on the basis of his juvenile record. We said there that '[w]e do not and need not challenge the State's interest as a matter of its own policy in the administration of criminal justice to seek to preserve the anonymity of a juvenile offender.' Id., at 319. However, we concluded that the State's policy must be subordinate to the defendant's Sixth Amendment right of confrontation. The important rights created by the First Amendment must be considered along with the rights of defendants guaranteed by the Sixth Amendment."

CASE SIGNIFICANCE: This case represents a classic confrontation between freedom of the press and a juvenile's right to anonymity in the name of rehabilitation. The Court said that freedom of the press prevails over the state's interest in protecting juveniles. Nonetheless, the Court emphasized that its decision in this case is narrow and must be so interpreted. It said: "At issue is simply the power of a state to punish the truthful publication of an alleged juvenile delinquent's name lawfully obtained by a newspaper. The asserted state interest cannot justify the statute's imposition of criminal sanctions on this type of publication."

What about prohibitions by the court, backed up by threat of judicial sanctions, against the publication of names in a juvenile proceeding? Most states have such a rule, which is sternly enforced by judges. Such rules are constitutional although they infringe upon the freedom of the press. This is because they are not considered punitive actions taken as a form of prior restraint. What a judge does, instead, is use the judicial contempt power to enforce court-mandated rules in an effort to maintain anonymity. Citation for contempt is not equivalent to a penal sanction for a criminal offense, although both can result in imprisonment. Generally, a court's contempt power is subject to fewer constitutional restraints and is not viewed as penal in nature. In sum, what the legislature cannot do by statute the judge can most likely do through the exercise of contempt powers.

II. LOWER COURT CASES

In re Smith
310 N.Y.S.2d 617 (1970)

It is unconstitutional to keep juvenile records when the petitions were withdrawn because of lack of evidence.

FACTS: Two juveniles, 14 and 15 years of age, were taken into custody during a demonstration that was held in front of a public school. Petitions alleging delinquency in the act of unlawful assembly and riot were filed. The petitions were withdrawn by the counsel representing the New York City Police Department because there was not enough evidence to make a prima facie case. The respondents asked that their records, both police and court, be expunged.

ISSUE: Is it unconstitutional to keep juvenile records when the petitions were withdrawn because of lack of evidence? YES.

DECISION: Keeping juvenile records in cases in which the petitions were withdrawn because of lack of evidence violates the due process and equal protection rights of the juveniles.

REASON: "While respondent's motion presents judicial questions of first impression, the handicap of a juvenile court record or a police record to a youth trying to gain a foothold in the job market, has concerned commentators on justice for juveniles and the underprivileged. The most frequent respondents in juvenile delinquency cases in New York City, as elsewhere, appear to be children of the minorities and of the poor, as indeed are the instant respondents. The Court obviously cannot determine this case on the basis of general social commentaries cited by respondents' diligent counsel. However, having considered the instant circumstances, the legal grounds for relief, and the jurisdiction of this Court, it has concluded that the motion should, with some modifications in the requested remedy, be granted.

"In sum, the Court and police records in their present form pose threats of injury to the respondents without justification in the public interest in law enforcement and indeed contrary to the public interest in helping deprived youths climb out of the poverty ghetto. Accordingly, a second and significant basis for relief for respondents is that the State's maintenance of the records constitutes an infringement of the constitutional guarantees of due process and equal protection of the law."

CASE SIGNIFICANCE: This case deals with the juvenile's right to privacy. The children in this case had delinquency charges filed against them, but the charges were withdrawn for lack of evidence. Because these children were not adjudicated delinquent, the issue of juvenile confidentiality shifts to the pretrial records of the juveniles. The question was whether the children could have their arrest and court records expunged. The court ruled that the juveniles' rights would be violated if their records were maintained. The reason is that the records might affect their future chances for employment and subsequent future success. The court held that the public interest in maintaining the records could not be proven, and thus must be secondary to the possible injury of the juveniles.

This case is significant because the court said that non-expungement of records in this case violated a juvenile's due process and equal protection rights. It made expungement a constitutional requirement in juvenile cases where charges are withdrawn for lack of evidence. Note, however, that this is a decision of a state court and has little value as precedent in other states.

In re J.D.C.
594 A.2d 70 (D.C. App. 1991)

A juvenile does not have to prove that continued exposure in the press would cause future harm before the press is excluded from the juvenile's hearing.

FACTS: J.D.C. surrendered to police shortly after the death of a 15-year-old boy. J.D.C., a juvenile, was charged with the shooting death, and a judge found probable cause that he committed the offense. He was ordered to be detained in a juvenile facility and his trial date was set. Before the trial date, *The Wall Street Journal* published an article that used the juvenile's name and also contained other information about the youth "which depicted him and his family unfavorably, and which related a number of facts of a private nature." The attorney for J.D.C. claimed that information in the article was incorrect.

Two days after the article appeared, the attorney for the youth filed an "Unopposed Motion to Exclude Media from all Further Proceedings." Reporters from the *Washington Post* and other newspapers were allowed to attend court hearings in the case, although the juvenile had objected to their attendance. *The Wall Street Journal* could not attend. Under Super. Ct. Juv. R. 53(a), each reporter agreed in writing that they would not divulge any information that would reveal the identity of the juvenile and the family.

On the scheduled day of the trial, the *Washington Post* ran an article titled "Printing of Daniel Suspect's Name Basis of Move to Close Trial." The story reiterated some of the information that had appeared in the original *The Wall Street Journal* article. J.D.C. filed a motion for reconsideration.

The judge held that "[w]ithout proof of a connection between these other readers or viewers and *The Wall Street Journal* coverage, the Court is reluctant, given Rule 53, to bar those members of the media who have complied with the rules. By not permitting *The Wall Street Journal* access to further proceedings, the damage done to respondent's interests can, hopefully, be minimized." A motion for reconsideration was filed. The concern was the overlap of knowledge that could be gleaned from future articles. The motion was denied. The judge stated that the harm was not in the presence of the reporters, but in the violation of Rule 53 to guarantee the confidentiality of the child and family.

ISSUE: Should the motion for exclusion of a newspaper have been granted? YES.

DECISION: The minor should not have to prove that the presence of the press would create future harm for him before a newspaper can be excluded. The judge's finding that the juvenile would not be further affected by continued media attention had not been supported, and therefore the judge erred in not excluding the newspaper.

REASON: "In the present instance, both the statute and the rule which implements it provide a substantial measure of guidance with respect to the weight which is to be accorded to various factors in the exercise of the court's discretion. The basic rule of the statute, repeated in the rule, is that juvenile proceedings are closed. The judge *may* permit the media to attend, but only '*on condition that they refrain from divulging [identifying] information . . .*' Sec. 16-2316(e) (emphasis added). Persons with a proper interest, including reporters, may be admitted to a proceeding, but only to the extent that the overriding policy of confidentiality is not compromised. If, in any given situation, adherence to this policy cannot be effectively accomplished without excluding the media, then the statute and rule logically dictate exclusion. Put another way, if there is no reasonable insurance that the admission of the press will be consistent with the protection of a juvenile respondent's anonymity, then exclusion may be the only alternative which will not compromise the legislature's paramount aim.

"Our statute and the foregoing authorities demonstrate that where, as here, a juvenile's identity has been widely publicized, the compelling interests posited by the trial judge are not equal. In the final analysis, at least on these facts, fidelity to the statutory scheme requires us to hold that the respondent's right to anonymity trumps the media's interest in attending and reporting on proceedings in a specific juvenile case. . . . Implicitly but unambiguously, the judge placed the burden on J.D.C. to show that the admission of the press to further proceedings in his case was likely to harm him.

"We hold that this was error."

CASE SIGNIFICANCE: This case features a confrontation between the freedom of the press and a juvenile's right to anonymity in the name of rehabilitation. In this case, the name of the juvenile had been published in violation of a signed agreement by a reporter. The trial judge felt that the situation called for excluding the reporter of the paper that had published the juvenile's name. He permitted the other reporters to attend the hearings. He also held that the juvenile could not prove that the presence of the other reporters and continued press coverage might have further negative impact on the juvenile. Even when a second newspaper printed information that might cause some to connect the cases being discussed, the judge did not exclude the newspapers.

This court held that the publication of the juvenile's name, initially, might lead to detrimental impact for the juvenile. It was not up to the juvenile to prove that it would cause him harm. The court held that in the conflict between the juvenile's right to confidentiality and the public's right to know, the juvenile's right to confidentiality prevails.

United States v. Three Juveniles
862 F. Supp. 651 (D. Mass. 1994)

The federal Juvenile Delinquency Act does not violate the First Amendment in mandating the closure of juvenile court proceedings.

FACTS: Three juveniles and an adult were arrested for alleged civil rights violations. The juveniles were charged under the Federal Juvenile Delinquency Act. Just before the July 20, 1994 arraignment, the *Boston Globe* moved to gain access to the arraignment and other hearings, as well as any documents in connection with the cases. On July 20, federal and state officials held a press conference discussing the investigation and arrest of the adult and the three juveniles. The newspaper stories focused on the fact that the arrested were alleged members of the Dawn Hammerskins, a white supremacist group. The newspaper reporters interviewed many people, including other juveniles reportedly members of the Dawn Hammerskins, and the arrested juveniles' names were given to the reporters in the interviews.

Three of the newspapers in the area published the names of the juveniles and at least one published a picture reportedly of one of the arrested juveniles. After holding an access hearing on the record, the court allowed the *Boston Globe* to "intervene for the limited purpose of seeking access, but denied the request for public access to the arraignments." The *Globe* did not claim that the Act, which protects the privacy of juveniles, was not valid, but they instead focused on the actions of the court and its discretionary power. Also, the motion contended that the First Amendment and common law "compel the court to balance the government's reasons for closure with the public's right to an open forum, permitting narrowly tailored closure only to the extent that it serves a compelling government interest." The *Globe* contends that it did not seek access to the names or any identifying characteristics of the juveniles, so closing access to remaining proceedings was inappropriate on the part of the government.

ISSUE: Did the judge's decision to block the *Globe* from further juvenile hearings violate the Federal Juvenile Delinquency Act or the First Amendment to the Constitution? NO.

DECISION: The Federal Juvenile Delinquency Act mandated closing of the juvenile proceedings. The Act did not violate the First Amendment.

REASON: "The starting point is the language of the Act itself. Section 5032 provides that a court exercising jurisdiction over a juvenile proceeding 'may be convened at any time and placed within the district, in chambers or otherwise.' Section 5038 further provides: (a) Throughout and upon the completion of the juvenile delinquency proceeding, the records shall be safeguarded from disclosure to unauthorized persons . . .

"The *Globe* argues that the statute does not require closure of the hearings, but gives the court discretion. *See PG Publishing*, 28 F.3d at 1361 (Section 5038(e) 'provides no evidence of a congressional mandate to close all juvenile delinquency hearings and seal all records.') The Act never expressly mandates a closed hearing for a juvenile proceeding. Rather, it states that a juvenile proceeding 'may be convened at any time within the district, in chambers *or otherwise.*' (emphasis added). While this provision, when read in isolation, appears to give the Court discretion as to whether to close the courtroom, it must be read in conjunction with Section 5038(e), which is direct and mandatory. It says that 'neither the name nor the picture of the juvenile *shall* be made public in connection with a juvenile delinquency proceeding' (emphasis added).

"If the courts were to permit public access to the delinquency proceedings where the juveniles appear, the result is ineluctable: the juveniles' names *will* be made public . . ."

CASE SIGNIFICANCE: In this case, some newspapers had published the names of the alleged juvenile offenders. When the *Globe* wanted access to the court hearings, the court blocked that access, but allowed that certain documents could be made available to the *Globe*. The newspaper appealed. The appellate court affirmed the decision of the lower court.

The reasons for upholding the court's decision were many, the first being that the congressional purpose of the Federal Juvenile Delinquency Act was to protect juveniles from the stigma and publicity that accompany criminal convictions. Again, in weighing the rights of juveniles to confidentiality and the right to freedom of the press, the courts upheld the juveniles' right to privacy as a tool to rehabilitation as the stronger right. Note that this case was decided based on the provisions of federal law and not because the juvenile has a constitutional right to confidentiality.

State v. Acheson
877 P.2d 217 (Wash. App. 1994)

Juveniles can be required by state law to register under sex offender registration statutes.

FACTS: Acheson, 14 years old, pled guilty in juvenile court to one count of child molestation in the first degree, having acknowledged that he had sexual contact with a three-year-old. At his disposition hearing, the court entered a sexual offender disposition in the case and ordered Acheson to comply with the Washington Sex Offender Registration Act, which required, in part:

> (1) Any adult or juvenile residing in this state who has been found to have committed or has been convicted of any sex offense register with the county sheriff for the county of the person's residence.

> (2) The person shall provide the county sheriff with the following information when registering: (a) name; (b) address; (c) date and place of birth; (d) place of employment; (e) crime for which convicted; (f) date and place of conviction; (g) aliases used; and (h) social security number.

Acheson's counsel objected and filed an appeal challenging the constitutionality of the registration requirement.

ISSUES:
1. Does the Washington Sex Offender Registration Statute apply to juveniles adjudicated delinquent for sex-related offenses? YES.

2. If yes, does the registration obligation extend beyond the age of juvenile court jurisdiction? YES.

DECISION: The Washington Sex Offender Registration Act included juveniles under the jurisdiction of the juvenile court. This interpretation is based on the inclusion of the word "juvenile" and the phrase "found to have committed" in the statute. Because the duty to register is a legislative mandate rather than a court order, it does not terminate upon the juvenile's twenty-first birthday.

REASON: ". . . [O]ur review of the language . . . leads us to conclude it was the Legislature's intent that the statute apply to juveniles under the jurisdiction of the juvenile court. Contrary to Acheson's assertion [the Act] does not require that the defendant be convicted of a felony. Instead the language of the statute requires, in the disjunctive registration by '[a]ny adult or juvenile residing in the state who has been found to have committed or has been convicted of any sex offense. . . . [The Act] plainly included juveniles who have been found to have committed a sex offense, and Acheson acknowledged in his guilty plea that he committed a sex offense by having sexual contact with a three-year-old.

". . . [A] juvenile's duty to register as a sex offender arises pursuant to the legislative mandate . . . rather than by order of the sentencing court. The sex offender registration statute contains no language requiring the sentencing court to order a defendant to comply with the duty to register. The court is simply required to give written notice of the duty to register . . ."

CASE SIGNIFICANCE: This case dealt with the issue of sex offender registration as it applies to juveniles adjudicated delinquent for sex-related offenses. The court interpreted the state statute based on its use of the word "juvenile" and the phrase "found to have committed," finding that the inclusion of those words clearly indicated the intent of the legislature to include juvenile adjudications in juvenile court in the registration requirement. The court further found that because the requirement was a result of state statute and not court order, the registration requirement did not expire at the juvenile's age of majority and in fact continued indefinitely into adulthood.

The significance of this case is twofold. First, offender registration in general is highly controversial, but with the inclusion of juveniles the registration provision runs counter to the philosophy of juvenile justice processing, which focuses on the best interests of the child. In this case, the public safety interest of the society won, with no attempt to balance the needs and rights of the juvenile delinquent.

Second, this blurring of minority and majority status represents a substantial intrusion into the basic confidentiality that has traditionally been the hallmark of juvenile justice processing. Requiring a juvenile adjudicated delinquent in juvenile court for a sex-related offense to register lowers the walls of confidentiality. Requiring the registration to extend beyond the age of majority lowers confidentiality protections even further and promotes greater inroads into the privacy rights of juveniles.

Index